LOOKING FOR...

LOOKING FOR...

Bollywood, Bachchan and Me

JESSICA HINES

BLOOMSBURY

First published 2007
This paperback edition published 2008

Bloomsbury Publishing Plc
36 Soho Square
London W1D 3QY

A CIP catalogue record is
available from the British Library

ISBN 978 0 7475 6862 9

10 9 8 7 6 5 4 3 2 1

Typeset in Rockwell by Palimpsest Book Production Limited,
Grangemouth, Stirlingshire

Printed in Great Britain by Clays Ltd, St Ives plc

Bloomsbury Publishing, London, New York and Berlin

All papers used by Bloomsbury Publishing are natural, recyclable products made
from wood grown in well-managed forests. The manufacturing processes
conform to the environmental regulations of the country of origin

www.bloomsbury.com/jessicahines

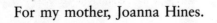

For my mother, Joanna Hines.

ACKNOWLEDGEMENTS

This list of thanks spans the writing of two books so it is rather lengthy.

First to my family who have been ludicrously supportive and never once suggested that I should give up and go get a proper job.

Thanks especially to my mother Joanna Hines without whose love, care and practical help neither book would have been written. Thanks to my father Derrek Hines for teaching me the importance of the absurd and for always seeing the world a *whole* lot differently than everyone else. Thank you to my grandfather Edward Hodgkin for teaching me about the importance of dancing backwards in high heels, being able to fight with furniture and that it isn't always open season on princesses.

My brother Peter Hines: quite the most lovely man on earth. And my other brothers and sisters, Alison, Alex, John and Sacha for keeping me inspired and laughing.

Thanks to my other brothers and sisters Daisy and Neula Dunlop and Luke and Sam Tinson with whom no explanations are ever needed.

My friends who have put up with so much, have helped me through the dark times and danced with me in the sunshine: Fanny Johnstone for staring steely-eyed into the bleak winds that blow across the tundra and always being there for a prance on the spongy permafrost, Mo White for keeping me stylish in the face of often insurmountable odds, Anna and Emma Lavender for all their loves. Richard Brooks for shared insanities. Fred Martinson for making me realise there is always a better party somewhere else in town. Goat Rampant! to Tamara Barnet-Herrin and Claire O'Brien for WGP exploits and, with Jay Basu, for childcare beyond the call of duty, Sweetie Kapoor for trying to make me cool, Arjun Kaicker for trying to teach me how to get on with everyone, Martino Sclave for demonstrating the importance of torque, Adie for escort services, Steve Tollervey: 800 miles and still running, who'd have thought it? Victoria Hull and Tom Hodgkinson for amused disbelief, Dr Jean Radford and Dr Luke Hodgkin for a place to stay and help with First Lines. Dr Simon Hodgkin and Dr Daniel Mortlock for answering endless questions and dancing like lunatics. Thanks to Chris Dwyer for appreciating the dull thud of the lone lentil. Thank you to David Spuring for inducting me into the Abstract Distractionalists.

Thank you to Louisa Gordon: acupuncturist, goddess, Millennium Falcon.

Big love and thanks to Jerry Pinto – I would never have fallen in love with Bombay if you hadn't shown me how.

My heartfelt gratitude to the man in the field of corn who loved, did not doubt and gave me the strength to start.

Thanks also to Los Bros Morani, my knights in shining Versace, for their support and help in India. Thanks to all those who have put me up and put up with me in Bombay – Udita Jhunjhunwala, Ajoy Kapoor, Jerry Pinto, and Manisha Koirala and for the remarkable Hajee family whose sincerity, warmth and acceptance made me feel part of their family. And to Charlotte for walks, coffees and talks/rants.

Thanks, I think, to Dr Rachel Dwyer for encouraging me to follow the white rabbit and handing out advice and Lucozade when the end seemed so far away.

Thanks to my agent Jane Turnbull for never failing to believe and being always so willing to don armour and fight my corner.

Thank you to Alexandra Pringle for her vision and to Chiki

Sarkar for 'getting it', imaginative editing and a shared love of aubergines.

Thanks also to Mary Morris who so courageously came in and took on the role of editor and supporter when Chiki left to rule the universe.

Thanks also to Joss Whedon and the cast and crew of *Buffy the Vampire Slayer*.

I wore chiffon.

A Cautionary Tale
or, what happens when you get too close to your subject.

PROLOGUE

*'One must have chaos in one to give birth
to a dancing star.'*

Friedrich Nietzsche

10 October 1942 (Brahma muhurata) Allahabad, Uttar Pradesh, India

Harivansh Rai Bachchan lies sleeping next to his heavily pregnant wife Teji. He has a vivid dream: he is back in his family's ancestral home and sees his father sitting in the little *puja* room where the household gods were kept; he has his glasses on and is reading from a religious text, the *Ramcharitramanas*. Harivansh and Teji sit outside the *puja* room listening to his father's recitation. It is the point in the story when the sage Manu and his wife Shatarupa are allowed to ask a favour from Visnu. Manu asks Visnu for a son like him.

> Feeling his faith, and hearing words so rare,
> The Fountain of Mercy allowed his pious prayer:
> 'Vainly one may search for my equal on this earth:
> Incarnate as your princely son shall I myself take birth.'[1]

---

[1] Harivansh Rai Bachchan, *In the Afternoon of Time: An Autobiography*, edited and translated by Rupert Snell (Delhi, Penguin Books India Ltd, 1998), p.308.

Teji wakes her husband to tell him that her contractions have started. It is the hour before sunrise, an auspicious time known as the *Brahma muhurata*, 'the hour of god'. The dream had been so compelling and real that Bachchan, India's much-loved poet, told it to his wife and then said to her: 'Teji, your baby will be a boy and he will be the spirit of my father reborn.[2]

The baby, born by forceps on 11 October 1942, was a healthy 8lb boy. He was named Amitabh, 'eternal light'.

<hr>

[2] *Ibid.* p.309.

Part One

MUMBAI

CHAPTER ONE

'Safety ... Obscurity ... Just another freak in the
Freak kingdom.'

Dead Kennedys, 'Viva Las Vegas'[3]

Monday, February 2002
Mumbai

Will meeting Amitabh Bachchan be the death of me? My rick-shaw is being driven by a crazy man so I can't help – ouch my butt – but have a fate-paranoia moment. What if everything I have done in life has been to bring me to this point where I die on a side road in Mumbai on my way to have dinner with the most famous Indian alive, Bollywood megastar Amitabh Bachchan?

Usually I can handle rickshaws, no problem *baas*; I have been to India twenty-three times so the odd loony rickshaw ride doesn't faze me. I would prefer to be driven by a sober, trusted family retainer in a plush air-con car but I don't have either so I've just got to do the rick thing.

I have been in Mumbai for a week but last night moved in with my friends Amin and Charlotte Hajee who have been kind enough to find a space for me.[4] I've spent the day hanging with them and the rest of their family.

---

[3] Nobody says Hunter S. Thompson's words better than Jello Biafra; that the American Dream is a lame fuckaround is a hard-won understanding.

[4] Amin and Charlotte met on the set of *Lagaan* ('Land Tax', dir. Ashutosh

I am still in my just-arrived-I-love-Mumbai-it-feels-like-home stage so I am happy to be hurtled along through Pali Hill and down Short Cut Rasta to watch Mumbai's evening markets coming alive. Mats spread out on the ground filled with fish, barrows full of fruit and veg that looks so much, well, *better* than any you get in Tesco.

If the barrows were a film set I would put money on it that there was about to be a fight and that they would soon be home to more than okra and aubergines. Oh yes, any minute now that nasty old *willain* is going to come crashing down on one.

Mumbai: a city with a genius for movement, for making money and movies. It's come a long way since the Portuguese gave it to the Brits as part of a marriage settlement in 1661. An unlikely city, grown out of mangrove swamps and salty, stinky creeks to become a hard-headed businessman whose backbone is the huge textile mills that emerged in the nineteenth century, but whose heart beats to *masala* movies, with their dedication to keeping it unreal.[5] It is a city whose inhabitants trade diamonds during the day, and then walk through the surf eating *bhel puri*[6] with their families, watching the blood-red sun sink into the sea.

The last hundred years have seen it become the city that personifies modern India: it is in touch with, but not ruled by, its roots and traditions; it is cosmopolitan – vast, crowded beyond belief – but it retains the feeling of a village. Within each social group everyone seems to know, or be related to, everyone else – quite a feat in a city of nineteen million. People here work hard and play harder than in any other city in the world – they make New Yorkers look like a bunch of slovenly wasters.

---

[4] *cont.* Gowariker, 2001) which required English actors to be the baddies. No change there then. We became friends during the film's promotion.

[5] '*Masala* movies' is the term given to popular films. They are mixed and spicy.

[6] A snack food.

Mumbai: home of Bollywood. Home of Amitabh Bachchan.

Ahh, Amitabh. How to describe him? You have to get quite excited to do him justice. It doesn't matter how many times I have written about him and tried to communicate just what he is, the sheer scale of what he means to people, in the end I can only do it by donning the mantle of *the fan*. You must be willing to pay homage and obeisance, for he is no ordinary man.

Amitabh Bachchan is the Living Legend of the Hindi film industry, unlike any other film star ever, more impressive and compelling than all of Hollywood's top stars even if you *could* smoosh them together to make an *Über*star. They wouldn't come close; Amitabh is in a whole different league.

Amitabh Bachchan, Superstar: The King of Kings in the biggest film industry in the world. On an average day, India releases more than 2.5 feature films; these are seen by at least fifteen million people a day in one of the country's 13,002 cinema halls, or projected on to a sheet in India's millions of villages. This industry is operating in a country with an average per capita income of about US$330 a year, one of the lowest in the world.[7]

Amitabh Bachchan – Top Hero numbers one through ten, *yaar*, demanding a lot of capitalisation of key descriptive words: Hero; Superstar; Urban Demi-God. So how to describe him? A cross between Clint Eastwood, Al Pacino, Elvis, but with more than a hint of John Travolta. Nah, that doesn't come close.

I was told once, with much conviction, '*Hero* is too small a word; he was a *superhero, bhai*. Perfect gentleman, a perfect

---

[7] Ashis Nandy, 'Indian popular cinema as a slum's eye view of politics', quoting 'Mass Media in India 1992' (compiled by India's Ministry of Information and Broadcasting) in Ashis Nandy (ed.), *The Secret Politics of our Desires: Innocence, Culpability and Indian Popular Cinema* (London, Zed Books, 1998), p.1.

gentleman I tell you, *and* he could beat twenty men in a fight, no problem.'[8]

And I am going to write his biography – if I can get through the next twenty minutes. This guy seems to want to test how fast he can go before we actually take off. Rickshaws are not the most stable of vehicles at the best of times and attempting to break the land speed record in one is not advisable. I would rather not be included in his death wish. But despite the jolts and alarming swerves I am happy.

Why would anyone want to write a biography of Amitabh Bachchan for a western audience? My choice of subject hasn't exactly made me a wow hit on the cocktail party circuit in London.

Party me: So, what do you do?

Party man: I manage hedge funds.

Party me: Oh, right.

Party man: What do *you* do?

Party me: I'm writing the biography of the greatest movie star in the world, Amitabh Bachchan.

Party man: Sorry, who?

Party me: He's a Bollywood film star.

Party man: Bollywood? That's really big, isn't it?

Party me: Yes. Hedge funds are *really big* too, aren't they? Canapé?

And then there is the problem that the whole of India believes they know all about him. *Ha bhai*, in a nation where everyone is more than happy to offer their opinion on anything, from how to get from North to South Mumbai, or how to get the best *malai*[9], the Amitabh Bachchan Story is everyone's *Mastermind* topic of choice.

Mumbai party me: So, what do you do?

---

[8]   Karim Hajee.

[9]   Cream.

Mumbai party man: I manage hedge funds.

Mumbai party me: Oh, right. Uncanny.

Mumbai party man: What do *you* do?

Mumbai party me: I'm writing Amitabh's biography for a British publisher.

Mumbai party man: Really? If you want to know anything about Amitabh Bachchan you come and ask me.

Mumbai party me: Well, alrighty then. If you need a hand with those hedge funds, you don't hesitate to call me, OK?

This is what I will be told:

The Amitabh litany

Amitabh Bachchan: son of Hindi poet Harivansh Rai Bachchan; childhood friend of the Gandhi kids Sanjay and Rajiv (sons of Indira Gandhi, grandsons of Nehru); educated at top private school Sherwood College in the hill station Naini Tal; spent six years as an executive in a shipping firm in Kolkata.

At the age of twenty-seven he left his safe, well-paid job at the insistence of his brother and went to Mumbai to join the film industry. His first role was a small part as an Urdu poet in a film by veteran film maker K. A. Abbas, *Saat Hindustani* ('Seven Indians', 1969). After the success of his second film *Anand* ('Anand', dir. Hrishikesh Mukherjee, 1970), in which he played the part of a doctor, his career languished for a couple of years during which time he got only gentle roles in 'flop films', dressed mainly in a *dhoti*. He began to despair that he would never make it big. Three years later he had his first hit, *Zanjeer* ('The Chain', dir. Prakash Mehra, 1973). That same year he married the film heroine Jaya Bhaduri, who subsequently gave up her own work, and they had two children, Shweta and Abhishek.

In 1975, he revolutionised what it meant to be a hero with

his portrayal of gangland boss Vijay in the hard-hitting, gritty, urban film, *Deewaar* ('The Wall', dir. Yash Chopra, 1975). He stalks like a hungry panther through Mumbai's underworld, dishing out justice; his heavy-lidded eyes spell danger and sex and d-e-a-t-h. Vijay is the kinda guy your mother wouldn't approve of (hell, his own mother doesn't approve of him). That same year he played the small-time crook turned people's hero Jai in the most successful Indian film of all time, *Sholay* ('Flames of the Sun', dir. Ramesh Sippy, 1975).[10]

These films rocketed him into the Number One slot and established him as the Angry Young Man (AYM). He was the man who fought against the odds, against the system, and won. He was ironic, hip and compelling viewing.

So from the mid-1970s he has been, Mumbai street patter and all, too kool for skool. His deep, rich baritone voice (oof, he made Barry White sound like a *hijra*[11]) fitted his standing as a colossus who bestrode Mumbai from Chowpatty Beach to Nariman Point. Nothing, and no one, could touch him. At one point in the late seventies he had eight different films running in eight different theatres, all 'House Full'. Amitabh Bachchan Superstar was hot, white hot, as hot as the tight white flares that he wore as he grooved and fought his way through the seventies. Famous not just because he looked so great fighting, but also because he looked tremendous singing romantic songs, dancing amongst the snow and clouds of Kashmir and, not least, because he could be very *very* funny. He has ruled, more or less, ever since. Sure, new stars come and captivate the Indian public for a time, but only Amitabh remains a perpetual star with the power to enthral.

---

[10] *Sholay* has been outdone in ticket sales by some films recently, but those have already faded while *Sholay* lives on and becomes more and more iconic every year. To me it is truly the most successful film of all time.
[11] Eunuch/castrato.

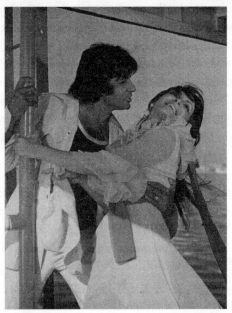

In 1982, Amitabh had an accident on the set of *Coolie* ('Porter', dir. Manmohan Desai, 1982). After being critically ill for a couple of weeks, he died. Then he came back to life. It was widely believed that the prayers of the nation brought about this miraculous recovery.

Two years later in 1984, after the assassination of Indira Gandhi, then Prime Minister of India, he went into politics at the behest of his childhood friend Rajiv Gandhi, but after three years resigned in protest at the allegations that he had taken kickbacks in the Bofors arms deal scandal. He went to court in Switzerland, Britain and the US and successfully cleared his family's name.

Amitabh won a national award for his role in *Agneepath* in 1990 and then took a break. He returned in 1994 having turned himself into a brand, the ill-fated Amitabh Bachchan Corporation Limited, and suffered a string of flop films. Facing bankruptcy and thought to be finally on the way out, he accepted the offer to host *Kaun Banega Crorepati?*, the Indian version of *Who Wants to Be a Millionaire?* It was a smash hit, and coincided with a return to strength in his film roles as the Stern Patriarch. He was, once again, King of the Hill.

In a nutshell? He is the king of infinite celluloid space, and of the hearts of millions.

Of course, what I tell them about hedge funds is between my broker and me.

I am here after getting a commission to write Amitabh's biography. A Big Respectable Publishing House thought my proposal – to look at Amitabh's life, his films and his star persona as a kind of running triage – suitably exciting and unique to give me cash to be hurtled through suburban Mumbai.

I grew up in a tiny hamlet on the Lizard Peninsula in Cornwall so there is no reason on God's good earth why Amitabh and I should appear in the same sentence. There has been nothing in my upbringing to draw me close to Bollywood, other than suffering through orchestral versions of the songs in Indian restaurants while eating bright red chicken tikka. After school I went to Canada and studied clown. When I came back to Britain I decided to study Comparative Religion. One of the courses I took was 'Cinema and Society in India'. I fell in love with the films. I just thought that they were brilliant; I loved the music, the stories, the melodrama and magical fantasy world of glamour and high romance. I was able to escape from my all-too-realistic damp Cornish upbringing into a glitzy world where more is more and people didn't just think pink, they thought pink with a gold lamé trim and red sequins!

Then I went to India and saw *Hum Aapke Hain Koun?* ('What Am I to You?', dir. Sooraj Barjatya, 1994) at the Raj Mandir cinema in Jaipur.[12] I loved the way people threw money at the screen when the songs were playing and how the audience grooved. I loved the whistling and the kids racing about, and what else would one want to eat during the interval but a samosa snack? But most of all, I loved what happened when a song came on: the lights that surrounded the *massive* screen started to flash. There was no turning back.

I am constantly being told that I am an 'Old India Hand', so I am determined to deal with this and be cool tonight when I meet Amitabh. We are going to set up a time to do the interviews for the book so I have to present my most mature and competent side. There has been a bit of a time-lag between getting the commission and arriving here due to the fact that I had to help turn Selfridges into Bollywood. So tonight I want to emphasise to Amitabh that I am back on track. As it were.

---

[12] A massive hit film about an extended family where nothing much happens except dancing and eating. The only event to speak of is when a young mother falls down the stairs.

The first time I met Amitabh I wasn't what one might call cool about it. I had seen his films, of course, and after watching *Hum Aapke Hain Koun?* had started to shift my degree around so that it fed into my study of Indian cinema. But I wasn't prepared for the effect that he would have on me. Nor did I have any inkling that just by meeting him I would step over the line and into the fantasy world of Bollywood.

OK, smooth bit of road. Let's use this opportunity to go back, back in time.

How it all started

29 October 1995
London

I was still in bed when the phone rang. I hauled myself reluctantly out from under the warm duvet to answer it.

'Good morning.'

'Hello. Can I speak to Jessica Hines?'

There is only one person in the world who has a voice like that. The world stopped spinning for a moment, the floor seemed very far away.

'Speaking. This . . . this is me. Speaking. It's it's it's Jessica Hines speaking,' I stammered, and gave a little high-pitched laugh just to confirm that I am, indeed, an arse.

'Hello. It's Amitabh Bachchan.'

'Oh! Right! Hi!'

'Hi.'

'Wow.' I sat down on the floor heavily and stared at my stack of *Love and Rockets* comics.

There was a pause, a brief pause; it felt like social death. 'Say something!' I scream at myself, '*Carpe* that bloody *diem* Hines, *carpe* forchrissake *carpe!*' I am in the second year of my undergraduate degree. In order to continue working on Indian cinema after the course finished last summer I have opted to do endless dissertations on the subject. This is my first. I didn't really have a clue how to go about it. I just thought it would be cool to interview Amitabh so I wrote to him, never dreaming that he would actually respond. Now I am at a total loss as to how to talk to him.

Amitabh came to my rescue:

'Er, I understand you wanted to interview me?'

'Yes, yes, I would love to interview you. I'm doing my dissertation on representations of masculinity in the films of Amitabh Bachchan, looking at the different ways in which masculinity is portrayed' – I suddenly realise what I am saying – 'by *you*, in, well, *your* films.' He might think that I am suggesting that he is sometimes *not* a man. 'I mean, heh heh, obviously you're always a man, you know, it's just a silly, you know, academic way of putting it.'

'Ri-i-ight.' He drew it out, his voice heavy with disbelief.

I could tell that he was suddenly thinking of all the other things that he could be doing on this crisply sunny autumn day.

'So when would you have some time?' I asked quickly, before he could change his mind.

'I'm free for an hour now.'

'OK! I'll be over in half an hour.'

He gave me the address, the Connaught Hotel off Grosvenor Square. I am in Islington.

'It might take me a little longer but I'll be there as soon as possible.'

'Please. I have to go to Birmingham to record an album.'

My head is filled with joy. He is an Important Man still making Cultural History – I am so *lovin' it*!

I put the phone down and stood up and screamed.

How to get there in half an hour? It is Sunday morning, ergo all minicab drivers will still be in bed after a hard night attacking lone women. My brain skids through my wardrobe like a needle across a record; I throw clothes around, phoning every taxi service this side of Luton. It took me almost the full half-hour to find one with a driver who hadn't got lucky the night before.

Amitabh Bachchan. Amitabh frickin' Bachchan.

I heard a car beeping. The international sign of *Cabus Minius*. Into the taxi I lemur-leaped.

'GOOD MORNING!' I sparkled at the driver. 'Take me to the Connaught Hotel as quickly as you can, my good man!'

'Whas tha'?' The driver sat and looked at me in the rear-view mirror. His large brown eyes are sunk above pouchy cheeks of grey stubble. He has that middle-aged Middle Eastern male gerbil thing bad. I think to myself, 'This is not one of life's go-getters; I can't imagine him ever getting lucky'. It looks like his arse has become one with his saggy ashen seat. Irrational irritation was rising:

'It's on the south side of Grosvenor Square,' I snapped.

He reached his concrete arm across to the glove box. The air in the front seats has Martian density; his every move is depressed effort. I didn't know his story. Surely very tragic: he was probably the Surgeon General in Istanbul, and driving a cab in London was psychological hell for him. Right then I didn't give a flying fuck, all I cared about was getting to see Amitabh before he took off to Birmingham.

Taxi guy took out an ancient, bollocksy *A–Z* and started to thumb through it, his finger smudging down the list of things beginning with G, his mouth working the word.

'Don't worry, I'll direct you. Drive to Oxford Street.'

'Hokay, ladi.' He sighed, put the *A–Z* back in the glove box, hauled his hands on to the steering wheel and laboured the car out from the curb.

Outside my grimy taxi window life was normal.

'Um, hello?' I thought, 'Oi! Sunday morning Islington people!

Over here! Yes yes, me in the Vauxhall Cavalier with the sad Turkish man driving and a plastic bag tied to the aerial. Do any of you have any idea how exciting and astounding it is that I am going to meet Amitabh Bachchan? Why aren't you all clapping for me? Why is no one waving Union Jacks and saying, "Yey, you go girl"?'

Cab ride agony evaporated when we got there. I trotted lightly up the smooth stone steps, tink tink tink! and was engulfed in Olde English Plush: deep red carpets, much polished wood and rich heavy chintzes. I felt a surge of inadequacy, so much the impostor.

I went to the reception, resisted the urge to tug my forelock, and asked the prissy imacuguy to call Mr Amitabh Bachchan. Gallingly – even allowing for regulation posh hotel sangfroid – he failed to register the slightest flicker of comprehension as to the importance of this meeting.

Amitabh told him to send me up. And up I went, my heart beating fast, so much blood in my eyes I could hardly see, I felt sick. I found my way to his door down a preternaturally hushed corridor. I knocked. I died, I ran back down the stairs, I stood still, I took deep breaths, I wished I was a different person. I heard him come to the door and pause, was he looking at me through the spy hole? I compulsively tucked hair behind ear, I mummummumed my lipstick, I died again, I levitated.

He answered the door:

'Miss Hines. Welcome. Come in.'

His voice is velvety with underlying danger and power: like a soft-spoken polite tiger.

'Hello!' I said, jauntily, swaying about a bit. 'Well, there we go', I thought, peering at him through bleary eyes, 'How about that: he is oddly *beautiful*.'

I walked past him into the drawing room filled with over-stuffed furniture, tasteful prints and heavily swagged curtains and was immediately caught up in his scent: 'What a fragrant fellow,' I thought.

He invited me to sit on the sofa. The cushions were so full of stuffing that my feet scarcely touched the ground. Infantilised, much. I stared at him. I couldn't help it. I couldn't stop staring.

He was older than I had pictured him in my mind's eye, though he looked younger than his fifty-three years. In fact, I couldn't tell you what age he appeared at all. Tall by Indian standards, but not as tall as all *that* (he is always talked about as if he is freak-of-nature tall). Intelligent hooded eyes, a fleshy generous mouth and an ample nose which drops into a kind of extra bobble at the end. They are all fairly odd features but somehow they worked together to create an attractive, middle-aged man. He is dressed in soft fabrics, a cream polo neck, brown trousers and ... oh, no! ... *blurgh* ... those slip-on Italianate leather shoes with little *tassels*. What up wid *that*? I want my AYM to be wearing biker boots at the very least (unashamed desire to indulge in homovestism, granted). 'But', I tell myself firmly, 'he's not the characters he plays in his films.' I know this.

Even with the vile footwear he was immaculately put together. The man oozed carefully considered taste. And he smelt so good.

I started to feel slightly giddy, stoned. Was this the effect of too much Chanel Egoist? I wasn't sure that I would be able to make my fingers do intricate tasks like set up the tape recorder. Keep me away from heavy machinery.

What do I say? Why is Amitabh having this effect on me? It's not because he is famous; I *have* met other famous people. And anyway, two years ago I didn't even know he existed, so it's not like I'm totally wigging out and imploding under the weight of years of worship made manifest. It's not like he's *Morrissey*. But there is something about him.

I wittered on about how pleased I was he was letting me interview him. He looked vaguely embarrassed and uncomfortable and stared at a point on the carpet to avoid my florid gratitude. I wished I hadn't covered my tape recorder in *Star Trek* stickers. For the first time in my life I wanted to be immaculately presented, like he was; to only use the correct procedure for all things, as I was sure he did; to laminate all important bits of paper before filing them neatly, as I imagine he does.

'So,' I began, hearing my own hesitant girly voice and wishing I sounded more Katharine Hepburn, 'what actually happened to you on the set of *Coolie*?'

I did the interview. I was banal and my questions were pedestrian; I was mentally flat-footed, my thoughts had no arches: What made you want to become an actor? Which heroine did you like acting with most of all? Which are your favourite films? Why did you become a politician?

To his eternal credit Amitabh never once made me feel like the fool I was. He was a total pro and treated me as though I was asking him piercing and incisive questions, ones that he had never thought of before, ones that made him look deep into his soul, his past and his crazy, madcap career. He was engaged and charming and we talked for almost two hours. His attention transformed me from gauche schoolgirl to grown-up researcher, neatly dissecting my subject into clearly defined parts in order to understand his inner workings.

At one point he asked me if I wanted some tea. I said yes. It was ordered, in due course arrived and was placed, with much flapping of damask napkins and straightening of silver pots, on the table between us. And there it sat. Steaming tea. Crumbly buttery biscuits. And it sat and it sat and it sat. After a time I began to be distracted from my Pulitzer Prize-Worthy Questions and his tales of mad fan adoration and political mistakes, as other Big Cultural Questions started to lumber into my brain: was it up to me to offer to pour the tea? Would this seem pushy and ungracious? Did being a star in India trigger off a chain reaction that resulted in one's losing the ability to pour tea? I started to tug at the hem of my skirt and dart looks at the cooling tea and the warming milk. Eventually Amitabh noticed and said something like, 'Ah, yes, the tea.'

'Heh heh, yes.'

There was a silence. What to do?

'Shall I be mum then?' I blurted.

'Yes. OK then.' He sounded relieved.

'*Mum*? Shall I be *mum* then?' I rail at myself. 'What sort of a dumb-ass comment was *that*? Amitabh is thirty years older than I am. Mum? . . . *Mum*?

He stared at me with a look of gentle disbelief. I didn't blame him; I was pouring tea like it was nitroglycerine. Neither of us breathed.

'Geez mista, mustya stare at my hands?' I think.

Too . . . much . . . pressure . . . can't . . . hold . . . out . . . much . . . longer . . .

My mind caved in, I started to drift away from the moment. Offering to 'be mum' to Amitabh Bachchan is not such a safe, cosy, tea-pouring job as it might sound. In his films he often dies long bloody deaths in his mother's arms.

Mum: much weeping and railing against all things worldly.

Him: stoic forbearance and scoops and scoops of pathos.

What if, by suggesting that I be mum, I triggered something in his brain? What if it sent him into a mental filmic flash-back loop? What if he suddenly lunged at me across the table, scattering the bone china and biscuits and landed between my legs, all covered in exploded blood packs and sugar lumps, his eyes already seeing beyond the veil, and said something like, 'I am not a gangster now, Ma. Forgive me, Ma.'

To which I would have no choice but to shriek, 'Nahi, nahi beta! *Beta*!'[13] And then a really high-pitched '*Nahiiiiii*' because, you see, although a bad sort, he had always been my favourite son.

---

[13] 'No, no son! *Son*!'

I looked up at him as I stirred in his sugar. He sat like a big solid brown bear after a very good feed on honey and salmon, waiting patiently for his tea. No lungeing into my lap to a background score of soaring strings. He was a wise middle-aged businessman in posh Euro casual, trying to explain to me how by turning himself into a brand would, in one fell swoop, sort out the lack of order in the Indian film industry.

The interview continued until the arrival of his occasional business partner, Kirit Trivedi, who was taking him up to Birmingham to record an album with British-Asian pop star Bally Sagoo. We parted company. I thanked him profusely. He said 'Not at all' a lot.

I went down stairs and into the bathroom next to the reception. A bathroom attendant filled me a little sink full of water and handed me some soap.

'Oh my god!' I gushed at her, 'I have just met Amitabh

Bachchan! Do you know who he is? He is like the biggest film star *intheworld*. He is, just, like, *brilliant*!'

She looked surprised at my outburst and murmured encouraging as-long-as-you-don't-get-weird noises.

I gripped the basin edge and allowed myself a little moment of unravelage: 'Ohmygodohmygodohmygod.'

The assistant looked at me warily and handed me a towel from as far away as she could get.

I scooped my mind out of the sink and squished it back into my head. OK. Ready to face reality. I gave the lady a quid and skipped out into the delightful autumn sunshine.

Now what was I to do? My mind played hopscotch over all the things that had happened that morning. I didn't want to be anywhere, I didn't want to see anyone I knew. I wanted to drift through the spaces that had opened up in my mind, I wanted to be in unreal London, Amitabh London. There were dishes at home, laundry, homework, friends all with expectations and limitations to tug me back to earth . . . But now I no longer felt on the same plane as them: I was gorged on Turkish Delight; my mind was full of another world. I drifted through Grosvenor Square full of big orange leaves fluttering about. Shopping? I had no money, but I did have some M & S tokens my Nan had given me. I drifted through Marks, brushing through the stay-press trousers like they were fur coats. I finally bought an outfit and forced myself to go home, but I was no longer really there . . .

The next day I realised that I had bought myself exactly what Amitabh had been wearing: cream angora sweater (OK, his wasn't angora, it was probably, if future jumper borrowings were anything to go by, TSE cashmere, darling) and what could only be described as brown slacks, neither items that I would ever wear.

Two days later I took them back and got knickers instead.

Bollywood and me

That meeting with Amitabh was the start. The rest, as they say, was his-story. My life has revolved, in some way or another, around him ever since.

After I wrote that first dissertation on him, he happened to be in London again and I contrived a meeting where I could give it to him to read. To my horror he proceeded to read it right there and then, *out loud*. I sat and squirmed under the uniquely exquisite torture of having my clunky unedited prose read to me by my subject. Has anyone else had this happen, I wonder? When he had finished he pronounced that my basic thesis was totally wrong. I writhed in my little Petri dish of embarrassment.

'So you are not the personification of the promise of the phallus to India's disenfranchised young urban males?' I squeaked.

'No!' he smiled, 'I *am* the phallus!' and he burst into sudden big booming laughter.

I sat exhausted by my ordeal, laughter seeping out of me like tissue fluid from a wound.

From that moment a strange friendship developed between the two of us. Every now and then, when Amitabh came to London, he would call me up and we would go out with some of my friends for dinner or a film. I managed to devise countless situations to justify going out to Mumbai to meet him. My friends couldn't understand it. 'Why would he want to be friends with you?' they asked, kindly. I would shrug my shoulders. I was as much at a loss to explain it as they were. But there it was and I got used to it.

I even had the dubious honour of appearing in the Indian gossip columns, once as 'Icy Spicy', and another time as an 'English Rose', both of whom were apparently leading Amitabh astray whilst he was in London. I was a bit thrown by this, but Amitabh sagely pointed out that he was news and if he had so much as coffee with someone it would get written about.

It was through him that my fascination with all things Bollywood took off. I met most of the industry in some way or another, and became friends with a couple of the young stars who had made their mark on Bollywood in the 1990s – Nepalese beauty Manisha Koirala and Mumbai's home-grown romantic hero, Aamir Khan. I guess I became kind of addicted to the whole Bollywood life thing. I needed the rush of extreme situations, of difference, of highly stimulating surroundings and the mass of incongruities that clutter every day spent in Mumbai. Being a student in London wasn't much competition.

I did a lot of things to create a world in which my addiction could be fed. After I finished my degree I did an MA at the British Film Institute, and in the summer term of 1998 I put on a season at the ICA called 'Bombay London', showcasing the best films of the nineties and the Asian underground music scene, and holding interviews with the stars. Of all my friends who had agreed to take part – Aamir Khan, Manisha Koirala and Amitabh Bachchan – only Amitabh actually showed. I tried and failed to produce a documentary on the making of *Lagaan*, a film about cricket that became the first Indian nomination for an Oscar since *Mother India* (dir. Mehboob Khan, 1957). I ended up just helping a bit with the pre-production and organising a screening of the film for the British media and Important Folk. I worked for the Clerkenwell Literary Festival in 2000 and 2001 and managed to give that hip rock and roll event a tinge of chicken tikka red when Bollywood came to town: Aamir Khan sang 'Chaudhvin Ka Chand'[14] to Blur's Alex James and the poet-turned-scriptwriter-turned-lyricist Javed Akhtar recited poems with my dad, poet and playwright Derrek Hines. The event was compèred

---

[14] One of the world's most romantic songs; the hero is looking at his beloved and asking her if she is the full moon or the sun, because whatever she is she's the most beautiful thing he has ever seen. From the film *Chaudhvin Ka Chand* ('Full Moon', dir. M. Sadiq, 1960).

by a not yet famous, still out of his head on drugs, but very sexy and funny Russell Brand. He kept having to disappear off to the toilet but it never seemed to matter. We all just drank and chatted until he came back and was funny and brilliant again.

The last few years have been unbelievably seductive and compelling, just knowing that at any moment I could be racing home to pack and be off to Heathrow Airport aka the 'Portal of Escape'. It is dangerously addictive, that rush of departure, and after a couple of years it meant that I felt justified in never committing to a job or a relationship in London because the most important thing in my life was to be able to take off on another trip to hang out in Bollywood. Home life became a half-life and only the high life felt like real life. I know that this isn't good, but I'm not ready to do the rehab thing.

And here I am, sitting in this rickshaw.

Crunch!

We have skidded into the back of a truck. This is enough. Even Old India Hand here is allowed to freak out now.

'You're insane! I want to live!' I shout in Hindi.

He turns and grins and waggles his head. The whites of his eyes are solid red. Great. He's trashed.

'Enough. I will take another taxi,' I say angrily, gathering up my bag and starting to get out. '*Kitna*?' I bark. He shrugs at Unreasonable Tourist Lady and looks at his rickshaw payment card.

The traffic has started to move and – oh God no! – so have we! The front of our rickshaw has somehow become attached to the truck and we are now being towed along with it.

'Stop!' I shriek in alarm. 'Stop! We have to get out of this rickshaw!'

'Why? We are moving, no?'

'And the petrol tank? Where is *that*?' I scream as we bounce about, holding on to whatever we can.

'*Aap ke neeche*.' He points to just below my bouncing arse.

26

That means if it explodes I will be the one doing the human torch impression? I start to wail. He laughs at my distress.

We come to a brief halt as the traffic clogs up again. I make an ungainly leap for freedom and almost fall on to a mat full of fish spread out by the roadside. The woman who owns it shouts at me angrily. I throw rupees at the driver, who laughs at me again before settling back to enjoy the ride as the traffic takes off.

'Sorry sorry sorry,' I apologise. I try to keep out of people's way and not step on their produce (sorry maa*ji*sorry oops! sorry), avoiding the traffic which is using the pavement as an extra bit of road for pointless overtaking. I look out for another rickshaw to take me to Amitabh Bachchan's '*naya bungalow, Shentaur ke baad*'.[15]

Mumbai. No matter how many times you come here it can undermine even the fiercest feminist resolve in an instant and, just as gallingly, undo the most carefully applied make-up *phataphat*.

I think I am doomed always to be uncool and crumpled when I meet Amitabh. Even if I am just coming down from my hotel room to meet him in the lobby, I get all rumply in the lift. This is an innate difference between us. He is never, ever rumpled, even if he has just executed a fight scene where he has been smashing men's heads into clay pots. I don't know how he does it: even his linens and silks obey him. My clothes look creased as soon as I put them on. But when he ushered me into his office that evening I was not just dirty and wrinkly; I was in shock. Amitabh is good in a crisis, and as ever he managed to get the right balance of solicitous kindness, gentle reprimanding and practical solutions (tea and delicious snacks).

---

[15] 'New bungalow next to the Centaur Hotel'. Everyone knows where it is. Mumbaiwallas often take out-of-towners on a tour past the houses of the stars.

Amitabh's office is a fortress of masculine wealth and power. It is on the first floor of his new home, Jalsa, and you reach it by going up a flight of stairs past walls hung with hundreds of photos of Amitabh and his son Abhishek (but mainly of Amitabh). Going into someone's house or office and being confronted by hundreds of photos of them might be alarming, but then Amitabh is often everywhere you look outside his house too so the whole continuous-flow effect works. In a little antechamber sit his secretaries Barbara and Rosie, and there you must wait until you are ushered into the inner sanctum.

A huge desk and an arch-villain-sized chair dominate his room. On the desk is a bang-up-to-date i-Mac. The walls are covered with Indian modern art, and on occasional tables placed at tasteful intervals around the room are books about him or the films that he has made. The most arresting objects are the fifty-plus fountain pens that sprout like sea anemones from silver tankards at the front of his desk, many of them Mont Blancs, their white snowflake splotches shimmering in the air conditioning – and the pistol on the wall . . .

'Nice gun,' I said when I had had a restorative cup of tea and some almondy snacks.

Just being in his cool, fragrant, bejewelled presence was enough to make me feel like nothing need ever be chaotic again. One of my friends recently asked Amitabh what made him smell so goddam good. He told us that he mixes his perfumes, having a different one for different parts of his body and a special one for his hands. This sounds foul but it works, in an Eastern Potentate kind of way. And being the most fragrant man on the planet goes with the whole Ming-the-Merciless-bling-is-my-thing look he has going on with gems the size of ice cubes all over his long, soft-looking fingers. He started wearing them when his business was going bankrupt and all hope was lost. When I asked him about them once he said that an astrologer had told him what to wear, and on which finger. I was sceptical, but must confess that since then his fortunes have turned about once more.

'The President of Afghanistan gave it to me when we went there to film for *Khuda Gawah*.[16] A couple of months later he was shot.' He looked at it grimly and then started to fiddle with the silver paper cutter in front of him.

'Wow. Cool. Gosh,' I say, intelligently. 'I loved that film. You look like you are having fun in it for the first time in years.'

'It was an amazing experience.'

'And the chemistry between you and Sri Devi is electric. It's so sexy.'

'It was a very sexy time.'

I look at him. What does he mean by that? He and Sri Devi finding a way to beat the cold? His expression is resolutely closed. I decide not to push it and just say, 'Well it shows.'

I look about a bit more. 'Can I have a copy of the book on the making of *K3G*?'[17]

'Of course. Haven't I given you one already?'

'Nope. Will you sign it?' I ask.

'Sure.' It doesn't surprise him that, even after all these years, I still want him to sign things. Everyone wants him to sign things.

'Do you want to borrow a pen?' I ask.

'No, I think I'll manage with my meagre resources,' he says smiling and plucks out one of the Mont Blanc tentacles. He writes incredibly neatly and then blows on the ink to dry it. I lean across to take the book.

'Wait! It isn't dry,' Amitabh admonishes. 'You are a very impatient girl.'

---

[16] *Khuda Gawah* ('God is my Witness', dir. Mukul Anand, 1992)
[17] This was the acronym given to *Kabhi Khushi Kabhie Gham* ('Sometimes Happy Sometimes Sad', dir. Karan Johar, 2001). There was a ruder one but I am not at liberty to divulge it.

'My turn to blow then,' I say and read what he has written: 'To Jessica – With love and great affection, Amitabh Bachchan.' Nice. I smile and pull the corners of my mouth down. 'Thanks!'

Amitabh shrugs and twiddles his pen.

Dinner arrives on a huge silver *thaali* full of different delicious vegetarian foods. There is even some chicken for me, damned meat eater that I am. After the horrid start it has turned into a lovely evening.

We talk about my book, when to do the interviews. He is really positive and helpful and says that we can start soon. But he also says that he would want to approve the text. I tell him that the level of approval he will have will be directly proportional to the level of help that he gives me. He seems to get that.

Due to my earlier trauma Amitabh was very sweet and drove me home. *Very carefully.* In his big silver Merc with two police escorts tooting and whistling all the nutters away. Mumbai is totally different when you are looking out at it from behind tinted glass, breathing air-con air and encased in leather.[18]

How to reach God

So how *did* I end up being asked by this urban demi-god to write his biography?

Hindus say there are many ways to God. Which is nice. But to descend from such lofty considerations for just a parsec and bring the conversation back round to me again, there are also many ways to understand why Amitabh would do such a rash and unlikely thing. The key lies, methinks, with my tutor at SOAS, Rachel Dwyer. Yes, it's all her fault, I am utterly blameless and innocent. And Amitabh? He, poor chap, is just a fashion victim. Allow me a moment to explain.

---

[18] The seat. Not my outfit.

Dr Rachel Dwyer was one of the first academics to get down and dirty with those high-stepping folk of 'filmi' Mumbai, and one of the things she undertook in her rigorous study of all things popular culture was a biography of the King of the Romance Film, Yash Chopra. Well, soon it became de rigueur amongst the good citizens of that imaginary country known to all as Bollywood to have your own academic. *All* the top stars had one. It was almost a better indication of social standing than the number of machine-gun-toting bodyguards you had cluttering up your driveway.

After I managed – despite my growing obsession with all things Bollywood – to get a first-class degree it seemed an obvious choice to continue with higher education. But once I had started my MA in Film and Television at the British Film Institute I quickly realised that, 'Bugger Baudrillard, fuck Foucault and sod Said, I am not meant for this sort of classy caper; I'm off to see a man about a dog.' I still had an aura of 'academic' about me: that intoxicating Eau de Bibliothèque is a hard one to wash off. Perhaps Amitabh just liked having his own academic around.

Year in, year out I took on still more projects that would enable me to travel out to India. Of course, for most people on the sets, it was still a bit of a mystery what I was doing there. Other than drinking lots of Pepsi, getting in the way of the lighting guys and occupying one of their precious white plastic chairs. Basically I just liked to hang out on the sets with Amitabh, but Amitabh is a polite chap and so when I arrived on another set with a new bemused director/producer/co-star, he would take great pains to explain me to the others. And since he couldn't say, 'This my academic. I know I know, she's last year's model and getting a bit rusty round the theory, but well, I don't like change very much so I'm going to keep her till she finally conks out,' we developed a bit of a double-act patter.

Gavin Fernandes

'This is Jessica Hines. She's from the School of Oriental and African Studies.' (This genus would change as time ticked slowly on and it became apparent that even I couldn't take that long to complete a degree. Eventually he began to say that I was a writer, but you could tell he was never happy with such an unprestigious designation.)

I would try my best to look friendly and unthreatening.

'She is completely mad,' he would go on and then, as if suddenly warming to his theme, he'd say, 'Do you know that in her thesis' – he never really liked the word dissertation – 'she dedicated a whole chapter to my wearing flares!'

The recipients of this piece of bizarre information would look suitably incredulous and I would jump in with: 'I thought that it was important to illustrate how you heralded the rebirth of urban cool. And anyway, nobody can wear flares like you can. Your long legs look great in white flares whereas most people look like egg timers.'

'See? She's mad. And she will drive you mad with her questions.'

So my right to clutter up the set would once again be accepted, and we would all settle back into our awkward silences on our white plastic chairs, until either someone could think of something to talk about with Amitabh or his next shot was called. Then he would spring forth from his little throne made of three plastic white chairs stacked on top of one another, as if being with us was the most socially difficult thing he had ever done, and take his place amongst the waiting extras and co-stars.

Also, let's face it, he must have quite liked me being around, all pink and flustered and eager, telling him that the shot he had just done was 'really great!' That old star ego is always happy for a bit of extra adoration after all. And I liked him; I liked being around him, even if he wasn't the easiest of men. Conversation did get more relaxed after a while, although I never stopped feeling like a construction worker perched high above the city carrying an iron girder and suddenly remembering that I suffered from vertigo. But that feeling was all part of the rush, part of the drug I'd started to crave.

All this bonhomie aside, eventually the question on every superstar's lips has to be: What does one do when one acquires the season's must-have item, one plump blonde academic? Especially once the novelty value has worn off and they show no signs of leaving? Like all film stars who have lots of servants and people hanging around them waiting to be told what to do 'in life', I guess Amitabh figured that it was his duty to tell me what I should be doing 'in life'. Little did he know that I would actually do what he told me to do 'in life'.

One day in 1998, on a shoot in Gujarat for *Sooryavansham* ('Descendent of the Sun', dir. E. V. V. Satyanarayana, 1999), I was sitting with Amitabh asking him about the fine art of film finance. He had adopted the defensive tone common to many people in the film industry when you ask them where the money comes from.

'You should write a book about the film industry,' said Amitabh.

'No,' I said. 'I don't know anything.'

'You are always hanging about asking questions I can't answer,' said Amitabh. Everyone else sitting with us laughed. The suggestion that there is a question that Amitabh can't answer is preposterous.

'I've only written about you. Over and over again. All my dissertations have ended up being about you.'

'Then you should write a book on me.'

'What, my experiences with you? A comedy?'

'Tragedy more like. I am a tragic figure, old and past it. A has-been,' Amitabh said smiling, and then suddenly looked sad.

I was not going to let this descend into a 'pat Amitabh's ego' session. I knew from past experience that he thinks he wants it, sets it up even, but then he gets awkward at everyone being nice to him and clams up, leaving everyone to wonder if they've said anything wrong.

'What, write your biography? Isn't Rauf Ahmed writing it?'

'He has been writing it for years. I am not sure he will ever finish it,' said Amitabh.

'Well, you're not dead yet, are you? I am not sure I could do it. My Hindi is so very bad.'

'Yes, it is. Very bad,' said Amitabh, supportively.

This needled me, and anyway, I was fed up with trying to get film stars to do things for British companies, who then didn't see the projects through properly. 'OK then, I will.'

'Good,' said Amitabh.

The next morning I woke up early and went for a walk through the neighbouring village as the morning prayers were being chanted at the temple. Every now and then the temple bell would ring as another devotee alerted God to his presence. I sat by the stream that ran between the village and the Palace Hotel and watched the production people rushing about, setting things up for the first shot of the day. A kingfisher was perched on a branch a little way off from me. I had never seen a real kingfisher and I stared at it, hardly daring to breathe. Suddenly it darted down into the water and caught a fish. It flew back up to its branch and sang such a happy, excited song at its successful catch. I was happy for it.

After that I went home and got myself a shit-hot agent, who got me a shit-hot contract with a shit-hot publisher, and now here I am.

OK, so it wasn't quite so simple a procedure (is it ever?), but do you really need the minutiae and the angst? Thought not.

That's enough for one day. A near death experience and a big meal have made me too sleepy to wait up for Amin and

Charlotte. Mumbaiwallas keep really late hours, and sometimes dinner isn't served till almost midnight. This, I have deduced, is because people don't do the whole let's-drink-wine-with-our-meal thing. Wine production in India is a relatively new thing: it's predominantly been a spirit/beer place. So they get all their alcohol in before trying to soak it up with lots of *dhal* and rice. Also, people work hard and late and then have long, stressful journeys home. It takes a little time for my constitution to get used to it. Anyway, enough with the pontificating already. Tomorrow I've got to start work.

Come on boys and girls, you want to get happy with me? Roll up those sleeves, find a big plump juicy vein and we can jack up Bollywood, just . . . one . . . more . . . time . . .

CHAPTER TWO

'Anything that raises the human spirit is basically good,
even if it is false.'

Joe Queenan on *The Oprah Winfrey Show*

Phoning film stars

Tuesday

This morning I began to call some of the people that Amitabh
has worked with over the last thirty years. The people who
inhabit the mythical world of Bollywood in North Mumbai are
the most wonderful, warm and giving people – as long as you
are sitting right in front of them. Move out of their sight and
you no longer exist, until the next time you meet when they once
again bless you with their gracious attention. That they live in a
constant present isn't their fault. The industry is set up in such
a way that to attempt any kind of long-sightedness is almost
impossible. So each time you meet it is often as though it is the
first. And in Mumbai trying to get hold of film stars by phone
is an exercise fraught with problems that can bring you to the
point of total breakdown. If you are unlucky enough to only
have a star's home number, you are doomed to failure. You will
never get through to some one who can understand heavily
accented Hindi, let alone speak 'Inglis'.

Two standard responses shouted by servants just before they

hurl the phone back at the cradle are: '*Saaar batroom mein hai*' or '*Saaar baahar gayaaaa*' ('Sir is in the bathroom' or 'Sir has gone out'). Once I got a 'Sir is taking his medicine,' which was a little alarming. I think there must be Star Servant Training Courses where the object of the telephone exercise is to frustrate anyone on the other end of the line to the point of apoplexy. Points would be given to the trainee servant who managed to make callers actually go purple, and first prize would go to the truly obstreperous who could make the caller collapse on the floor sobbing, having lost the will to live.

If you have their mobile number then you're in with a better chance. Although if the star doesn't recognise your own number they won't answer or, worse, fob you off on their *paan*-chewing make-up artist. You won't be able to understand this person because they have a mouth wadded full of dripping red betelnut, which makes them slurp at you as they ask your name. This confuses you. It also confuses them, so they hang up. The best thing to do, I think, is to call all numbers and leave messages with anyone who answers. Or get really stroppy, hold the phone away from you and shout that you are calling from England, or demand to talk to someone who speaks English. It is very stressful and pressurised: it is horrible to feel like a rude bolshie mentalist, but trying to get to talk to stars is like cutting through loft insulation with a pair of nail scissors.

Today wasn't too painful. I got a few interviews set up with some of the directors and actors that have worked with Amitabh over the years: Shashi Kapoor, Neetu Singh, Rishi Kapoor, Yash Chopra, Prakash Mehra. I left messages for Rekha, Bindu, Sunil Dutt, Hrishikesh Mukherjee and Parveen Babi. Not surprisingly no one was free today itself, so I cut my losses and took off into town to meet up with Jerry Pinto for lunch.

Jerry Pinto – mathematician, poet, journalist, raconteur and bon vivant – has been my closest friend and ally in Mumbai since I first came to the city in 1996. He is the person that I use as a sounding board for all my crazy theories and my frustrations, and with whom I share my triumphs. Checking in with him is essential; I don't feel I have arrived in Mumbai until I've seen Jerry. I also don't feel I have arrived unless I have been to the Britannia Restaurant to eat their outrageously creamy and addictive Chicken Berry Pulao followed by Crème Caramel.

Mumbai

Mumbai is built on a long, thin spit of land, a series of islands really, separated from the mainland by brackish creeks and rivers. The film industry is at the north end; everything else is in the south. The dividing line is Worli: South Mumbai folk get nervous travelling north of Worli without a passport and, by and large, filmi folk only emerge out of the celluloid-saturated suburbs for 'phunctions'. People who live in Bandra or Pali Hill (like Amin and Charlotte) feel superior due to their equidistant position between the two. As a visitor to the city it's more fun to stay in South Mumbai (more sh-sh-sh-shops! for a start), but if you are working on anything to do with film, it's better to stay in the north. Cutting down travel time is essential, primarily because it limits the amount of pollution you inhale each day.[19]

If you travel from north to south it feels like you are going back in time. In Juhu stand the solidly confident film star bungalows built in the 1970s, when land was still relatively cheap – now, remarkably, it is the second-most expensive real estate in the world, after Tokyo. I make my way down through Bandra past the crumbling Portuguese-influenced villas that seem to be held up with their own dust and ghosts, and on through the

---

[19] I once spent so long in traffic trying to get from the studios to the south and then back up north for the evening that I went temporarily blind for a good five minutes. It was extremely scary.

huge, abandoned textile mills which gave the city its first rush of crazy prosperity during the American Civil War, when the world looked to India to supply its cotton. Now they are covered in creepers and inhabited by trees, but somehow they still smell of dye and sweat and are full of the shadows of thousands of migrant workers. Just looking at them makes me feel the bone tiredness of manual labour and gives me backache.

Then you pass the racecourse that sits just north of Haji Ali Mosque, just before you reach South Mumbai proper. The racecourse is a Mumbai miracle. A huge, green space, open to all, right in the heart of some of the most fiercely contested real estate in the world. For a while I stayed with friends at Kemp's Corner, just south of the racecourse, and we would come running here first thing in the morning. India is at its most magical just before dawn and at sunset. Running around the often quite wild-feeling track through the pinky, pearly light as the racehorses were exercised on the track next to you was, well, special.

Finally you come down the hill from Kemp's Corner along Hughes Road, and turn a corner on to Marine Drive, curving along Back Bay, lined with bougainvillaea on one side with the sea on the other. In front of you lies downtown Mumbai, *just like I pictured it, skyscrapers and everything*. The architecture switches abruptly from ornate Indo-Portuguese buildings, with their delicate carved wood balconies, to the clean elegance of 1930s deco. Once you are in the centre of town you are surrounded by the high tropical Gothic of the Raj government buildings, the law courts, the schools and club houses, Victoria Terminus a crazy kedgeree of different coloured stones taken from all corners of the empire, and finally the Gateway of India, where my grandfather landed to take up his first billeting during the war, and instantly had his suitcase nicked.

Mumbai, where my heart feels at home . . . for at least two weeks before the pollution gets to me.

Usually, when I drive through Mumbai, I see it as a backdrop to films. This way it comes alive and is at the same time familiar and magical: the big bungalows house the hero whose rich family don't understand his love for the poor girl, the beaches are full of women in big floppy hats singing that they love you, and here, on Marine Drive, is where fifties superstar Raj Kapoor first met Nargis, the woman who would become his great love and the heroine of what many believe to be his best films. I wonder if there is any truth in the myth that she had been cooking and, when she answered the door and saw it was *him*, wiped flour in her hair.

The city resonates with Amitabh's films, they pulse and morph in and out of the everyday present: there is the place in front of the Gateway of India where he danced in *Don* ('Don', dir. Chandra Barot, 1978), and behind those gates are the docks where he beat up Peter's gang in *Deewaar* ('Deewaar', dir. Yash Chopra, 1975) and danced with Kimi Katkar in *Hum* ('We', dir. Mukul Anand, 1991), squirting her with a big hose. Once Rachel and I went to the top of the Oberoi Hotel and acted out a scene from *Deewaar* where Amitabh buys the building his mother laboured on – it was a moment.

Over lunch Jerry Pinto and I gossiped a lot and then made a programme of what I want to get done during the rest of my time in India. Obviously I need to a) talk to the people who made films with Amitabh, but Jerry thinks that I should also b) make a couple of little biographer pilgrimages to places where Amitabh has lived. He is probably right: I have just read *Flaubert's Parrot* by Julian Barnes and this is what biographers seem to do; go to old houses and schools and stuff. So I could go up to Allahabad, and Naini Tal to see where Amitabh spent his early childhood and where he went to school. Plus, according to the *Lonely Planet*, in Naini Tal I would have the possibility of hiking up a glacier. Because I am such a mountaineer. Oh yes, back in Britain I am up a Welsh mountain every weekend, me. So perhaps that bit will remain in the realms of fantasy, like most of my outward-bound projects.

But the idea of clean crisp mountain air is very welcome right now – Mumbai is getting *hot*.

There is so much information about Amitabh: the amount of people he has been on and off screen, the sheer amount of *stuff* that there is, the volume of material that I could use (both primary and secondary) to write this biography. It causes me to suffer from acute overwhelmshon. I see myself as a tiny humanoid beneath a vast cliff made up of bits of paper and studded with mouths all talking in Hindi.

Before I came over this time I asked biographer par excellence Caroline Moorehead how she wrote her biographies. She alarmed me by saying that it only takes her a week or so to write each chapter. She does the research then gets all her notes ready and just cracks on through. I am hugely impressed by this. I keep thinking about the card index boxes on her neat desk in her elegant sitting room in Chalk Farm. Perhaps that is what I need. Card index boxes. Caroline would *for sure* go on biographer pilgrimages. But if someone were to want to write a biography of me I can't imagine what they would get out of going to Tregarne and hanging out on the old milk-churn stand, squishing pennyworts and guessing what type of tractor it was coming around the corner. Or maybe they would? *There ain't no rocks on my arms, 'cause I'm just Jess from the farm.* Sista.

I don't think that if I went to Allahabad I would understand Amitabh's childhood in 1940s India. Perhaps I lack the empathy real biographers have. I need to be an empath like Counsellor Troi on *Star Trek: The Next Generation*. Or perhaps biographers just project wildly like the rest of humanity and then claim that they are empaths and that their interpretation is the right one because they *empathed* it.

After lunch Jerry took me to a photo studio on the side of the road and we had our photos taken with cardboard cutouts of the stars.

I can't work out why I have an almost physical aversion to the idea of going to Allahabad. I think it's because that is not the kind of biography I want to write. I am not, in case you hadn't noticed, Julian Barnes. Or, indeed, the ever impressive Caroline. I want to somehow write a biography of Amitabh that does justice to the overblown insanity that he has lived through, and to some extent created. Amitabh on set is remarkable. Amitabh on film just eats up all your attention. I want to tell his life story a different way, and show how the facts have been refracted through his films. But also I want to incorporate how his star persona has shifted and changed over the years and how this in turn has affected who he has become. I just don't think that my noodling about Naini Tal will help.

Also, what Amitabh achieves each time he steps up to the camera and does something extreme is much underrated. Sure, Hindi films are now much discussed in academic circles, much used in advertising in the west, but no one really gets just how hard it is for the actors to do what they do.

Once, in early 2001, I got a line in a film. It was about as unglamorous as one could possibly imagine. I was in Mumbai with the BBC reporter Imran Khan and photographer Gavin Ferna..des, securing photos of stars for a book commissioned by Alex Proud (who set up *Dazed and Confused* with Rankin and Jefferson Hack) which was never published. We arrived at an abandoned house in Versova in North Mumbai where two top stars Anil Kapoor and Rani Mukherjee were shooting *Nayak* ('The Real Hero', dir. S. Shankar, 2001). We wanted to try to talk them into sitting for us. The scene being shot was the one where the press mobs Anil as Rani looks on adoringly, and as a result it was even more chaotic than usual, with hundreds of extras all psyched and ready to rumble. As soon as we arrived, Imran and I were handed mikes and told to get in there and hassle him too. The film unit – totally insular like all film units around the globe – just assumed that we were there as white

44

extras. We sat in a room on the ground floor of the house with the rest of the guys with mikes until we were called to the shot.

Anil and Rani looked amazed to see me.

'I'll be with you in a minute Rani Mukherjee!' I shouted, feeling for the first and last time like Cary Grant in *Bringing Up Baby*, as we were dragged into the

Gavin Fernandes

thickest part of the mob. I was told that when Anil tries to achieve some order I had to shout, 'Please Sir, just one more question.' Ha, OK *bhai*, got it. Years of expensive education had equipped me for just this sort of challenge.

Imran and I had a great time jostling and yelling – it was like being in a mosh pit – and then it was my moment and I shouted in as pushy and hard-bitten international reporterish away as I could:

'Please Sir! Just one more question!'

Anil turned on me and shouted:

'Be quiet!'

There was real anger burning in his eyes as he delivered his speech. I was genuinely shocked. I wanted to remind him that it was really only me, remember me? Jess who had been over to his house a couple of times for lunch, who he had known for such a long time? And then I remembered that he was acting. Doing an intense scene of love and despair well isn't half as hard as doing a flip scene well. I first realised that Amitabh was a great actor when he jumped out of an Easter egg in a top hat, tails and a monocle and made it look like the most natural thing in the world. In the West being a Bond girl is seen as a simple task – you just simper and say 'Oh James' a lot. Halle Berry made it look simple. Madonna showed us just how hard it is.

Is Hindi film escapist? Sure as hell is for me. Surely *all* cinema is escapist in some sense, enabling you to disappear into another world where time is speeded up and multiple worlds unfold around you. It doesn't really matter if it is Mike Leigh or Manmohan Desai, Lukas Moodysson or David Dhawan: they all present other worlds where things just don't happen the way that they do in real life – but perhaps should. What is wrong with affirming the possibility that good might well triumph over evil, and that given the right conditions people might just burst into song in the mustard fields of the Punjab and kids might grow wings and play football on the roofs of Russian tower blocks? We all have times in our lives when we want to leave the reality that we live in and let our minds escape into other possible realities, be it at the Curzon Soho in London or the Eros Cinema in downtown Mumbai. For the rickshaw driver whose life is endless traffic stress, abuse and exploitation, what could be nicer than seeing an ordinary man take on the world and win both respect and the girl? I have often escaped into five-star hotels, exiting my life in London and entering the sparkly world of the famous where everyone is beautiful and shimmers. My friend the insane rickshaw driver from the other night gets to enter a plush Art-Deco air-con world and bask in the warmth of the light that is reflected off the screen. His face glowing red from a woman's wedding sari, his heart strengthened by the right guy winning. We all take a little of the energy of the film we have seen out with us, making the world we live in just that bit more bearable for a while. Of course, it needs topping up as the harshness of life crashes down again upon our heads, but is this such a bad addiction? Surely being taken out of yourself is what art, be it popular or high, is all about? High art. Ha. White lines don't do it.

Film City

Wednesday

I went and saw Amitabh on set today. Since we didn't pin down exactly *when* and *how* we are going to do the interviews when we had dinner together, I wanted to ask him face to face. It's been a long time since I sat on plastic in the sun, getting sweaty thighs and waiting for Amitabh to invite me into his trailer/dressing room. It made me almost nostalgic for the days when I was content to sit for hours and watch the film unit bustle about. Amitabh was shooting in Film City, an area of land set aside by the government in the 1960s for film production, so I made the Big Schlep out to the suburbs, to beautiful, sunny Goregaon.

Mumbai has spread north from the original port area where the British built their fort, through the Victorian Indo-Gothic buildings of government and dominance, along the Art-Deco apartment blocks that line the seafront at Back Bay, up through Worley, across Mahim Creek and into the leafy hills of Pali Hill and Bandra. Now it moves relentlessly forward, out from Juhu into the mangrove swamps and drying fish of Versova, and beyond into the scrubby hinterland of Goregaon. Here thickets of new super-high-rise apartment blocks zoom up thirty floors, condemning more housewives to struggle to make their lives meaningful in a sterile box in the sky.

The area has changed even since I started to go out there back in the mid-nineties: then, you still felt like you were on the fringe of the world. Now massive high-rises form a thicket of extreme architecture and throng right up to the gates. In the late sixties it was so far from anything even remotely resembling civilisation that the stars would say a little prayer for their cars before they left work in the evening, asking the gods to protect them from breaking down on the way back to town.

Getting *into* Film City has become harder. I used to be able to just tell the guards that I had an appointment with Amitabh and they would wave me through, but now . . . now it is a battle of Wit and Righteousness over sheer bloody-minded petty authority. Today I couldn't be dealing with talking to every policeman within a five-mile radius and explaining again and again what I was doing, so I called Amitabh and got him to speak directly to the guy. That worked a treat.

When the taxi was finally let through the gates and was speeding along practically the only road in Mumbai without potholes, down the hill and through the rolling green hills, I got the old familiar feeling of flying, of being let out of a cage and into a world where fantasy and imagination rule. Anything is possible here. As we drove, with the open, empty road in front of us, I was pleased to see that the funfair was still waiting to be used, the temple was still waiting for a god, and the heli-port on top of the highest hill still rose above the rest of the landscape – without a helicopter in sight. There are lots of films being made in amongst the trees but you can hardly ever see the work in progress until you get right up close. This adds to the feeling of stumbling upon Fairy Revels.

It is this sensation – of being in the presence of such a large number of people in the midst of creating; be it toe-tapping tunes, the right lighting that will bring out the magic of a moment, or even the brown liquid that purports to be tea and on which the industry runs – that gets into my heart and makes me happy. Everyone, from the star who makes you believe in Truth and Beauty to the guy sweeping the sets, is engaged in an act of creation, which produces a certain insanity, a certain febrile energy that I love. This Bollywood addiction thing hasn't only been about hanging out in five-star hotels drinking cold coffee (although I have managed to do a startling amount of that). Oh no. I have also craved this – to be on the sets, to witness the acts of creation.

The decrepit entries to two of Bombay's largest film studios.

Having said that though, life on the sets is hot, dusty, dirty and often boring. In the studios of North Mumbai, everything is very dilapidated and sometimes the buildings are quite literally falling down. The dressing rooms for the world's most glittery of glitterati are shocking: cheap whorehouses, but without the pride – stains on the carpet, dirty sheets on the sofa beds, mould on the walls, grime encrusting everything. The stars often sit in full make-up and silks on plastic chairs, shaded from the sun by just an umbrella, surrounded by the detritus of a hundred years of non-stop film making, like humming-birds on a rubbish dump.

Over the past few years it has not only often been boring on the sets, but it's also sometimes been alarming. For example, once I was watching the filming of a dance sequence. The female star stood on the middle of a dance floor surrounded by men all done up to look like extras in *Ali Baba and the Forty Thieves*. The music blared out from huge amps. The lights came on, the camera rolled. The lights started to swing about to create a disco look. But instead of using big rotating lights, tiny men were swinging about hanging lights from precarious boards high up beneath the baking-hot studio roof. The smoke that swirled about the stars' feet was made by more tiny men carrying huge trays of hot coals that they flapped at frantically, whilst trying not to let any fall on their toes.

The complete disregard for the safety of the lowly workers was brought into harsh relief on another set where huge pyros shot into the air as dozens of dancers in plastic did their best to look techno and not melt.

'Are there any safety precautions? Fire extinguishers?' I asked the director.

'Yah,' he said, pointing at a bucket full of sand studded with *beedi* ends,[20] so old it had gone solid. 'But a man's destiny is

---

[20] Cheap Indian cigarettes.

written here.' He waggled his finger back and forth across his forehead. 'You cannot control what fate God has for you. If you live, great. If you die . . .' He shrugged his shoulders.

The music started up again. Flames exploded up into the lighting tracks. Chaos engulfed the sets with everyone rushing to and fro. Ah, fate – what is written in your destiny. How convenient that God's will dispels the need to fork out on crash mats and insurance.

Today I track down Amitabh in one of the studios. I am absurdly proud of my ability to find my way about Film City. It is a hard-won knowledge that has come from many frustrating journeys to the wrong bit with taxi drivers from the Maharastran heartlands who can't believe they're actually in Film City and so drive about randomly, gawping.

When I went inside the studio to find Praveen, Amitabh's valet, or 'man Friday' as they are called round these parts, I saw others setting up the tracks for the camera to roll along. The camera itself is a beautiful, huge old Arriflex: stately, solid and serious. It is built like a tank, it can withstand extreme heat and cold, and is therefore perfect for the unrelenting Mumbai climate of humidity, dust, heat, torrential rain and sea salt. It was being cradled carefully by the cameraman's assistant, and only when the track is laid and the dolly rolled back and forth along it, making sure there are no bumps and jumps, is it placed back on top. Then the cameraman, who looked like he should be a cattle rancher in Argentina, portly with a leather jerkin and a cowboy hat (why is cameraman fashion universally odd?) got up on to the seat to compose the shot, shouting angry instructions at the scurrying men.

There are a lot of scurrying men on a film set in Mumbai. In fact there always seem to be about ten times the necessary number. All thin little men carrying impossibly heavy and awkward bits of equipment, their voices drowned by the throbbing hum of the generator, rushing on and off the set. Today these mini-men carried huge reflectors made out of tin foil and giant lights, shouting, '*Shide shide shide*', which roughly translates as, 'Get the hell out of my way! This thing is so heavy that if I break my pace things could get ugly.'

Amitabh calls to Praveen and I am shown into 'the Bus'. This is a motor home which, having been made in the late seventies, is quite remarkably ugly – a beige corrugated-metal box on wheels. It was a gift to Amitabh from director, producer and friend, Manmohan Desai. Desai was the creator of some of the world's greatest absurdist cinema and would use only Amitabh in his films. He died in the early nineties when he jumped from the roof of his house. For sentimental reasons, Amitabh has refused to ever get a new van. Every time he sees the Bus he thinks of his friend. It also has the added attraction of being familiar and homely. I have travelled to and from sets in it with Amitabh for many years and feel a deep affection for it myself.

Inside the Bus it is, as always, dark and freezing. Amitabh sits in a chair on one side with a little table in front of him; it comes out of the wall like tables in trains. There is another seat opposite him and against the other wall is a built-in sofa bed. There are curtains on the tinted glass windows made from the same brown paisley-print fabric that covers the chairs. Outside looks a long way away, as if the warm, richly scented, film set hurry-scurry is happening on telly. Amitabh is dressed in a dark blue double-breasted expensive-looking suit and he is looking at me. I try to read his face. Is he pleased to see me? He isn't exactly wild with excitement. I shiver. I have been sitting under the icy blast of the A/C.

'Hey, you know cryogenic freezing only works after death?'

My joke falls flat like a belly-flopping fat kid, making me wince as it hits the carpet.

I know from this start that any attempt to bring up the interviews is not going to get anywhere. So I try to make small talk in an effort to draw him out which, when Amitabh is being all broody and closed like this, is like trying to convince Mr Kurtz to leave the jungle.

He was in an odd mood today and no mistake. If past experience is anything to go by, this means that something major is going down in his life that I will be told about later. At times like this it is best just to be supportive and not be another person making demands, however legitimate. I am, I like to believe, first and foremost his friend. Any work that we do together comes as an adjunct to this. I think that I have become fairly adept at working with him and juggling the two, but every now and then he just shuts off for no apparent reason. I call this phenomenon 'the Glass'. You can be wandering along happily in an interview, whistling a nothingy, sunny sort of tune and then Boink!, you hit an invisible wall.

'Youch!' you cry, more from shock than pain. You call out to him but the sound doesn't seem to reach him. He has sunk back down into the swamp, only his eyes showing above duckweed.

After lunch the director suddenly announced that it was pack-up. No time watching him on set today. So Amitabh drove me back to Juhu in the Bus. I attempted to ask him what he thought would be the best way to go about finding time for the interviews. He said that he would work something out and then sort of sunk into himself. I did get a bit frustrated by this today so I stood up and postured a bit, telling him how frustrating it was when he wouldn't engage with me.

He stared at me. Amitabh has a uniquely paralysing quality of stare. It's like being stared at by a cross between a monitor lizard and Paddington Bear; your limbs get all heavy and it suddenly becomes more difficult to breathe.

'Perhaps you should write about it then. In . . . your . . . book,' he said, and waded back out to sea, disappearing beneath the waves like Godzilla.

'I will,' I said. I can't have him doing this now. I need him to be cooperative and supportive. After all, *he* suggested that I undertake this crazaloid endeavour.

Well, there's always next time. Amitabh has always made good his promises.

Girl talk

Thursday

After doing some more calls to set up the meetings (each one can take anything up to ten calls), I went and met up with Manisha Koirala. I have been to many film sets and met many people but a couple of times stand out. One was the night that I first met Manisha Koirala.

It was during the filming of what turned out to be possibly one of the worst films of Amitabh's career, *Lal Baadshah* ('The Red King', dir. K. C. Bokadia, 1999), in Jaipur. Amitabh was there to shoot a song sequence at night in one of the palaces. His co-star, rather improbably given their age difference, was Manisha Koirala. I had been very impressed with Manisha's amazing performance in a film about interfaith love set against the communal riots that shook Mumbai in the early nineties called, aptly, *Bombay* (dir. Mani Ratnam, 1995), and I was looking forward to meeting her.

We all sat around on our white plastic chairs as the dancers practised their steps and the lighting guys made the palace all lumièred, and Amitabh tried to ignore the thousands of men who had gathered at the gates of the palace, hanging on the railings about twenty feet away, screaming for his attention. At one point he stood up and waved hello, a slow regal wave – the crowd went bananas. The rather lackadaisical police hit a few people's hands with their *lathis* and told them all to pipe down. One guy would not be deterred though and just kept hollering,

'Amitabh! AMITABH! AMITABH!'

Eventually Amitabh turned to him and said:

'Ha? *Bolo beta.*' (Yes? Speak son.)

The man looked as if he was being strangled by unseen hands and fell back into the throng, who all laughed good-naturedly as they caught him.

I had just cut my hair extremely short and, in the presence of Manisha's stunning beauty and femininity, I felt like a rad seventies butch dyke. Amitabh did his little introduction and to both our amazement Manisha just said, 'I love your hair. I would love to have my hair like that. It's so cool.'

'Really?!' Amitabh asked.

'Yes, I think it looks great.'

Amitabh pulled a face. I told her, 'He thinks it makes me look like a drug addict.'

'Yes,' said Amitabh, 'you look just like an addict.' He emphasised the word 'addict' in a staccato way that only people brought up on Hindi's plosives can.

Manisha faltered a little, 'No, not at all! I would love to cut my hair like that.'

I looked at her lovely, long, thick glossy hair all tied up and bedecked with jewels. It was to die for. I decided that she was OK.

'Well, thank you,' I said, 'I wish I had hair like yours!' She smiled the easy careless smile of someone who gets compliments all the time. We all fell back into silence.

Now the place has been lit up and one of the extras stands in an alcove so that his friend can take his photo. The harsh uplighting makes him look like a gargoyle. Amitabh points it out, laughing.

'Put that one in a frame!' he says, and we chuckle in a faintly superior way.

The local bigwigs have been allowed on to the set, and one of them comes up and introduces his whole family to Amitabh and Manisha, who nod and smile politely at them. One man tries to touch Amitabh's feet and Amitabh, in a rare off-camera burst of speed, catches his hands before he manages to reach them. A mother pushes her four-year-old son forward. He is wearing a mustard-yellow double-breasted suit that is made entirely of polyester and is so boxy and stiff that it sits several inches out from his body. He solemnly walks up to Amitabh and silently offers his tiny hand to him. Amitabh solemnly reaches out and shakes it. The boy walks silently back to his overjoyed mother. They all ask to 'click one photo' with the stars and are allowed to. Then they leave.

After a while a little girl in a cheap printed dress with greasy pigtails, who has somehow got into the shoot and has spent the last half-hour devising ways to get past the police and the crew, makes a final dash past the assistant director and sprints up to Amitabh and Manisha. I cheer her arrival. They smile at her and when she requests an autograph Amitabh asks her name. She mutters something that I can't hear above the noise of the generator. Amitabh asks her again and she tells him. He asks if that is a pet name or if it is her real name. He nods at her and tries to give her his signature on a cheap piece of paper that has been held for so long it is shiny. The pen refuses to work so I produce another piece of paper and pen. Amitabh signs his name. She stares at his hand. Then she takes the paper to Manisha who also signs it and chucks her under the chin, telling her she is a cutie. People always stare at a star's hand when they sign the paper, as if by doing so they can somehow keep the physical presence of the hand there. I guess that is what makes an autograph special, the fact that the star must have had contact at some time or another with the thing that is signed.

After the girl leaves I say, 'Well, she really deserved that autograph! She worked hard to get it.'

Amitabh turns to us and says, 'Her name was Pepsi.'

At that point one of the wooden boxes used to house the plugs caught fire. A few people noticed and there were various opinions on what should be done about it, so they stood about and discussed them. Eventually one of the *lathi*-wielding policemen came up and whacked it till it went out. The people standing round it chuckled with the policeman at a job well done. No one from production came over and attended to it. The generator still hummed, the lights still ran, the music still blared through the dewy night.

'Did you see that?' I asked. Amitabh was deep in thought so didn't respond. Manisha rolled her eyes and giggled a yes. I searched for something to say but couldn't think where to start.

Amitabh and Manisha are called for their shot and they go and groove together on a grassy knoll, do a couple of little steps, wiggle their hips back and forth and then nod their heads together smiling blissfully at each other as fountains explode and the dancers leap about behind them. Hundreds of men go wild with enthusiasm at the gates.

After that shoot Manisha and I have kept in touch and meet up whenever we are in each other's city, cook for each other and bitch about men. I mean, what else in life can be as important as having a girlfriend in every port with whom to enjoy these two fundamental activities? It was cathartic to do this today. Manisha made me pasta which was really very good. It is always a bit tricky attempting to cook the food of another culture without the right ingredients, but some pasta dishes can be re-created quite well in Mumbai.

Manisha is going to have a party for Holi[21] so we spent a long time working out what type of party it should be. A good one, was the decision.

---

[21] Hindu festival of colours.

CHAPTER THREE

'Truth is unobtainable; humanity does not deserve it.'

Sigmund Freud in a letter to Arnold Zweig

Yash Chopra

Friday

Yash Chopra is the single most successful director and producer in Bollywood's history. This is not to say that he hasn't had his slumps, the mid to late eighties were a low period, but then they were for most people. (The 1980s were not Bollywood's finest hour; all shite disco music, absurd violence and no stories.) But in the early seventies Chopra teamed up with the hot young scriptwriting duo Salim Khan and Javed Akhtar[22] to create Amitabh's famous Angry Young Man (AYM) persona. The Angry Young Man felt fresh, relevant and proactive. Amitabh interpreted this character in such a way that, for a heady few years during the seventies, he made the rest of the actors wish that they could keep it as real. There is a nice irony to this in that Chopra is not a born tough-talking director of gritty realist films. His natural tendencies veer towards what he describes as 'glamorous realism'. (He is the Indian Richard Curtis but,

---

[22] They entered the industry when 'scriptwriter' as a job title didn't really exist as such.

thankfully, without the comedy swearing – you won't hear anyone saying 'Sod a dog' in a Chopra film.)

He is also a consummate businessman and after the runaway success of *Deewaar* he recognised that this new type of hero was what the audience wanted and went on to make the next two films in the AYM trilogy, *Trishul* ('The Trident', 1978) and *Kaala Patthar* ('Black Rock', dir. Yash Chopra, 1979). He didn't turn his back on his true calling though, also making the two films that came to define Amitabh as a romantic hero, *Kabhi Kabhie* ('Sometimes', 1976) and *Silsila* ('The Affair', 1981).

For Amitabh, teaming up with Salim-Javed[23] and Yash Chopra was the best thing he could have done. Salim-Javed were at the height of their scriptwriting skills and Chopra's technical skills were some of the best in the business. Plus, his sensitivity towards his characters allowed him to exploit the emotional side of the AYM which would probably have been overlooked by a regular action director. Of course, when Amitabh went stellar the magazines wanted to know why he was working with *them* and not the other way round, and he replied that it was because they had rescued him when it was looking like his career might flop. 'That's why given a choice I'd opt for them. What happens when they flop? I'll flop with them – who bothers!'[24] He didn't realise then that these words were prophetic.

Chopra's office is in a cul-de-sac off the crazily busy Juhu Road, deep in the filmi heartland. Once you go through the gate you are in an oasis of calm green and huge houses. The office feels rather cramped for the locus of a multi-million-pound movie empire, but this is always the way in Mumbai.

---

[23] If there is a duo in scriptwriting or music direction that works together all the time, their names are shortened to a combination of their first names.
[24] Raju Bharatan, 'How I came to play Haji Mastaan', *The Illustrated Weekly of India*, 18 May 1975.

Very rarely do you get something that really shows the true scope of the industry. When I have taken different film crews and photographers around Mumbai, *one* of their complaints is that it is impossible to get anything that captures its size. They have been impressed at its colossal might in a land that prides itself on its extremes. But how are they going to show this enormous scale, this legendary glamour, when all they get to shoot are dusty run-down studios, Stone-Age technology and extras in tacky costumes?

You cannot photograph obsession. The workers create magic cinematic moments without the latest in technological advancements. They often create great films, and the industry *is* enormous even if you can't find one thing to photograph that shows it. The ladies and gentlemen of the Mumbai film industry have cinema in their veins. Most of them *have to* create; then are driven to direct, write, act and produce by more than just the lure of money. The richness and diversity throughout the history of Indian cinema is a real testimony to the nation's ability to tell cracking stories. The industry has created cinematic legends and has produced a pantheon of stars whose glamour and allure the west hasn't achieved since the 1950s.

And the man who has been doing it for forty years is Yash Chopra.

I am told to go to his office and I make my way up the narrow stairs past posters of his, and now his son's, hugely successful films. He is sitting behind his huge desk surrounded by a forest of Filmfare awards and other honours, and many statues of Ganesha, the elephant-headed god who is Mumbai's unofficial patron saint. The famous Indian painter-turned-film maker M. F. Husain did a painting just for Chopra of a Ganesha in a Bavarian forest, after visiting him when he was filming *Dil To Pagal Hai* ('The Heart is Crazy', 1997) in Baden Baden. There is even a plaque from the Swiss tourist board thanking him for his services to Swiss tourism. This may sound a little odd, but Chopra was one of the pioneers of filming song and dance sequences in foreign locations. When the troubles in Kashmir got really bad in the late seventies, Chopra upped stumps and went to find romantic mountains elsewhere. He found what he was looking for in Switzerland and shot so many films there that Rosennear Lake is now known in Mumbai as Chopra Lake.

'Hello Sir,' I say.

Chopra gets up and comes over to greet me. We shake hands. He has a deep voice with such a thick Punjabi accent that I often have a hard time understanding him.

We exchange pleasantries. He asks about my old teacher and his biographer, Dr Rachel Dwyer, or 'Ratchel' as he calls her. I tell him that she is well.

'Jessica,' he says, 'I know that you have friends here in Mumbai.' He gives me a quick sidelong glance. 'But if you need anything, any help, you just ask me. I am your friend too.'

'Gosh, thank you so much Sir. That's very kind of you.' I am, not to put too fine a point on it, gobsmacked: this is an extremely generous offer from a very powerful man, and I am touched. I think it probably has more to do with the fact that I am Amitabh and Rachel's friend rather than with any innate worthiness on my part, but I am not minding much.

'Anything you need – just ask.'

I thank him again. And then realise that this particular bit of the conversation is closed. So I move on to my book and ask him if I can start with the interview.

'Of course. I will do anything for Amitabh. It is an emotional bond that we have.'

This is something that people tend to say in Mumbai: 'We have an emotional bond.' Or, 'He is like an older brother to me'; 'I think of him as my son,' that sort of thing. People in India like to make everyone part of an enormous psychological extended family which, at its worst, can be a little stifling and render all the claimed relationships a bit meaningless. But with the Bachchans and the Chopras there is a genuine warmth and love that has lasted for thirty years. Chopra elaborates:

'One Holi he had his arms around my wife Pam, Jaya and I, and was telling us that he loved us with tears in his eyes. (He used to drink champagne in those days.) Once we all had dinner with Anupam and Kiron Kher[25] and we were talking about the good old days. It was as if we were seeing just them, as if there was no one else there – it was just the four of us – so in the end Anupam and Kiron went away.'

I ask Chopra if we can talk about the AYM films first. He agrees.

'Zanjeer[26] had become a big hit and Amitabh and Jaya had got married. Pam and I were on the same flight as them when they went to London for their honeymoon and we were going there for our annual holiday. I said to him that I would like to do a film with him when we got back. I planned to make Kabhi Kabhie and had narrated the story to him.[27] He agreed to do it but then Salim-Javed came to us with Deewaar and narrated the story with all the dialogues. They said that I should take Amitabh for the role. Amitabh

---

[25] Anupam Kher is one of India's best-loved character actors. Best known in the UK for his roles as the dad in Bend it Like Beckham and Bride and Prejudice.

[26] ('The Chain', dir. Prakash Mehra, 1973). The first hit film that shifted people's perception of Amitabh from gentle middle-class boy to lithe, vaguely menacing man.

[27] It is one of the unique things about film production in Bombay that up until recently, there were no complete scripts ever. Directors and producers would go and narrate the story to the star and they would agree or disagree on the strength of the director's narration. Then the star would be given his lines on the day of the filming. Amitabh had to beg director Hrishikesh Mukherjee to give him the climactic death scene in Anand in advance, to allow him to prepare.

said to me: "*Paaji*[28] we should make this, it is very powerful." We made it in ten months and recorded and picturised four songs, ultimately. We had passion, it was a focused thing. We also all became very very close with Shashi [Kapoor].[29] Then we went on to make *Kabhi Kabhie* almost simultaneously. These two films are hugely different things for an actor and a director, and no one could have done the roles like Amitabh. You could feel the irony of the thing: *Deewaar* got seven Filmfare awards but Amitabh didn't get best actor.

'In *Deewaar* there were lots of sequences with Parveen Babi at the Oberoi. Amitabh would shoot all night and then go to Bangalore and shoot for *Sholay*. He stayed at a party of Javed and Honey's[30] until 4 a.m. so that he could catch the morning flight and be at the shoot on time. He did this for a week.'

'Really? He must have been exhausted.'

'Yes, but with Amitabh you can be sure that he will come on time. Amitabh is never late for professional work and he won't change the dialogue – usually when actors become stars they won't say certain lines. He would never do that, he is very disciplined. I remember when we were shooting for *Kabhi Kabhie*, I met Amitabh and Shashi coming into the hotel one morning in their suits. They pretended that they were ready for the day's shoot, that they weren't coming in after a night on the razzle. I told them they were needed in an hour. They weren't late – they had no choice but to go straight to the film, snoozing in the breaks.' He chuckles.

'Shashiji and Amitabh sound like they were a lot of fun to work with.'

Chopra nods and says, 'During the *Kabhi Kabhie* shoot in

---

[28] A term of endearment: 'elder brother' in Punjabi.

[29] Shashi Kapoor is one of the Kapoor film dynasty. More about him later.

[30] Javed Akhtar's first wife was the actress Honey Irani. His second wife is the actress and political activist, Shabana Azmi.

Goa, Amitabh and Shashi disappeared one day. Shashi would never shoot on Sundays and one Sunday he said, "OK, you shoot with the others, we're both taking a holiday." They didn't show up that night, we were all really worried, we didn't know which beach they had gone to. Finally they came home very late and drunk. They had got drunk and fallen asleep on lilos and only woken up when they heard the noise of the rescue helicopter!'

We laugh: me in amazement, Chopra in delighted recollection.

'Do you think he changed after the accident?' I ask.

I have this idea that the key to understanding Amitabh lies in the accident that happened during the shooting of *Coolie*. A while back I asked Amitabh what he thought of this. I had been thinking about him dying, his body packing up, and wondered whether this would have caused some sort of brain damage. Amitabh told me he had lost 50 per cent of his brain. Oh how we laughed, but wind-up aside, he agreed that he had changed after the accident. And you can see it when you watch his movement in the later films.

Chopra puts it down to the fact that the accident was like nothing else in cinema history – the country went insane at the idea of his death:

'I have never seen such adoration as there was after the *Coolie* accident – millions of letters,' says Chopra. 'My son, Aditya Chopra, wrote him a letter and Amitabh replied when he could hardly move. When I left my house one morning I was stopped by a small boy who begged me to use any of his limbs if it might help Amitabh. You see these things in our films but to experience it in real life was very powerful. He is not living one life, he is living many lives. It is His [God's] will that he survived. But his will to work is something very powerful.'

I nod in agreement. Amitabh's hunger to work, to live his life to its maximum limits, to push himself constantly, even when ill, is quite extraordinary. He has an insatiable appetite for life and for work and, most importantly, for success.

Because it was Amitabh, the accident that took place on the set of *Coolie* was no ordinary accident: it was a defining moment in the history of post-Independence India.

The Accident

In 1982, Amitabh was shooting a fight sequence in Bangalore. It was a pretty standard fight; Amitabh was getting the crap kicked out of him by the baddie, but would soon rally and give better than he had got and all would be A-OK. Amitabh was known for his superior fight scenes. Ever since he had arrived as Hero Number One, fights had become much more frequent in films, so doing a fight sequence was no biggie for the Big B. But on this fateful day Amitabh fell awkwardly on a table corner and crumpled to the ground in agony. The director congratulated him on his realistic acting. Amitabh wasn't acting. By the next day he was in hospital, unconscious and with a stomach that was as stiff as a board. Eventually someone noticed on the X-ray that he had a rip in his intestines, the contents of which were seeping into his abdominal cavity – if this continued he would die. They operated immediately, as soon as they could airlift him to the better-equipped Breach Candy Hospital in Mumbai. There he underwent more operations as, one after another, his vital organs packed up on him. For more than a week, it was touch and go whether he would live or die.

The country went into shock. Indira Gandhi, Prime Minister at the time, came to see him and her son, his childhood friend Rajiv, cut short his American trip to visit the hospital. Thousands of fans underwent penances and made pacts with their gods.

The show ran and ran, weeks went past with the situation developing hourly and keeping everyone gripped, glued to their radios. Amitabh told me of a guy who promised to run backwards from Baroda to Mumbai, a distance of 425 kilometres, to say prayers in a particular church if Amitabh got through. He succeeded, and was rewarded on this plane by being met there by the man himself.

Today Chopra looked out of his window at one of the last remaining mangrove swamps that lies between Juhu's main drag and one of Mumbai's north–south trunk roads and concluded:

'He may be up or down but the people outside his house is never less.'

Chopra has had his ups and downs but today he is one of the most important men in the business, not just because of his almost uncanny ability to produce hit film after hit film in a notoriously fickle industry, but also because of his sheer longevity. He is the only film maker Amitabh worked with during the seventies who is still making films today. He is one of the few who know how physically and psychologically hard it is to keep going, day after day.

How did he put it? . . . the people outside his house is never less.' There was an almost alchemical transformation that occurred to Amitabh after the accident.

During his time in hospital, communal prayer meetings were held where fans could pray together for his survival. When he finally did pull through there were banners proclaiming, 'God is great! Amit Lives.' I sometimes wonder if that level of devotion can change you physically?

From then on he was no longer just a film star. He had been transformed by the intense interaction between him and his fans. As soon as he returned home from hospital after his accident, past all the banners, the fans began to come and collect on their debt. They would gather each day outside his house for *darshan*.

Darshan is a practice that is at the heart of popular Hinduism. It involves seeing and being seen by the gods in the temples, but this is a special kind of seeing, a very physical act, a kinetic exchange between the viewer and the viewed. It is as if the gaze flows from the eyes of the gods in a kind glittery stream and touches the worshippers. The verbs in Hindi are *darshan dena* and *darshan lena* – to give sight and to take sight. When you go into a temple in India you ring the bell to alert the gods to your presence, so that they can bless you with their benign gaze. It is a practice that is not just confined to statues of gods but also to the gurus who impart religious teaching throughout the Subcontinent. Special people have a special gaze; you can gain something from being on the receiving end of it. Amitabh once said:

> It's very peculiar because it wasn't there before the accident. I feel it is pure curiosity, nothing permanent. It's uncanny – even if I go away it starts the very day I return. It keeps happening because I do go out and see them. There is nothing wrong in waving or smiling at them is there? Surely every actor, all of us know that this will disappear the day that there is someone better.[31]

Quantum physicists have realised that by looking at an experiment people affect the outcome. If you fire a particle and then look at it midway between two points, you affect where it goes. It is not your will that affects it; you can't change its direction by thinking 'Go right! Go right!' really hard, but simply the act of observation affects the way it goes. And so you can only ever know either the direction *or* the position of a particle at any one time. Although Amitabh Bachchan is slightly more complex than an electron, and the forces working on him are rather more complex than a lone photon and the beady eyes of an experimental physicist, the effect of being watched is not to be underestimated. We all act slightly differently if we know we are being watched, and for Amitabh the change from being almost entirely viewed as the characters in his films to being

---

[31] Khalid Mohamed, *The Times of India*, 10 April 1983. It must be pointed out that no other actor has had the masses gathering for *darshan*.

watched all the time must have been not a little disconcerting.

The next twenty years of his life were going to be even more of a roller coaster ride than the forty years that had culminated in the accident. On awakening from his illness he found himself strapped into a roller coaster car. Amitabh would have to learn over and over again how to manipulate the inertia as he hurtled first skywards and then back down towards the concrete, his knuckles whitening as gravity left his gut in the air and sucked him downwards towards the crowds who never tired of staring at him – mouths open, ice creams melting. Just as he could smell the sweat and polyester he would be flung back up to suck in the ultra-violet tang of ozone . . . Up and down, up and down. It was as if, in the moments that he was dead, God, amped up Hindi film style to the point of distortion, had yelled at him through the void: 'Scream if you wanna go faster, *yaar*!'[32]

Once I went to see Amitabh when he was shooting in the basement of the Airport Centaur. Even uglier than the Juhu Centaur (think tropical social-realist bling), this one looks like a medieval keep done on the cheap with substandard Lego. They were shooting near the huge kitchens and the room had that foetid and clammy feel that is common to all commercial kitchens. Amitabh was waiting to do his shot and was presented with a huge plate of delicious steaming samosas.

He took them and thanked the man who had given them to him whilst stopping him from touching his feet. Quite a tricky manoeuvre to accomplish without the samosas rolling off the plate. He took a bite of one and then offered them to me. I readily accepted. They were delicious.

'These are from a man who made his fortune selling samosas in the interval at cinemas,' Amitabh told me. 'He found that when it was one of my films playing he could charge more for

---

[32] 'Yaar' in Hindi has a similar feel to the liberal use of 'mate' at the end of English sentences.

his snacks. When I was in hospital he promised God that if I survived he would donate a truck full of samosas to the poor. After I came out he arrived at my house with the truck for me to bless. Now he gives me samosas.'

'Cool.'

He looked at me: 'Yes. Cooooool.' He said it like he was advertising mints.

Then he was called for a shot where he had to poke his gun through a hole in a door. Waiting for the shot to be ready he stood behind the door and poked his finger through instead and wiggled it around like a little worm. I laughed and ate another blessed samosa.

On the way back from Chopra's office I saw a taxi with a huge stone Shiv lingam roped to the top. It was filled with guys and careering through the rush-hour traffic, beeping its horn crazy style. I had to laugh out loud. I know that most men see their cars as some kind of penis extension, but not many can honestly claim to be transporting the phallic god of sex and death.

I called Amitabh to find out when I could come and hook up with him again. He sounded tired.

'I went to see Yashji. I had a good interview with him,' I offer.

'What did he have to say about me?'

'Oh, you know. Stuff. He told me that you shot for *Deewaar* and *Sholay* back to back, doing one during the day in Bangalore and then flying back to Mumbai to do the other. Is that true? That's crazy behaviour!'

'Yes!' He perks up. 'By the end of the week I was in hospital on a glucose drip . . . But it was such fun!'

'He also told me about you and Shashiji getting a little bit merry and falling asleep on your lilos, drifting out to sea, and getting rescued by a helicopter.'

'A rescue helicopter?'

'Has Yashji created a Hindi film moment?'

'There were no rescue helicopters! It was a tugboat chugging by. We had drifted into the shipping lane.' He sounds a bit uncomfortable.

I pushed on, 'What's it with you and water? I read that when you were in Calcutta you used to tie yourself to posts in the Hooghly River and wait for the boar-tide wave to crash into you?'

'Yes.' He studies his fingers.

'You were young! No one is going to think badly of you if you got a bit happy and did silly things.'

'Yes but I don't drink now, that's not who I am, it's who I was for a very short period and its being sensationalised isn't right. If it's mentioned in the press now it becomes the focus of the whole article rather than a couple of insignificant moments in my past. It's lazy.'

I felt a bit bullish when he said this and shrugged, thinking 'Why would he mind his youthful high jinks being written about? What else is he going to mind me writing about? Does he think that this is going to be yet another hagiography?' and left soon after.

But on reflection I have to say I am sympathetic: god knows I wouldn't want all my, erm, 'youthful high jinks' to be discussed and published. It is best for all involved that a tidy veil be drawn over those. It is a huge double standard that writers are guilty of. We are happy to dissect and regurgitate other people's failings and foibles safe in the knowledge that our own are never going to see the light of day. Perhaps it is a form of passive-aggressive behaviour: we could fall asleep on a lilo and get rescued by jive-talking-afro-wig-wearing aliens who impart to us the secret of peace in the Israel/Palestine conflict as they gently place us back on the beach but the general public still isn't going to give a fig. Whereas these folk that we write about need only take a different route to work and everyone wants to know why. Our obsession with the 'sensation' helps us trivialise the famous and thus affords us some sense of superiority.

Amitabh the Fun Guy

One thing everyone agrees on is that before the accident and his subsequent foray into politics, Amitabh used to be a really fun guy. I think this is mainly because he just loved acting and being an actor. I read an interview with the actress Raakhee that paints a very different picture of the young *ingénu* in film land from the man we see today.

Before shooting started for *Reshma Aur Shera* ('Reshma and Shera', dir. Sunil Dutt, 1971),[33] Amitabh was in Delhi staying at his parents' home. Raakhee would go on to play opposite him in some of their greatest hits, but at the time they were both struggling and penniless. She remembers their first meeting when he accompanied her on a group outing to see the Taj Mahal, when they were normal middle-class Indians. It was winter; the Mumbaiwallas were not dressed properly and were feeling the cold. Not so Amitabh who was dressed in an enormous Afghan coat. Unfortunately this coat stank and everyone begged him to take it off. He refused, so they threatened to push him out of the car. When all their pleas failed they emptied their perfume bottles over him in an attempt to make it more bearable. The stench of old, damp Afghan and cheap perfume must have been quite over-whelming.

The stinky coat notwithstanding, Amitabh seems to have made friends easily on these early films. During the shooting of *Reshma Aur Shera* he seemed to be having a ball. Sunil Dutt had definite ideas about order amongst his cast and crew. The

---

[33] Amitabh, whose deep baritone would soon rumble its way into the hearts of India's females, was playing a mute. This has become one of the greatest casting jokes of all time, up there, for the Bachchan fans, in the absurdity stakes with him being turned down for the job as broadcaster for All India Radio.

filming was taking place in the deserts of Rajasthan so there was not much to do. Raakhee describes the shoot:

> Since all of us had minor roles in the film, we had a lot of free time on our hands, but no freedom. Dutt*saab* was a strict disciplinarian and everyone on the unit was expected to be in costume on the sets irrespective of whether they were required for a shot or not. Still young we resented his authority and preferred to be in each other's company. Everyone in the unit was provided with a horseshoe-shaped tent and a personal camel to move around the location. We had strict orders to be in our tents before dusk and to make sure that nobody broke the rules. Dutt*saab* personally took rounds at night to check the tents.[34]

The novelty of having your own camel must have worn off after a while, especially if you weren't allowed to ride it and had to sit about on set in your costume while it glared balefully at you. Amitabh and the other junior male actor Ranjeet Kapoor got up to all sorts of mischief-making, including stealing beer (although, apparently, they put it back soon after) and carrying the sleeping cameraman in his bed and placing him outside the tent so that when he woke up after being in the frozen desert night air with a fever he had to cancel the day's shooting.

I think this is a bit of an odd sense of humour myself, but I guess you just had to be there.

Amitabh can still be a funny guy. Not so long ago I went to the Filmfare Awards party at the new *enormous* Mariott Hotel on Juhu. I was rocking in the free world with the guys from *Vanity Fair*, laying down some seriously great moves to some filmi song or other and, inexplicably, clearing the dance

[34] Bhawana Somaaya, *Amitabh Bachchan: The Legend* (Delhi, Macmillan India Ltd, 1999) p.82.

Call it evolution, transformation or a conscious duckling-to-swan (or vice versa!) process. Change, whatever its name, is integral, unavoidable, even desirable at times—a part of the filmi game, or more specifically, of the filmi face.....

In the following pages, Zeenat Aman, Parveen Babi and Shabana Azmi present themselves in their multi-faced splendour—a panorama of their individual and unique evolutive growth from the day they stepped into the industry, to now, at the peak of success.....

Who says Rekha has the monopoly of facial and other physical versatility?

CHANGING.....
CHANGING.....
CHANGING.....
FOR THE BETTER AND/OR
THE WORST!

Shabana Azmi, Parveen Babi and Zeenat Aman holding what appears to be a coven meeting.

floor. Abhishek came up, stood on a little step next to me and smiled in amusement. I laughed back but suddenly Amitabh was standing next to him staring hard in a pointed way at me. Then they did this father and son staring thing, managing to move their heads and eyes in sync, which totally fried my synapses. 'Argh!' I cried, covering my face, 'I can't deal with Double Bachchan Action!' and fled to the other side of the dance floor. They stood and laughed at me.

So he is still able to have moments of levity. He is just also prone to bouts of glumness. But then I think most stars of his generation are. I guess it's a cumulative thing; they have been through a lot by this stage in their lives. Especially the women, the heroines. When I went to meet up with Amitabh on the set of *Ek Rishta: The Bond of Love* ('The Bond', dir. Suneel Darshan, 2001), I sat and chatted for a bit to Raakhee. In her films she always comes across as a bit depressed. Perhaps I don't get her sad poetic beauty because I am not Bengali. But that time she seemed just depressed – either that or she didn't want to talk to me!

Life has not been kind to many of the heroines of the 1970s. Shabana Azmi has done well though.[35] She married Javed Akhtar and lives a good productive life as a political activist. When I went to see them last spring she was endlessly amused by my need to find out stuff about Amitabh.

'I just want you to know that I think your outfit in *Amar Akbar Anthony* ['Amar Akbar Anthony', dir. Manmohan Desai, 1977] – you know, the flared trousers and the flowery shirt – was totally great!'

Shabana laughed and rearranged her hand-woven cotton *kurta*; she is a long way from that particular polyester dream.

---

[35] Daughter of poet Kaifi Azmi and heroine of the 1970s art cinema scene, she also made the odd Bollywood film. Daring to be part of both scenes was frowned on in those days – now everyone is at it.

'Can you believe, I designed the yellow bridesmaid dress I wore at the end myself!'

'*No!*' I am slack-jawed with amazement.

She is humoured by the effect this has: 'Yah, I was jealous that Parveen had that lovely big white dress so I put all the extra flowers on. I wouldn't be outdone!'

That evening we all went to an award ceremony together and she fussed over Javed*saab's* outfit, adjusting his shawl in a fond amused way. In the car on the way there he told us about his early days in Mumbai helping out at the Filmfare Awards. After the ceremony he was in the fifties screen legend Meena Kumari's dressing room and held her award for Best Actress.

'I decided then that one day I would get this award,' he declared

'What for? Best Actress?' I quipped.

He chuckled.

'Cheeky girl,' clucked Shabana.

Mumbai again

Saturday

I have spent the day in taxis. I feel sick. I have ingested so much lead from the pollution that I think I might weigh more than when I started out this morning. My arse hurts from the anti-suspension fitted as standard in all taxis. My breasts hurt from being boinged about over the potholes. I want to lie under a waterfall and be cleansed, both physically and spiritually, and then be massaged by lots of attentive and kind men.

At one point today my taxi ground to a halt at some traffic lights. As is their wont, the other drivers started to beep their horns. Sweat was dripping into my eyes.

A handful of beggars took this opportunity to race over to my car. Some kids started to sing a street version of 'Jingle Bells' but changed the words to 'Jangle bells jangle bells Santa Cruz' (Santa Cruz is an area in the suburbs). I handed out small change and fights broke out. A man came over and flopped what looked like a loaf of bread into my open window. It was in fact a huge growth coming out of his gut.

Gavin Fernandes

I couldn't help but recoil. *What is wrong with him?* I winced. I am not good with too many degrees south of normal.

I gave him some money. He took it and heaved his stomach-loaf out of the window and wended his way back through the line of cars. I am ashamed to say I breathed a sigh of relief.

The practice of maiming children so that they are better equipped to be the object of sympathy, and therefore better beggars, is one that is particularly hard for me to deal with. I was in Mumbai once with a couple of guys from England. One was finding the whole experience way too much. And, as is the way of such things, he seemed to attract all the most horrific cases: I have never seen so many truncated limbs and mutated growths as I did when travelling with him. One journey from North to South Mumbai was so extreme I was beginning to think that there was a beggars' convention in town. There were about three seriously maimed and handicapped people at each traffic light, jostling for space with all the butchest and most aggressive *hijras* in north India.

The poor guy was a wreck and I was just praying that he would be able to hang on till we got to my friend's place on the top floor above Woodlands at Kemp's Corner in South Mumbai, where we could whisk him up out of the chaos and get him a beer. But at the traffic lights at Hajji Ali a man came over and dangled his wrecked body across the front window. He had had his limbs broken so often that he was forced to move about like a spider. It was a shattering sight even for the taxi driver . . . That night my friend decided to go for a walk to clear his head: he was attacked by one of the packs of terrifying wild dogs that roam the streets. Mumbaiwallas steer well clear of them. It was pitch black, and in his terror to get away he ran over a whole pavement full of people sleeping who, not surprisingly, all set upon him. The next morning we sent him to the beach across the bay at Alibag for some R and R. This city is *ek dum maha hard core*.

Everything in Mumbai – even the simplest thing, like a taxi ride – is fraught with the possibility of difficulty and frustration. This city is chaos theory in action, anarchy in its purest form, self-organised, self-regulating and with apparently little outside intervention from the state or services. There is no direct 1-2-3, A to B linear-shlinniar movement and the only Newtonian rule of physics that seems to apply here is the Second Law of Thermodynamics and the principle of entropy, the tendency of all things to decay into disorder, randomness and nonsense. But most of all it's the human suffering and misery that crashes in huge waves around your head as you move about the city, the unrelenting flood of humanity that presses up against you whenever you leave your house or hotel. In Mumbai 'personal space' is simply not having someone stepping on your toes rather than, as I am used to, having your own cliff top.

'Bombay is a crowd,' wrote V. S. Naipaul.[36]

'Mumbai is apocalyptic insane-o-ville,' thought our young heroine as her taxi finally started to lurch across this peninsular town, from sea to polluted sea.

At this moment I am unable to remember what it is that I like about Mumbai. Or Bollywood.

What is Bollywood anyway?

The director John Ford said, 'Hollywood is a place you can't geographically define. We don't really know where it is.'[37] I guess that pretty much sums up Bollywood too. Bollywood resists definition – it is whereever the power happens to be concentrated that month, that year, depending on which producers and directors are making hits, which actor is currently number one, which actress can claim to be Queen Bee. But most of all, it is a state of mind. If you drive north from the Gateway of India, once you hit Bandra most thoughts revolve around the film industry in some way. It is a world unto itself, with rights and rituals as arcane, as seemingly meaningless as the Masons'. It operates in a more or less closed ecosystem, and can only be negotiated with a finely developed transactional mentality. A endless round of gift

[36] V. S. Naipaul, *India: A Million Mutinies Now* (London, William Heinemann, 1990).

[37] John Ford on BBC TV, 1964, in David Bordwell, Kristin Thompson, *Film Art: An Introduction* (New York, McGraw-Hill, 1979) p.xiii. It is a tribute to the power of Bordwell and Thompson's film studies classic that the programme on which this was said is not mentioned and has ceased to be relevant.

giving, favour providing and favours owed means that all business is conducted on a personal level, and all relationships are based in business.

Bollywood: it's a whole world, an addictive imaginary space.

Sunday

Last night we sat on the roof of Amin and Charlotte's building and ate pizza. We looked at the big fat moon that hung over the ocean. The warm sewage sea lapped the rocks and the few remaining palm trees rustled listlessly. They live in the little fishing village of Chimbai, squashed between Bandra and Pali Hill in mid-central Mumbai. Chimbai clings bravely to the edge of the land, refusing to disappear under the waves despite the huge lumbering high-rises that push and jostle for space at its back. Mumbai has an insatiable hunger for space, and profit wins over history and the poor every time. I breathed deeply.

'Tell me a story about Mumbai. A tale that sums up Mumbai for you,' I asked Amin. He drew himself up so that his barrel chest stood proud in the moonlight and, after thinking for a moment, produced an almost perfectly circular sentence:

'I can say one thing, not about Mumbai, but about life: dreams come true. Now, you won't understand what I mean if you don't understand what I'm saying. But you *will* understand what I'm saying if you know what I mean. Dreams come true.'

Dreams come true? Is this a story of Mumbai? Is writing a book on Amitabh a dream? Is the life of Amitabh Bachchan a story of dreams coming true in Mumbai?

It may just be that I am still feeling sick, but I am suffering from extreme overwhelmshon. Writing Amitabh's biography is an enormous task. The amount of information it would be possible to gather is quite staggering. I could, potentially, interview people who worked on every film he made. Each film always has stories attached and Amitabh has made more than 120 films. A book has just come out about *Sholay*. *A whole book on just one of his films* . . . Writing biographies today is so different from what it was in the days when Virginia Woolf called it 'the most restricted of all the arts'. She called it that because it had to be based on facts gleaned from letters, diaries, writings, and verified by family and friends. Which makes it sound nice and orderly and populated by decent chaps in tweed. Print media has gone bananas since then, and the amount of possible places from which to glean these facts grows exponentially almost daily. And so far I haven't met one chap in tweed, decent or otherwise.

Can you get claustrophobia from someone else's life? Perhaps knowing your subject well as a person is somehow detrimental to the biographical project? What if you admire someone as an artist and as a star and decide to write about them, but then, through the process of getting to know them, become totally cheesed off with their behaviour as a human being? Surely that must necessarily interfere with your ability to write about them *at all*?

As a professional biographer I should take my subject's foibles in my stride, and somehow maximise all situations. Or is this why so many biographies are of dead people?

OK, focus on the positive, Jess. *Sholay*. Can't get much more positive than that.

Sholay

I met Ramesh Sippy, director of *Sholay*, the best Hindi film ever, at a screening at Ad Labs in Film City a few years ago. I can't remember for the life of me what it was for. It must have been an Amitabh film because he and Jaya were there. I had come with a group of people including Aamir Khan. In the interval while we ate our snacks I somehow found myself

talking to Sippy. I caught sight of Aamir watching me nervously. Someone more distinguished came over and Sippy turned his attention to them. I went back to my group.

Aamir said, 'Do you know who that is?'

'Yes. Of course I do. It's Ramesh Sippy.'

'It's Ramesh Sippy, Jessica,' said Aamir, repeating the obvious just to make sure that I understood, as he is wont to do. 'He directed *Sholay*.'

'Yes, Aamir, *I know that*,' I hissed.

'I hope you were respectful.'

'Naturally I was respectful.'

'But you didn't look nervous. He was laughing.'

'Well, I wasn't nervous. I was funny. What to do?'

'He directed *Sholay*, he's a very senior member of the industry.' Aamir wasn't convinced. I rolled my eyes at him. Luckily the second half of the film started and the conversation was terminated.[38]

But he was right. Sippy is a director to be treated with respect. *Sholay* was without a doubt the high point of seventies cinema in India and the most successful Bollywood film of all time,[39] and yet there is something else that sets it apart

---

[38] This conversation was mirrored at the Marrakech Film Festival when I found Aamir chatting nonchalantly to David Lynch.

'What did you talk about?' I asked, breathless from being star-struck in the solar plexus after being introduced to Lynch, one of my big heroes.

'I told him what film to make next.'

'*You told David Lynch what film to make next? But you've never seen any of his films! Do you realise how important he is?*'

'You told me about his films. So I suggested he should make a film of *The Gypsy's Curse* [a novel by Harry Crews].'

'Hmm. Not bad. Not bad at all,' I conceded grudgingly.

'He was very surprised that I knew who Crews was.'

'I *bet* he was!'

[39] Until being overtaken recently by the jingoistic *Gadar* ('Mutiny', dir. Anil Sharma, 2001).

from the rest: a whopping dose of celluloid magic that everyone strives for and yet no one can manufacture.

We can say that technically it is a very accomplished film, made by a director at the height of his creativity and drive, or we can point to its fabulous script written by Salim-Javed in a frenzied two months of sweet tea and cigarettes, inspired by the unromantic revisionist Westerns by directors such as Sergio Leone and Sam Peckinpah. We can praise the performances and the ever-rocking soundtrack by the great R. D. Burman, but deciding *why* it is such a captivating film has to be the prerogative of each of its fans. It is a world as fantastical as other Hindi film worlds, and yet it seems as if it is more real than the world in which we live.

The main relationship in the film is between two buddies, misguided petty thieves who are brave and would risk everything for each other, as in *Butch Cassidy and the Sundance Kid*. Amitabh's character, Jai, is painfully hip, ironic and sexy. He was a mystery man; where his character came from was never made explicit. He was held perfectly in the moment, he appeared to have no desires for the future or gripe with the past. He was captivating because you had no clue how he would react to a situation; each time he reacted as his gut told him to. Amitabh got the role against all the odds – in the early seventies, when the casting was taking place, he was a flop actor. Yet now the idea of any-one else playing the role is ludicrous. Amitabh has said about it:

Veeru had all the punch lines while I was the brooding one.[40] We were bracketed eventually as a likable duo. We were crooks but merry crooks. We'd indulge in petty crimes but never in

---

[40] Veeru is Dharmendra's character.

killing or bestiality.[41] We walked into a job out of curiosity, without realising what we were getting into.[42]

The story is a revenge plot between ex-policeman Thakur Baldev Singh (Sanjeev Kumar) and a bandit, Gabbar Singh (Amjad Khan). Thakur hires two crooks, Jaidev and Veeru, to hunt down the heinous Gabbar Singh. The first half contains two flash-backs: one shows Thakur deciding to hire Jaidev and Veeru and recounting how they helped him defend a train against an attack by dacoits, deciding to go to jail rather than let Thakur die. The second shows Thakur hunting down Gabbar and sending him to jail. Gabbar then escapes from jail and massacres Thakur's entire family apart from his youngest daughter-in-law Radha (Jaya Bachchan, née Bhaduri), who was at the temple. The rest of the film is of Jai and Veeru defending the village, hunting Gabbar down and, naturally, falling in love: Jai with the widow Radha, and Veeru with the chatty *taangewalli* (driver of a horse-drawn cart used as a taxi) Basanti (Hema Malini). In the end Jai dies saving everyone's life and Thakur pounds Gabbar into submission with his super-powerful kicks.

One of the more delicious facts of Hindi film history is that when the film was released it was a flop. The public flocked in for the first weekend's shows, but to the consternation of the cast and crew, there was no reaction, no clapping or laughing or hooting, or any of the usual chorus of accompaniment to films. What was going on? Complete silence was not an option for a Hindi film audience. Panic set in. The

---

[41] I believe he means the second definition of bestiality, behaving in a way that is more appropriate to an animal than a human being, rather than the first, engaging in sexual activity with animals.

[42] Khalid Mohamed, *To Be Or Not To Be* (Mumbai, Saraswati Creations, 2002).

Sippys had pumped almost all their money into this film; if it flopped they would be ruined. The industry and the critics who saw the film at the previews and the premiere were harsh in their criticism. People love success, but they also love to destroy someone who seems preternaturally successful. Mr Ramesh Sippy was a cocky young director so they went at it with gusto. One top industry figure said wisely: '*Hindustaniyon ko aisi picturein nahin achhi lagti hain*' – 'Indians don't like films like this.'[43]

At an emergency meeting held at Amitabh's house options were aired. One thought was that Amitabh had suddenly become too big a star to die in two films (*Deewaar* had been released in January) so close together. Perhaps they should reshoot the end again over the weekend and have Amitabh and Jaya riding off into the sunset with their chums Dharmendra and Hema Malini; a job well done and love ruling supreme. The script writers Salim and Javed said absolutely not, they were still convinced it was going to be a massive hit. Ramesh Sippy decided to listen to his heart and go with the film as it was.

But by midweek the box-office receipts were down to 50 per cent and it was clear to Ramesh that he had, for the first time in his life, failed. He told the people making the prints, '*Printing band kar do. Abhi kuchh samajh main nahin aa raha hai*' – 'Stop printing. I don't understand what's going on.'[44]

But then a curious thing happened. Although there was little advance booking the theatres were full, and one cinema proprietor told Ramesh that his film was a hit. Ramesh asked how he could say that? The proprietor replied, 'Because the sales of my soft drinks and ice creams are going down. By the interval the audience are so stunned that they are not coming out of the

---

[43] Anupama Chopra, *Sholay: The Making of a Classic* (New Delhi, Penguin, 2000), p.161.
[44] *Ibid.*, p.163.

theatre.' Finally Ramesh understood why there was no reaction. People were overawed by what they were seeing. They needed time.

After this there was no, and I mean *no* looking back. *Sholay* ran and ran and ran and ran and ran and five years later was still running. Countless stories surround the reception of the film: of the black marketeers who bought property and put taxis on the road from the money they made selling tickets for *Sholay*; of the girl who prayed to Sai Baba to have her sight restored so that she could watch it, and by the interval was fully sighted.[45] The music company Polydor quickly caught on to the audiences' repetition of the dialogue and put out a record. They recognised that the character audiences loved to hate, who anyway had some tip-top lines, was the evil Gabbar Singh. Soon the dialogue:

'Arre o Sambha, kitna inaam rakha hain sarkar hum par?' – 'Sambha, what reward has the government put on my head?' 'Poore pachaas hazaar.' – 'A full fifty thousand.' 'Suna? Poore pachaas hazaar.' – 'Hear that? *Fully* fifty thousand.'

became to India what Clint Eastwood's 'Do you feel lucky?' speech in *Dirty Harry*, Robert De Niro's 'You talkin' to me?' in *Taxi Driver* or, for those of us who are slightly younger, most of *Star Wars'* truly abysmal but oh-so-great dialogues were in the West.

Quite simply, there is no other film in the world like it. It has a visceral, immediate quality that takes you by the scruff of the neck and pulls you in. There is never a moment when something isn't happening, when your attention is allowed to wander. You exit the theatre stunned, unable to connect to the world around you for a while. And Amitabh? Amitabh just eats up the camera – every time he's on the screen, he is all you look at. And why not? Amitabh Bachchan:

---

[45] OK, I made that one up.

A Devi Rana number inspired the hit song 'Mehbooba'

Helen, nicknamed the H-Bomb, seen here dancing a famous sequence in *Sholay*.

tough, sexy, ironic and brooding in dirty denim. What's not to love?

It worked! I feel much more positive!

A brief note on violence

There is something about Amitabh and the way he fights that sets him apart from other action heroes. I like to think that he accesses some well of primordial male energy, but maybe I just need to take a cold shower. Once in Jaipur I watched Amitabh doing a fight sequence. He punched and kicked and flew through the air in a way not perhaps, as he would put it, 'commensurate' with his age. I was standing behind the camera with the rest of the crew as Amitabh took out a few dozen clay pots with a stunt guy's head. Shards flew and the men around me laughed and shook their heads.

'*Dushum dushum*,'[46] said one.

Amitabh asked the guy if he was OK. He bounced up all smiles. Everyone carried on chuckling. Amitabh waggled his eyebrows at the stunt guy and slapped him hard on the back in a 'masculine mates' way. Everyone was happy. Violence rocks.

Amitabh, or rather, the Angry Young Man, is often credited with introducing not only anger but also violence to Hindi films. This is of course nonsense.

Throughout Indian cinema history the heroes have walloped the dastardly: sixties star Shammi Kapoor regularly beat up the baddie before handing him over to the cops; in the fifties Dev Anand wasn't above an almost effete but still effective punch or two. People want the hero to dispense justice; indeed 'fight master' Mahindra Varma thinks that a hero isn't actually a hero until he does this in as violent a way as possible: 'Until the hero beats the villain into a pulp, the audience doesn't enjoy a film', he says.[47]

In Amitabh's films, however, the violence became a justified means to an end rather than the last resort of a patient man right at the end of the film when the villainous bugger deserves it. In Amitabh's films the villainous bugger seemed to deserve it straight off. Throughout the seventies and eighties his physical prowess went from strength to strength, till he became able to execute moves that Spiderman would be proud of.

In *Zanjeer* in the early seventies he had a fight with Pran which left them both exhausted, both feeling the pain, and both respecting the other. By the time *Trishul* rolls around in the late seventies

---

[46] The sound foliœed in for the fight scenes sounds like *dushum dushum*, so that is what action films have become known as.

[47] Nasreen Munni Kabir, *Bollywood: The Indian Cinema Story* (London, Channel 4 Books, 2001), p.81–2.

the fight is heralded by Amitabh arriving at the scene in an ambulance. He tells the baddies that it is for them and sure enough, at the end of the fight, he piles the bodies into the back and sends them off to get medical treatment. In *Mr Natwarlal* 'Mr Natwarlal', dir. Rakesh Kumar, 1979) during the same period, he is first seen helping himself to someone's safe. The gang arrives and they tell him that this time he will not escape. The lights go off, and when they are switched back on again by a confused peon he discovers the whole gang bound and gagged by Amitabh 'I know Kung Fu' Bachchan. As his star persona grew, as he became a super-hero, the violence became less and less real, but more and more fun.

My favourite fight scene is in *Kaala Patthar* ('Black Rock', dir. Yash Chopra, 1979). It is not as iconic as the fight in the *godown*[48] in *Deewaar*, but to my mind it should be. The difference between the fights is that you are worried for Vijay in *Deewaar*; in *Kaala Patthar* you worry for his opponent – but not too much.[49] Salim-Javed keep us waiting till we are desperate to see Amitabh pound the crap out of the villain Mangal Singh (Shatrughan Sinha's character). For a good half-hour Mangal Singh has been winding up Vijay, being deliberately irritating and provocative, like a younger sibling who is determined to get under your skin. They are all set to fight, but then the cops arrive so the fight is postponed. The tension mounts. Mangal Singh is a loud-mouthed bully – will he be too strong an opponent for our thin, sensitive hero?

---

[48] Warehouse.

[49] Film stars in India tend to have a couple of names in films. Raj Kapoor was almost always Raj; Amitabh was most often called Vijay – it instantly denotes that his character has similar traits to those he had played in the past e.g. anger.

The next scene opens with Vijay walking towards Mangal, who swaggers towards him. Vijay then breaks into an easy run and as he reaches Mangal does this massive leap, arriving at a right angle and planting both feet on Mangal's chest. They fall heavily to the ground. A cheer goes up from the audience (me). It should end there. It doesn't. It's only begun. The fight is on. Raaaa!

Amitabh's image of a tough man doing the job in hand was enhanced by his insistence on doing all the stunts himself. Yash Chopra told me that he asked Amitabh to use a body double for one action sequence in *Kaala Patthar*, but Amitabh had felt that this would make the shot less effective because they had to shoot it with four cameras, 'The water used to throw him against the wall and he would fight against the water.'

Amitabh's physical ability, with acrobatic fight sequences that were developed especially for him, did of course set him apart. Shashi Kapoor could match him kick for leaping kick, as he does in *Trishul* and *Shaan* ('Destiny', dir. Ramesh Sippy, 1980), but there was an ease and a grace to Amitabh's fighting that made it look almost effortless. In the fight scenes in *Mr Natwarlal* Amitabh often arrives from the top of the frame, in a huge arching leap from God knows where, presumably in a gravity-defying spring from the ground, enabling him to take out a whole army of men with guns on horseback. In *Don* ('Don', dir. Chandra Barot, 1978) and other films, Amitabh often does a backwards somersault uphill, or on to a platform. While for us cinema-savvy folk it is obviously film played backwards, for those less versed in the technical possibilities of film, it must have been remarkable. Amitabh's fights in the late seventies and early eighties are a celebration of the power of the male body; a delight in the possibility of flight.

Monday

Went to see Amitabh again today. He was surrounded by people demanding his attention. We formed a little line of hopeful supplicants on our white plastic chairs outside The Bus. Flapping ourselves with bits of paper, trying to edge our way into the shade. I was happy to sit in the sun for a bit, being a mad English lady and knowing that I was a lunch appointment and so wouldn't have to wait *for ever*. Amitabh has started to have very modest light lunches of soups, which is good for my waist line. I always put on weight in Mumbai because I just eat so goddam much. My favourite thing is being able to have a *dosa* for breakfast.[50] I remember telling Rani 'perfect figure' Mukherjee that I liked a *dosa* with my coffee and she just looked stunned and horrified by my gluttony. Anyway, Amitabh told me over soup that things were really crazy at the moment, but that he was working out when we could do the interviews. It might be best not to do them in Mumbai but to wait till he goes 'out station'. Basically I am only going to get some proper time with him when there is a shoot happening some place other than Mumbai. I guess this means that I will just have to spend more time talking to the good folk of Mumbai.

The taxi driver who took me back into town asked me what people always ask me: 'What is he like?' I used to try to answer this honestly, but now I just say, 'He is a good man.' I mean, it's not as if I'm lying, and saying that he is a 'good man' seems to fulfil some deep subcontinental need that I don't quite understand. How does Amitabh describe himself? I once filled in a UK entry card for Amitabh. Under 'Profession' I didn't write Urban Demi-God like I wanted to, but 'Actor'. He took the card back and read what I had written. Looked at me like I was a total muppet, sighed in a pointed way as

---

[50] Fried pancake with a spicy vegetable stuffing.

only he can, neatly crossed out 'Actor' and wrote, 'Film Artiste'.

I laughed.

'What is so funny?' he asked.

'Not sure,' I admitted.

Tuesday

Today I got cancelled by Shashi Kapoor. I am fine with being cancelled by Shashi Kapoor a couple of times. He is a star. Stars cancel. It's cool.

So I called Jerry and told him to hold the front page, I was taking him to lunch. I picked him up from his office at Famous Studios and we drove into town. At a traffic light a woman came up and pushed her baby against the window. I suddenly couldn't breathe.

'That baby is dead,' I whispered. Jerry nodded. I found his hand and held it tight. The woman was saying something that I couldn't understand.

'What is she saying?'

'She's saying that she begged for money for food but no one would give it to her. Then when her baby got sick she begged for money for medicine but no one would give it to her. Now that her baby is dead she wants money to give it a proper funeral.'

'Oh, God.' I reached into my bag for my purse, fighting back tears.

'It could well be true, but there is a trade in dead babies from the hospitals for this sort of thing,' said Jerry, holding my shoulder. We looked at each other. Could it get any worse?

'But that isn't really the point, is it?'

He agreed and rolled down the window as I gave the woman some money.

After that I needed to get out of the taxi fast so he directed it to Swarti Snacks and did his best to cheer me up with a funny story. He had been asked to write an obit for Spike

Milligan. He wrote something really silly:

'Spike Milligan died of kidney failure. He had been trying to get them to pass their exams for some time but to no avail, so he gave up and died.'

The copy came back to him as: 'Although uneducated, Spike Milligan . . .' To have your own bad jokes come back to you as false facts! Terrible.

It reminded me of when I was living in Canada and my rib popped out from my spine after I'd given a drunken naked yoga demonstration. I had been waitressing while I completed my clown courses, but while my back was healing I couldn't hold the trays. So I went on Welfare. When they called me up to book a time to come and see the house, they asked if I had any contagious diseases.

'Only a contagious sense of humour!' I quipped (with apologies to Oscar Wilde).

The day before they were due to come I got another phone call.

'Apparently someone in your house has contagious eczema?'

I explained that I had said sense of humour and not eczema but they were not convinced and called my partner and me into the office, explaining that they didn't want to risk their worker's health. When we arrived we were put in a room with double glass between us and the interviewer. I felt like an Irish peasant arriving at Ellis Island, dehumanised and freakish.

'This is really silly,' I told the pretty young blonde woman who arrived in front of us, gesturing at the iso-cube we were in. 'I said sense of humour not eczema.'

She didn't crack a smile; her neat bobbed hair was smooth and didn't move much as she got out my forms. 'I'm getting married this weekend. I can't risk catching anything. Your name?'

My partner and I started to laugh, 'Oh well, if you're getting married you'll need a sense of humour! Come, let us breathe on you!'

No smile. She stared at me. 'You want to *breathe on* me?' She looked back at her door as if about to summon security.

'No, no,' I said. We needed cash. 'My name is Hines,' I said, resigned.

The translation of information is so fraught with all kinds of danger at the hands of copy editors and petty officials. But we also change stories as we tell them at different points in our lives. The past dramas are constantly reinterpreted according to what is going on in the present. We shift emphasis, we colour differently, we pick out different key events, and slowly the event that acted as a starting point is lost, is no longer relevant.

When I met with Yash Chopra, we talked about all his films but now looking back over what he told me I realise I have read it before, mainly in Rachel Dwyer's biography of him. I don't know how I could have got him to remember other stuff. I think he enjoyed his interview with me as it was a time to sit and reminisce, but I did get the feeling that he was just rolling out his 'Amitabh stories'. Really need to think about how to get behind those stories. Is all else just forgotten, or not in the right pattern in the brain to be recalled and told? Memory is very odd, she said, sagely.

Shashi Kapoor

Wednesday

I saw Shashi Kapoor on film for the first time when I was still a student at SOAS and Rachel was starting the research for her book on Chopra. I would go round to her place and eat her consistently exceptional food and lounge about watching films. One afternoon we watched *Waqt* ('Time', 1965), the first film Chopra directed, which stars, amongst others, a young

Shashi. In one scene he wears a starched white chauffeur's outfit. Rachel and I started to squeal with delight.

'Flippin' heck! He should need a licence to go out looking that sexy!' said Rachel.

He was, to my mind, the best looking of all the male stars of the seventies. The youngest son of cinema legend Prithvi Raj Kapoor (and brother of the screen gods Raj and Shammi Kapoor), Shashi was acting in films from early childhood. In his late teens he joined up with the Kendal family who needed a young hero to tour with them around India. He fell in love with Jennifer Kendal, they married in 1960 and quickly had a son. Shashi left theatre and joined the film industry primarily, he says, for financial reasons. But he had been making movies with his friends at weekends since he was a child. Well I mean why not, his brother owned a studio! Even though he was one of the top stars of the seventies, everyone got eclipsed by Amitabh. By the late seventies Shashi would often be playing Amitabh's younger brother or friend. But then, so was everyone else.

Today I went to talk to him about Amitabh. We met at Prithvi Theatre, built by Shashi to honour his father's memory after he died in 1972. I was running a little late and the taxi was inching its way to Juhu in first gear. I explained to the taxi driver that I had an appointment with Shashi Kapoor and would it be possible for us to go any faster.

'Ha, OK, I will go faster,' he agreed, and then continued at exactly the same pace but just moved the steering wheel about, his hands going up and down and up and down a bit, as they would have if we had been really pelting along and he was trying to keep control. His taxi must be ancient and its steering totally fucked, as this didn't make the slightest bit of difference to the direction we were moving in. I asked him how long he had been driving a taxi.

'Thirty years,' he told me, not taking his eyes off the road ahead, concentrating hard on his imaginary Monte Carlo experience. 'Ever since I arrived in Mumbai when I was twenty.'

Was I understanding him correctly? He looked seventy if he was a day – his face was shrivelled and deeply lined, a piece of old shoe leather.

'How old are you?' I asked him.

'Fifty,' he said. His kept his eyes fixed on the potholed tarmac as we overtook Schumacher on the corner and took the chequered flag at the traffic lights.

And people wonder why I make such a big deal about the pollution in Mumbai.

I bought Shashi a big bunch of pink roses that a little girl was selling to the cars at the traffic lights. When he arrives at Prithvi Theatre (thankfully a bit later than me) he is taken aback:

'Girls aren't supposed to give the flowers. I should have brought you flowers,' he smiles, the banter coming easily to him. His eyes still sparkle. So many people who worked with Amitabh in the seventies have lost the sparkle in their eyes.

'Oh, I figured that I was allowed to bring you flowers. I wanted to show you how much I appreciate you meeting me, and I knew that you'd understand that English girls like to do things differently.' He nods, still smiling, and hands them to one of his entourage.

'Let's have some lunch, shall we?' he asks as we settle down at a table under the trees.

Prithvi Theatre is one of Mumbai's oases. It is calm, civil and you feel a million miles from the hectic streets you travelled to get here. It also does a mean line in kebabs. I knew I had made the right choice in meeting up with Shashi at lunchtime. The Kapoor family are film royalty and have always appreciated the finer things in life. They also tend to swell beyond all recognition as they get older. I think it is because they are all so beautiful and talented; they somehow go into self-sabotage mode – the Marlon Brando syndrome.

Or it could be that they just eat and drink too much. Whatever the reason, the fringe benefit for me today is that I get to eat lots of spicy meat dishes.

I had of course come to talk to Shashiji about working with Amitabh, but as we sat there I realised I just wanted to talk about him, about his own extraordinary life. It was nice to be transported into his world and not be obsessing about Amitabh for a couple of hours. I did manage to ask him a couple of pertinent questions though, for example what Amitabh was like when he arrived in Mumbai. He started to laugh and said that one of the first times he met Amitabh he chucked him out of a film:

'I was filming *Bombay Talkie* with Ismail Merchant and James Ivory in 1970. There is a scene where Jennifer's car has to stop for a funeral procession. Amitabh was one of the actors in the crowd of men. I told him to leave the set and not do this role. He was upset, saying that he would lose out on earning Rs 50. I told him that he was going to be better and bigger than this.'

I raise my eyebrows at him. 'It must have been hard for him

to believe that at the time, having just arrived and not getting any work.'

'Yah, he was annoyed.'

Later on I told him that the stories I had heard about Amitabh being wild during the mid-seventies all started something like, 'Shashi decided' or 'Shashi suggested'. How did he feel about being such a crazy influence on Amitabh?

He shrugs and smiles, 'We became friends during the shooting of *Deewaar*. We had a lot of fun together. One time we were called to Pune to judge a beauty contest with Zeenat Aman.[51] We got quite drunk and couldn't decide which of the women we liked best – they all looked lovely to us. We thought they should all get prizes. Zeenat had been a beauty queen so she took over the proceedings and made the choices for us.' Shashi was undoubtedly wild in his youth, but now there is a mellowness tinged with sadness about him that makes me feel oddly safe. I don't often feel safe. Very strange.

I ask him what he likes about Amitabh.

'I like his clarity. He has a determination about him. He knows his strengths and his weaknesses, and he works very hard. He pushes himself. He is a masochistic Libran, always hurting himself physically and emotionally.'

After lunch Shashiji drops me back to Pali Hill. In the car I ask him why he likes Mumbai.

'People leave you alone to run your own life,' he says. This is a bit odd coming from someone who has had their own life scrutinised by millions. For most people, though, this is true. I tell him that I like Mumbai too, that I love its energy, although I find the pollution a bit much.

'Mumbai will never be clean,' he says with gentle, bemused amusement. He lifts his hand up and drops it again on the armrest. 'I am not sure why.'

---

[51] One of the top heroines of the seventies.

CHAPTER FOUR

*'Truth is contrary to our nature, not so error, and this
for a very simple reason: truth demands that we
should recognise ourselves as limited, error flatters us
that, one way or another, we are unlimited.'*

Johann Wolfgang von Goethe

Prakash Mehra

Thursday

Today I met with Prakash Mehra. As one of the most successful directors of the seventies and eighties he, along with Yash Chopra and Manmohan Desai, made Amitabh Bachchan the all-singing all-dancing Angry Young Man we know and love. Most importantly it was Mehra who, in 1972, took a chance on a flop actor and cast him in the lead role in *Zanjeer* as a policeman who goes outside the law to bring his parents' killer to justice. It was a gamble, but it paid off big style for both director and actor and heralded the birth of the new type of hero, one that Amitabh came to personify.

Mehra's office is in the Kings International Hotel. This squat, unimpressive low-rent place is overshadowed by the hulking shell of the Hotel Horizon, a concrete monstrosity, shipwrecked on Juhu beach. Hotel Horizon never fails to frighten me a bit with its empty rooms, blackened eye sockets staring into the past, at the glittering seventies and eighties when it was illuminated by filmi parties and weddings. It is nothing but ugly; it has no redeeming features. I don't know why it is empty but it is, spookily void.

I sat and waited for him in his office which is lined with wood panelling that has been made to look like bits of caramel waffle. How did they do it? Was each panel carved out of a single piece of wood, or is it strips that have been joined? No joins visible. I squinted at it, wondering if I would have time to get up and inspect it before Mehra arrived. But I didn't think it would do to be caught fondling his walls.

The furniture would sell for a fortune in the retro shops of Shoreditch: taupe leather and tubular steel chairs – small, squashy and rounded. And with a desk to match of smoked glass, leather and steel. All it needs is a couple of guys with 'nohawk' mullets in skinny-arsed hipsters and slightly too tight shirts, drinking pints of Kronenbourg, and I could be back home in Hoxton.

There are lots of little shelves displaying the usual array of awards and commemorative plaques of his big films: 'Seventy-five Weeks' for *Namak Halaal*, '*Laawaris* Golden Jubilee', a huge bottle of Vat 69 – the ubiquitous drink of all film villains and no hope drunkards – to celebrate '*Sharaabi* Golden Jubilee'. And, of course, there are lots for *Zanjeer*, the film that propelled Amitabh into the big time.

Prakash Mehra comes in wearing shorts and a T-shirt; he has a hugely distended belly which sits on top of his very skinny legs. The effect is quite alarming; he looks off balance and I fear topplage any moment.

I explain I am writing Amitabh's biography.

'That only his wife can do,' he tells me emphatically.

'You're right,' I agree, smiling. I don't bother arguing the point. 'But would you be so kind as to help me have a stab at it?'

MAY 31,1984

TODAY

AMITABH BACHCHAN

PRAKASH MEHRA

FILM INDUSTRY

MANMOHAN DESAI

THE
BIG BUDGET
SURVIVORS

LARKINS SPY CASE : NEW DISCLOSURES
UTTAR PRADESH : PRIVILEGED MLA'S · TAMIL NADU : TEMPLE POLITICS

'Yes, yes,' he agrees affably. We start with *Zanjeer*.

'The movie made him,' he says, 'If it wasn't for that film he would not be who he is today. It happened by the grace of God, who is the one to make someone or destroy him. It was destiny.'

'Indeed. But why did you choose Amitabh in particular?'

'I saw him as per the script. I liked his voice and eyes, this worked with the character – a cop who speaks very little and has all his expressions in his eyes. I had seen *Bombay to Goa* and had liked one particular sequence, the action sequence with Shatrughan Sinha.'[52]

Bombay to Goa. Who would have thought this unassuming, charming cautionary tale of what happens when nice middle-class girls get involved with the film industry would have had such a knock-on effect for the whole of Indian cinema history? *Bombay to Goa* happened at a time in Amitabh's life when he was pondering his options as an actor and not liking what he saw. He told his mother that he might have to consider becoming a character actor.

Saviours rarely ride in on a white charger. They infrequently swoop down on a rope to whisk you away from danger; they hardly ever appear with a steely look in their eyes, accompanied by a stirring background score. You can seldom swoon against their manly chest, knowing that everything will be all right now that they are there. And there sure as hell ain't no happily ever after, with the two of you blissfully futzing around the castle. But while Amitabh was hanging around on pirate ships, batting his eyelids hopefully at the big producer/director teams of the day who he thought would be his saviours, his real knight in shining armour was entering stage left, in a dwarf outfit. S. Ramnathan, a diminutive film director from Madras was making a low-budget film called *Bombay to Goa*, and he needed a hero.

The reason that this film is now legendary is because it

---

[52] *Bombay to Goa* (dir. S. Ramnathan, 1972).

contains a fight sequence that convinced Salim-Javed that Amitabh should be used in their tough cop flick *Zanjeer*. They recommended him to Prakash Mehra. I watched this fight recently to see if I could see what it was that they liked. And – can you believe it? – I could. As soon as it starts there is a definite change in Amitabh's quality of movement. Up till then he has been trying to do a cheeky-chappie hero and looking really uncomfortable doing it.[53] When the fight starts he suddenly relaxes; he looks focused and physically engaging. It's like the weight shifts out of his head and into his pelvis. It is, of course, easy to see this in hindsight but it was very perceptive of Salim-Javed to notice it despite the awkward romantic hero act he was doing for the rest of the film.

The film was a hit, and after the success of the next film in which he used Amitabh, *Hera Pheri* ('Funny Business', 1976), Mehra decided that there was only one actor for him. He says that when people came to narrate scripts to him he would tell them: 'If it is for Amitabh Bachchan then please narrate it, if it is not then please don't bother.'

'I was having an obsession with him. The movies were not for the high-class gentry; they were for the masses,' says Mehra. 'After *Laawaris*[54] Amitabh gifted me two watches and said: "I must admire your confidence; you knew this was going to work."'

Mehra shifts in his chair and looks at the awards on his wall. 'Then I wanted a comedian and I made *Namak Halaal*,[55] in which he is a buffoon. It took him three days to memorise the "English is a very funny language" speech. He said, "You have to do this sync, I will not be able to dub it." I had five cameras running because I didn't want to take any chances.'

---

[53] Rajesh Khanna was the reigning hero of the time, the best chocolate-box romantic hero ever.

[54] *Laawaris* ('The Orphan'/'The Unwanted', dir. Prakash Mehra, 1981).

[55] *Namak Halaal* ('The Faithful One', dir. Prakash Mehra, 1982).

Personally I find *Namak Halaal* almost impossible to watch: I can't bear Amitabh's imbecilic character, but the 'English is a very funny language' speech really is very funny. Amitabh is desperate to prove to his boss that he is good for the job as part of a hotel's housekeeping staff. The manager says that he has to be able to speak English. Amitabh replies that he knows such good 'Inglish' that he can leave the 'angrez' (English) behind. And then in English with a super-strong accent he says, 'I can waaalk Inglish, I can taaalk Inglish, I can laugh Inglish because Inglish is a berry phunny lanuguage.' And then he launches into two lengthy speeches about cricket with lots of play on words. The thing that makes me laugh is Amitabh's serious face when he has delivered this rant, and then the question, 'Do you have any comment to make on my general knowledge?'

I realise that Mehra only remembers what was important to him: why he chose Amitabh; the fact that Amitabh could turn his hand to anything; the broad definition of his films – is it a comedy, is it a tragedy? I wanted to discuss the finer points of the concept of Angry Young Man, but Mehra is a practitioner who doesn't really give a damn about what his films signify, unless we are talking box-office returns. So I take a different tack and go back to my favourite question:

'Did you notice a change in Amitabh after the accident?'

'He was more humble after the accident. Nowadays he is totally different to what he was; so humble and so nice.'

'What are you working on now?' I ask.

Mehra shifts forward in his seat and places his hands on the clouded glass table, staring at his feet through the murk:

'I haven't made a film in thirteen years because I have diabetes. My wife had a brain haemorrhage and has been in a coma for the past year and a half. An air hostess who is a family friend and was there with her when it happened told me, "Keep your heart strong and listen to me. You are going to lose your wife." My wife has had nine operations and I have kept saying to her,

"Please don't leave me please don't leave. I am here with you."'

I am silent, stunned by his reality.

He looks down at his hands, turns them over, and then turns them over again. I want to say something that will offer some hope to a man who suddenly seems so lost. The waffle walls seem to be very close.

'Amitabh says that he will do another film with me. I will only make a film with him,' he offers smiling but, I think, not really believing what he is saying.

I look about me at the memorabilia of his past successes. They are all wrapped in a protective plastic covering to defend them against the relentless Mumbai climate. The plastic is old, brittle and discolouring. They are dead lumps of wood and metal – detritus washed up from the other side of yesterday, specimens in dirty jars of formaldehyde, suspended in death.

Prakash Mehra has stopped reminiscing about the good old days. We are definitely in the harsh light of the present day. It is a long time since Amitabh gifted him two watches. A man enters the room and Prakash Mehra nods his head at him. He tells me that now he must go for his work-out. I nod and thank him for his time. Back out in the warm evening air I feel as if I have escaped.

Amitabh relaxing on set with Prakash Mehra and Parveen Babi.

Friday

Felt quite depressed by my meeting with Prakash Mehra yesterday. Felt unable to face yet more calls so went and bought myself some curtain material.

This film industry is so harsh. OK, all film industries are harsh. A couple of years ago I wanted to make a documentary about how hard it is to be a Bollywood film star. I told Amitabh, declaring that most stars of yesteryear are either dead or mad.

'You can't say that,' he exclaimed. 'You'd get killed!'

'But it's true, isn't it?' I insisted.

He stared out of the window.

'Isn't it?' I tried again.

He looked at me blankly. 'What?'

Saturday

I couldn't sleep last night so I got up, crept out of the house (leaving a note), went and woke up a taxi driver and persuaded him to take me into town.

Dawn at Baanganga in Malabar Hills. A tank[56] lined with old temples where old sadhus pray to the rising sun is one of my favourite things in the whole wide world ever. I love watching the city

Gavin Fernandes

---

[56] This is the term given to the many 'enhanced' pools of water all over India; they are often flanked by one or more temples.

come to life, everyone doing their thing, people walking walking walking through the night from miles away to the Siddhivinayak Temple every Tuesday, doing a bit of yoga on a roundabout, wheeling their fruit and veg stalls, trying to hold life together whilst sleeping on the pavements. I asked the driver to take us under the flyovers. I like the whole *Blade Runner*, post-apocalyptic urban thing you get there. It is all hazy and dark, with this weird half-light that filters down from the bright lights that line the highway. There is a definite two-tier city around these flyovers – below them the lower-middle classes continue to struggle through life in the grimy smoggy dark, and above rich Mumbai whizzes over and onwards. Baanganga on the other hand, just beyond the Hanging Gardens and the Towers of Silence, is timeless ancient India.

Apparently on this spot Lord Rama rested when he was exiled from Ayodhya. His wife Sita was thirsty and so he fired an arrow into the earth to summon the Ganga to give him fresh water. Jerry took me here on one of my first visits and, ever helpful, told me that if I walked clockwise round the tank, all my sins would be washed away. So I do this now every time I come to Mumbai, but it seems a little easy. Quite frankly, I don't think I am going to be able to perambulate my way out of my bad karma. It will be more a question of thousands of years of harsh penance on top of a mountain. But still. Going there feels spiritually grounding.

I managed to talk to Amitabh briefly today. His father is very ill again; they are going to have to send him in for more surgery. I didn't ask him about the interviews. He *knows* what is needed, after all, and I just want to be a supportive friend right now.

N. C. SIPPY PRESENTS
HRISHIKESH MUKHERJEE'S

MILI

EASTMANCOLOR

Hrishikesh Mukherjee

Sunday

Today I called Hrishikesh Mukherjee, father of what became known as 'middle-class cinema',[57] and asked if we could meet up, but he just hollered at me that he was an invalid and couldn't possibly see me. So there we go, no interview with him. Poor chap, I think he has arthritis. It is a shame not to be able to see him, but people have warned me that he has become quite reclusive. That is so typical. The guy has a crippling disease but because he isn't seen he gets labelled as reclusive. Mukherjee was the man who gave Amitabh his first hit, *Anand* (1970).

The most important thing about *Anand* for Bachchan was that he got to play alongside the reigning superstar of the time, Rajesh Khanna. Mukherjee's use of Khanna in *Anand* and in *Namak Haram* ('Traitor', 1973) is similar to the use in 1990s British films of glamorous American heroines (e.g. *Four Weddings and a Funeral* and *Notting Hill*) in otherwise quite low budget films. Khanna's presence allowed the film to appeal to the mass-market audience – who were all swooning over him after his 1969 hits *Aradhana* and *Do Raaste* – as well as the middle-class market.

Mukherjee is by all accounts an intelligent and thoughtful man who has worked in a different way in an industry that almost demands homogeny. From what I have read I get the impression that he was something of a father-figure to Amitabh in the early days. Sad that I can't talk to him.

The other reason I wanted to talk to him, of course, is because

---

[57] A series of films in the seventies that went some way to bridging the gap between the realist art house and the unrealist popular fare. Broadly speaking, it explored the personal individual space of its middle-class protagonists.

it was on the set of his film *Guddi* ('The Darling One', 1971) that Amitabh first met the woman who would become his wife, Jaya Bhaduri.

Jaya Bhaduri

Jaya Bhaduri graduated from the newly created Film Institute in Pune as a Gold Medallist in the late sixties and then came to Mumbai. The directors and journalists took to her immediately and she was often referred to as 'fresh' or 'different'. She is small and has a determinedly natural air about her. She doesn't seem to suffer from the neuroses – the please-please-will-you-all-love-me vibe – of most other film stars. Jaya exudes self-possession. She certainly didn't fit into the look of the heroines of the time – the great bouffant hair and winged eye make-up just didn't suit her. Luckily for her there was the newly emerged middle-class cinema for her to act in and she, au naturel, became their favourite heroine.

Jaya Bhaduri is one of those women that people tend to become very devoted to. She has a loyal coterie of friends and supporters. I remember once talking to some of Amitabh's fans who had just come from Mumbai where they had met with her. They called her Jaya*didi*, giving her the title of older sister to show their respect (another example of the need to make everyone part of your family). They said that I would become much more a fan of hers than of Amitabh. 'Everyone does,' they assured me. 'She is so kind and generous.' Jaya is someone who can create a sense of intimacy and make people feel special and at ease.

I have met her on only a couple of occasions and she was always polite and kind, although I think she found me a little rambunctious. At a screening of *K3G* (Karan Johar's sumptuous family drama *Kabhi Khushi Kabhie Gham*) I was one of the first

people out in the interval. (I wasn't, like most, trying to sop up the tears with shredded hankies and regain some composure before having to talk with people. That was one sob-fest that left me cold: too picture perfect, too sterile – like a really long Coke ad.) Amitabh and Jaya were waiting to greet their guests. I barrelled forward out of the auditorium, heading for the sandwiches, and almost ran straight into them. I skidded to a stop.

'God, Amitabh you are so mean to Jaya in this film!' I said, probably a little too loudly. I turned to Jaya: 'I think in the second half you should divorce him for mental cruelty.'

They both smiled politely.

'Yerrrs,' said Amitabh. 'The sandwiches are over there.'

I don't want to interview Jaya Bachchan until I have got the interviews with Amitabh over with. Partly because I am not sure what to ask her and how to do it. She is so good at being Mrs Bachchan. People always ask her about Amitabh, or about her life before she got married. They never ask her about what else she does or thinks about other than her husband and her children. This is of course very Indian, but I am not sure how to get to the other stuff. I guess I need more time to think it through. Perhaps she wouldn't want to talk about it. I mean, I don't think that being Mrs Bachchan can be the easiest job in the world, but at least she has a smoke screen to hide behind when it comes to interviews. It is by reading interviews with her that I have gleaned most of the information about the start of their relationship. Amitabh is not often asked why he fell in love with Jaya, or about their first meetings, etc. probably because gender stereotyping assumes what women want to talk about, e.g. relationships, and what men want to talk about, e.g. not relationships.

The shifting allegiances of the press have been more damaging to the portrayal of Amitabh and Jaya's courtship and marriage than to any other aspect of Amitabh's life. It is now very difficult to get a sense of the relationship that lies beneath the cobweb layering and the wildly diverse accounts offered by journos according to whatever attitude they had towards the couple that particular month. This ranges from the destructively slanderous in the late seventies to the blindly reverent today.

Jaya's description of their courtship on the sets of *Bansi Birju* (dir. Prakash Verma, 1972) and *Ek Nazar* ('A Single Glance', dir. B. R. Ishaara, 1972) reads to me like a chapter from *Lessons in Dealing with Difficult Men for the Modern Woman*. She says she quickly realised that Amitabh was a brooder rather than someone who shouted:

> To make matters worse, we had a scrap on the very first day. That too over something very silly. I always carry an *elaichi*[58] box in my handbag. So on the sets, as I was offering *elaichi* to everyone, I offered it to him as well. He looked at the box, at me and then turned away. His attitude made me mad! Irritated, I turned away too. But by temperament, I am not the brooding kind, so after keeping quiet for a few hours, I dropped my defences and got chatting with him . . . Again, he snapped at me. I tried asking him what the problem was, but he refused to answer. Exasperated, I decided to leave him alone.[59]

Ah ha! Early evidence of the Glass! So it is not just me that triggers this! It can't have been that easy for Jaya, feeling like she was constantly negotiating some unknown assault course blindfolded. She goes on:

> We were together all the time, spending almost all our free time with each other, but we never extracted promises. I was aware of his preoccupations. He had this unique way of judging situations, resolving conflicts. For instance, in a given situation,

---

[58] Cardamom.
[59] Bhawana Somaaya, *Amitabh Bachchan: The Legend* (Delhi, Macmillan India Ltd, 1999), p.40.

he'd say, 'If she says this or if she does this, she's my type.' And as it happened, I always did that. I sometimes feel that he married me because I did all the right things. He wasn't an easy boyfriend. Introverted and hypersensitive, but because I knew him as well as I did, I coped.

Unequal success or wealth between two people in a relationship can be a strain. Jaya was much more successful than Amitabh at the start of their courtship. In 1970s India it must have been especially difficult: the man was still supposed to be the main provider, and be better off financially. It can't have helped much that when the relationship finally did get off the ground the gossip press unfairly suggested that they were together because Amitabh was using Jaya for her success and contacts.

But there is a gentleness between them in the films that they acted in together. People are always looking for an on-screen chemistry between people who are involved with each other in real life. I see an understanding and a certain sympathy that isn't present in Amitabh's dynamic with his other heroines. I have to say though that I don't see it in *Silsila* or *K3G*. Giving up acting after she married, becoming a mother and being jolly good at being the wife of the most famous man in India is going to change you. She went from being the bigger star to being, in a way, the guest appearance in her husband's films.

Mumbai

Monday

It is getting very hot. Everything is covered in dust and looks exhausted – and it's only March! Months till the monsoons. It feels like the whole city is just gritting its teeth, putting its head down and getting ready to battle through the next couple of months. This evening, on my way back to Amin and Charlotte's, my taxi stopped on the Bandra Causeway. The stench from Mahim Creek was startling and made my eyes water. I once asked Jerry what made it smell so much. First he tried to blame dead fish, but after I squawked at him not to be so absurd he admitted that the river flows down from Pune through some of the most industrialised areas of India. He then told me that a friend of his had once been on an over-crowded commuter train and had been unfortunate enough to get squeezed out as the train crossed the Creek and fell in. He said that she actually turned green and spent years trying to get over the multitude of diseases she got from the toxic sludge. In the end though she succumbed. Jerry said, 'Her innards collapsed and she went home and died.'

The blocks of flats next to the Creek used to be blackened concrete corroded by the fumes; it was as if they were wilting from the stomach-churning reek. But now they have all been painted bright colours and they no longer look quite so post-apocalyptic. On the other side of the road lies the sea, edged by a broad beach. Here the big boats belonging to the Koli fish-ermen are drawn up, one of them covered by a huge film hoarding, like an enormous tent. It is somehow absurd that they still live there, almost exactly as they always have done. It's like having a little enclave of working farms in Belgravia. I have been told that they have their own system of self-governance, and that the police very rarely interfere in their world.

From my taxi I watched a small boy sitting on the ledge that runs alongside the road, edging the beach. A man came up to him. They had a short wordless exchange and he followed the man off, his shoulders slumping slightly as he went. I shud-dered at the howl of desolation his skinny little back gave off as they disappeared amongst the evening crowds and I felt sick-eningly sure that the guy was not his father. He was a customer.

What should I have done?

Happy family: Amitabh, Jaya and their two children.

Tuesday

Today I once again attempted to see scriptwriter Javed 'suddenly difficult to reach' Akhtar. I think I know why he is playing hard to get. I think he is still angry at me for just missing him at Heathrow when he came over for the Clerkenwell Literary Festival last summer. As I was waiting for him at the barrier, I got a text from Aamir Khan (who was also in London for the Festival) asking me to pick up some cigarettes for him. I popped to the newsagent's, got back and waited and waited, but no Javedsahib. He had come through while I was getting the fags and gone on into London. Luckily there were other friends meeting him too, but the whole thing was just awful. I have apologised over and over again but I think I lost all my Akhtar privileges that day. Which is gutting because he was a great guy to hang out with every now and then.

I remember one day going to a studio where they were recording one of his songs. We were, perhaps unsurprisingly, running a little late. As our car made its way through what used to be virgin mangrove swamps, now a big extended building site, Javed got a call from the music director who was already at the studio. After he hung up he turned to me and said with delight:

'They want to know, "Where is the poet!" Where is the poet, they cry! I assure them that I am on my way and they are satisfied.' He raises his hand as if he is delivering a particularly poignant couplet.

'I can't imagine poets being held in such high regard in Britain,' I tell him. 'Audiences at poetry readings usually look as though the poet is trying to infect them with a virus: defensive with all limbs crossed.'

Meeting up with people to discuss Amitabh is hard work. Everyone is really busy or really not, and either way they don't have very much time. Getting people to commit to a time here is a bit like running in dreams: I am working away and running and running but my limbs aren't moving and I am not moving.

The Angry Young Man – Amitabh Bachchan. I used to believe that I understood what this meant. He was someone who expressed the anger and the frustration of a new nation that no longer believed in its vision of a better future.

Ever since Independence in 1947, India had been enjoying the pine-fresh air of the moral high ground, but by the 1970s unemployment was rising, standards of living were falling, in Mumbai one third of the population lived on the streets, India had been to war with her neighbours twice and nobody seemed to have any answers to the country's problems. Amitabh's characters were members of the appallingly treated underclass who, rather than being crushed by the state or gangland dons, took them all on and won. He was the hero upon whose bashed but triumphant figure all the hopes and fears of India's disenfranchised young urban males was focused.

But this is so far removed from the person that he is.

Amitabh once told me about his time in New York during a sabbatical at the start of the 1990s. He was happy and just mooched about a lot. He learned how to cook for himself (you buy the box, pierce the lid and put it in the microwave).

But, he said, he hadn't liked the fact that he had been mugged a couple of times. I confess that when he told me this I just started laughing, which upset him a bit. I quickly stopped and said that I found it hard to see him, Amitabh Bachchan, the guy who can take on several people in a fight and win, getting mugged.

He frowned and tisked at me. I immediately felt stupid; I had made the unacceptable mistake of equating him with his screen personas. As a friend I was no longer supposed to do this.

'How did you deal with it?' I asked, chastised.

'I recited speeches from my films as I walked along at night. People just thought I was insane so they stayed away!' he laughed.

I looked at him with awe. Can you imagine coming across Harrison Ford in, say, Shanghai, walking along and reciting his lines from *The Fugitive* or *Witness*. What a trip that would be!

'Did you bump into any Indians?' I asked. 'They would have thought that *they* were the insane ones.'

'I can't remember,' he said, irritated with me again.

Feeling a little panicky about what I am not getting done, but I am not sure how to be pushier. I guess I would be if I had to do it for someone else, but it is different if you have to do it for yourself.

Later . . .

Just been for a run.

I love love love Jogger's Park. It's a little park that was built on a reclaimed rubbish dump at the edge of the sea at one end of Carter Road, looking across to Bandstand. And it's magical; an oasis full of trees and different tracks that run in concentric ovals separated by hedges. Its outer edge has benches for people to sit on, and then there is a broad oval to walk and jog around. This is surfaced with red earth, which is lovely to run on – it seems to push you forward – but it means you leave the park covered in a fine layer of dust. In the middle there is a playground for the kids. The lights are shaped like mushrooms, which adds to the air of unreality. It's like a little fairy den. I have never stepped off the red running track for fear that it might all disappear, turn back into a rubbish dump, the sound of children's laughter echoing in my ears as bits of old paper go flapping past. Today as I joined the groups of people going around and around I had to fight an uncontrollable urge to put my arms out and go *nerrrrrahoao* like an aeroplane. I realised what it felt like – like being part of the dust clouds that swirl around the outside of a spiral galaxy, the lights as big stars, the play areas and benches for old people and lovers as miniature solar systems. Love it, watching the moon grow fat over the sea and the teak trees and palm trees catching the ocean breeze. Once I saw a guy walking around the track being followed by two guards carrying AK47s. Only in Mumbai.

I met with Amin and Charlotte afterwards and we went to get coconut water with lots of yummy *malai*: coconut flesh so tender it has the consistency of phlegm, only way tastier. Amin pointed to another parklet (more a roundabout with a fence) in front of Jogger's.

'This is where the Laughter Club meets each morning,' Amin explained. 'They sit and laugh for about an hour. And clap. But mostly laugh, or they would be known as the Clapping Club.'

Wednesday

I had lunch with Manisha today. We bitched some more about men. It is amazing how this topic seems never to be exhausted! She is quieter than when I first met her years ago. I worry that the bullshit that everyone has to go through is getting to her. I think she should get out now, before it overwhelms her. The industry is so pressurised and false. As I was once told, no one is your friend or your enemy for long in Mumbai.

One thing coming out in the interviews is that people are not sure how Amitabh has coped with the phenomenal pressures on him. The nature of these pressures has shifted over time, but the main pressure of being so bloody famous that anything you do or say is seen as front-page news has remained constant for more than thirty years. In addition there have been moments of intense stress. Miss World was one such moment, and I was there to witness it.

One of Amitabh's less brilliant business decisions was to have his company host Miss World in India. The event crippled the company financially, but that was not the only thing they had to deal with. The pageant became a flash point for all the political parties and everyone was eating his brain about it one way or another. I went to Bangalore – it seemed the thing to do. Different right-wing groups claimed that such an event was degrading to Indian ideals of womanhood; some got so worked up that they threatened to immolate themselves if there was too much flesh exposed. The media caught on – nothing sells newspapers like a good immolation juxtaposed with a scantily clad lovely – and every tiny demonstration was photographed and reported to death.

At one point I watched a reporter from *Time Magazine* get a call on his mobile saying there might be petrol pouring nearby. Off he set at a run, his flak jacket flapping behind him, his Hush Puppies easily navigating the potholed streets to his hotel car. I followed in an auto rickshaw and arrived to see him walking away from what had turned out to be just more men ranting, looking distinctly cheesed off.

My favourite absurdity was when one politician, in a bizarre appropriation of imagery, threatened that if the event went ahead, 'rivers of blood would flow'. Perhaps right-wing bigots have a book of useful phrases, and 'rivers of blood' is the entry just before 'taking our jobs'.

The whole *tamasha*[60] placed massive stress on Amitabh as the one person who could make the event happen. The threat of possible violence affected ticket sales. And then even the police turned against him; on the eve of the event they demanded that he pay Rs 2.5 crores immediately, or the gates wouldn't

---

[60] Show, spectacle.

be allowed to open the next day. I know this is beginning to sound like the script of a particularly hackneyed Hindi film, but Amitabh had to beg and borrow the money and get it to the Police Commissioner by dawn the next morning. For an event that was due to go out 'live' the loss of prep time for the technicians could have proved fatal. But in the end, literally against all the odds, Miss World 1997 went off fine.

After the show I thought I would go over and congratulate Amitabh on a job well done. There was no chance of getting anywhere near him. He was being mobbed by respectable middle-class men, all hurling themselves at him in a mass of Raymond Suitings, ecstatic that he had pulled it off. To their minds, he had saved India's face in the eyes of the world.

I have decided to get out of Mumbai and go to Pune to do some work at the film archives. I have run out of Mumbai steam. You need to hit the ground running here, and after a while the initial momentum is just worn down. I don't have enough energy to push for everything about a hundred times harder than I would have to push in London. I don't seem to be getting anything new from the people that I am interviewing. Everyone is just repeating their 'Amitabh stories' over and over again. Crucially though, no one wants to tell stories on record that might piss him off. When I first got to know Amitabh he was in a downward slump – looming bankruptcy, flop films, business mistakes, etc. – but nowadays he is becoming more and more powerful.

It's a bit unnerving actually. How will this regained position of strength and respect affect our relationship? Will he still want to be friends with me, or will he have less need of a supportive chum? Will it affect how he feels about the book? I would like to think that he would remember things as they actually happened, and that if I could just pin him down to do the interviews I would get *the truth*.

Part Two

PUNE

CHAPTER FIVE

*'This is the West, Sir. When legend becomes fact,
print the legend.'*
The Man Who Shot Liberty Valance (dir. John Ford, 1962)

Monday, February 2002
Pune

I arrived in Pune this morning on the 6.40 train from Mumbai.
The train has some special name but I can't remember it, so I
am telling everyone back home that it's 'the Deccan Queen',
because it's a cool name and they are not going to know the
difference. I had to travel backwards so arrived feeling most
sick. It's a nice journey though, two hours inland from Mumbai,
up over the impressive and dignified Western Ghats, stopping
at Khandala, the Brighton of Maharashtra, to let off young
couples.

I am here to do research at the film archives. This is where
I believe, with my quaint western faith in print-bound linear
narratives, that truth is stored. In my mind's eye, biographers
spend lots of time in libraries sifting through boxes of precious
primary texts.

'Ah ha!' they cry when they stumble across some long-forgotten
letter to a long-forgotten lover. 'That's why he only painted in
cow shit for a summer! The Whitbread Prize is mine!' Cackle
cackle.

Archives are repositories of great clots of knowledge just

waiting, like a trilobite in a limestone cliff, to overturn outmoded beliefs and the established order. Research is ordered, methodical and grown up. It requires commitment, diligent reading and notetaking.

Problem hai bhai, is that I'm not here to look for the truth, I am here to read the gossip magazines: lies, rumours, malicious gossip, I love it all – bring 'em on boss. Amitabh is a little irritated at my decision to come to Pune.

'Why are you reading the magazines?' he asked. 'You're going about this the wrong way. The magazines contain nothing but lies and rumour.'

I then explained why I want to be here: I keep getting confronted by so much rumour and supposition that I want to find the root of these myths. They do, after all, constitute the public idea of Amitabh Bachchan's life so far. He just shrugged his shoulders. I need to figure out how the different parts of Amitabh's star persona were born, and what survived each stage to create the Ultimate Mythic Movie Star we know and love today.

So here I am in Pune. I am not sure about Pune. Everyone in Mumbai seems to regard Pune as a kind of green haven of civility and calm. To me it just looks like small-town India, as noisy and dirty as Mumbai but without the energy. I am staying at the Boat Club, which isn't very swanky, but it does have a view of the river. It also has a swimming pool so I have got myself a modest Maharashtrian lady's swimming costume. It almost comes down to my knees. I need to do lots of exercise if I am going to be here, on my own, going faintly insane as I get more and more obsessed by the minutiae of Amitabh's life. I might as well go mad and thin at the same time.

After I dumped my bags and signed in to the hotel I went to the archives. They are housed in a large, surprisingly agreeable, concrete building and surrounded by huge bamboos. It is a pleasant space, set back from the road in a compound full of trees, with lawns of that weird ebullient bumpy Indian grass.

I had an appointment with the director who was very sweet and basically told me just to get on with it. So I did. I have decided to read all the *Stardusts* from its birth to when Amitabh had his accident on *Coolie*.

Gossip magazines

So, why *Stardust*? Because it was the bitchiest and most fun gossip magazine of the seventies and the one that led the anti-Amitabh freeze-out after 1975. Nari Hira, an advertising executive, started it in 1971 as an outlet for advertisements of his products. But before long he had succeeded in creating a totally different type of gossip magazine to all the others that were around at the time. These, such as *Filmfare* and *Star and Style*, were very conservative and didn't reveal much about the stars that they didn't want known. The headlines were things like: 'Asha Parekh reveals, "My mother is my best friend!"' Hira decided that he wanted *Stardust* to be more like the famous gossip magazines of 1950s Hollywood, *Photoplay* in particular.

His stroke of genius was to promote one of his copywriters, the self-assured, glamorous ex-model Shobhaa De, to be his editor. De had a healthy South Mumbai dislike of all things filmi and thought the stars were talentless jumped-up *vernie*[61] trash who had all slept their way into the movies and whose houses were made almost entirely of polyester (and why not? After all, as the ads in the magazines kept telling them: 'It's a Beautiful Glamorous Age: the Age of Rayon'). De refused to meet any of them, sending her subs out to trek around the film sets and wait endlessly outside dressing rooms, gleaning rumours from the set hands. She found them absurd and almost physically repulsive whenever they turned up at the *Stardust*

---

[61] Vernie is from 'vernacular' and refers to people who don't speak English.

offices (dubbed 'the Cat House'), and she had no problem trashing the 'star bores and star whores' every month.

It is one of the things that makes Amitabh's story so unique – that at the height of his fame he fell out with the press, and for the next seven years they didn't communicate with each other. It's like the press deciding not to write about Tom Cruise or Brad Pitt. But the fans, hell almost *everyone* read those magazines, even if they were just something to flick through at the beauty parlour. And although they apparently didn't mention him *directly* I know that they talked about him *in relation to other people* i.e. his wife Jaya Bhaduri or, more often, his alleged mistress, Rekha. So, whether Amitabh likes it or not, they played a large part in creating the star we have today.

Since I am having so much trouble finding the real Amitabh I might as well have a go at finding the origins of the false Amitabh.

Archiving for beginners

So, after figuring out how the little card reference system worked, I ordered some magazines from 1970–71. The librarian took my list and said, 'I'll need two to three hours for this.'

I stared at her. Was she joking? It was only about ten folders of magazines; I could *see* them in the back room. I am the only person using the reference room. She stared back. Not joking.

I went to the newspaper cuttings room down the hall, run by two women sitting at their desks surrounded by what seemed like just lots of *stuff* but I think should be calling *ephemera*. They looked relaxed and happy, slowly sorting through the piles of clippings and lobby booklets. Front-line archivists, living the daily battle of sorting and numbering. Respect. I introduced myself.

'Ahh yes, how interesting', they chorused, 'a book on Amitabh Bachchan!' They have his file ready for me and one of them gets up and fetches it.

'He is a great actor,' she said. 'What a voice!'

I agreed. What a voice.

'And do you know what his first film was?'

'Yes, of course, *Saat Hindustani* in 1969 directed by veteran film maker K. A. Abbas and co-starring his first friends in Mumbai, Anwar Ali and Jalal Agha.' I am pleased with myself; I know I aced that one.

'No, it wasn't,' the woman holding the box says. 'In his first film he played a mute! Can you believe it! Amitabh Bachchan was made to play a mute in his first film!'

'I don't think that was his first film,' I mumble with an apologetic smile. I am suddenly unsure. I still assume that everyone with even the vaguest connection to the Subcontinent knows more about Amitabh than I do.

'Yes, it was *Reshma Aur Shera*. He plays a mute,' she asserts firmly. She looks at me suspiciously and holds on to her box file. Is she thinking she won't give it to me now that I have failed the obligatory Amitabh Bachchan pub trivia quiz? *But it was like his third or fourth film . . .*

'Ah, right, yes, what madness!' I say, rolling my eyes. 'That was some casting mistake!'

We laugh together at the follies of the past and she hands over the box.

I go back to the main library and open it up, excited at the prospect of what I might find: chaos. The material hasn't been in any way archived; it's just lots and lots of newspaper clippings, tons of material, all shoved into the box file. No date order or anything. I have a moment of Dewey Decimal System envy and, resisting the urge to just read, start to sort the clippings into five-year periods.

Indian food

Tuesday

It was very hot today. I had lunch in a little restaurant down the road from the archives. A guy came up to me and said, 'How will you go back to eating bland food after this?' He was genuinely concerned. The Indian belief that theirs is the only food of any merit, and that the ingredients (say spinach or potatoes) are no good on their own without two gallons of oil and a shed-load of spices to make them taste OK, is irritating.

'I'll manage,' I said icily. My cutting irony was lost on him. He smiled sadly at me and walked off shaking his head as he considered my tragic, flavourless fate.

Once I was on the set of *Ghulam* ('The Slave', dir. Vikram Bhatt, 1998) visiting Aamir Khan and was invited to join him for lunch. While we were waiting, Aamir impressed me with his plate-spinning and his ability to put matches out on his tongue. The food arrived on the buffet table – vast cauldrons of different curries swimming about beneath huge slicks of oil. I delicately picked out a chicken drumstick and drained the oil on the side of the cauldron. The villain of the film was watching from his place in the queue behind me.

'Quite a lot of oil!' I say merrily, trying to keep my drumstick from falling back into the pot. 'Not really used to it.'

He stares at me: 'If you don't have oil, then how do you have taste?'

I stare back at him, not sure where to start with that one, and move on the chapattis. 'You don't need oil for flavour,' I say hesitantly.

'Yes, you do.' He clearly thinks I am a bit simple and that my cooking must be disgusting.

I feel beaten by the yawning cultural void between us so I just smile and shrug and go and sit down on my white plastic chair next to Aamir, who is telling everyone about how he almost died playing chicken with a train in order to get a realistic shot. I am impressed; being with him is like hanging with the characters in a real life Boys' Own Adventure Book. I repeated what had just transpired at the buffet table and got treated to a lecture on how Indian food is the best in the world.

'Can you cook Indian food?' asks a woman playing one of Aamir's friends in the film.

'Apparently life's too short to stuff a mushroom, so I'm hardly going to spend six hours making biryanis, am I?' I retort.

When I came back after lunch the library staff were all having their tiffins and chatting. As I started to plough through the material they sat back and started to snooze. The room was so hot that I had a hard time concentrating on Amitabh's words of wisdom. Libraries are so *meant* to be snoozed in. I was a member of the London Library for a while, and by 11 a.m. each morning the reading room was filled with the gentle breathing of the resident old men slumbering peacefully in the leather armchairs. But I didn't think that it would be very professional to be caught slumped across my clippings, drooling into my secondary sources, so I went and got myself a cola. What cola to choose has become quite complicated. There was Amitabh, Pepsi in hand, smiling at me from the stand – an obvious choice surely? – but then there was Aamir, merrily 'cheersing' me with his Coke bottle from the sign swinging above the store. I feel guilty whichever one I get these days, worried that I am not being a loyal friend. Which is stupid, because I am sure neither of them gives a figgy duff what I drink. I avoided choosing between them and got myself a Thums Up. Never mind *thanda* I want my thunda. Ha ha ha.[62]

---

[62] Aamir Khan came up with an advertising campaign for Coke that equated it with 'thanda' or cold. When you ask someone what they want to drink

Afterwards I sat and faced the mounds of old paper clippings all afternoon. There is something about all this old print that makes me really depressed.

Mosquitoes and yoga

Wednesday

My room has really bad mosquitoes. I am finding it hard to sleep at night because of them. I am not a mozzie-phobe, and if there are only one or two I can usually sleep through without minding the odd bite on my arm. If they wake me up I lay a trap for them: I put my head under the sheet with one arm out, artery side up, and my other hand poised. If one lands on my exposed wrist, I splat it and go back to sleep, exultant. But sleeping in a room overlooking the river has its downsides – the mozzies seem to see the Boat Club as their own private members' club. It is Mozzie Central here. When I go into the bathroom in the morning the taps and sink are thick with them. If I have left my suitcase open and then go to get something out of it, great clouds of them rise up. It's a bit demoralising and I am not really into hanging out here in the evenings.

This afternoon I went to the Iyengar Yoga Centre to see what they recommend I do to continue my yoga practice. I can't go and do it there because I'm not an Iyengar Lifer – they only consider your application if you have done something like two hours practice a day for ten years. I am only a

---

[62] *cont.* in India you say, '*Chai ya thanda?*' (tea or something cold). All of Aamir's ads were about how it should be obvious that when you ask for a cold drink, what you want most is a Coke. Thums Up, *the* Indian cola before Coke was allowed in the country, had a rather esoteric catch phrase: 'I want my thunder!' This is an example of how humour, especially wordplay, doesn't travel across cultural boundaries.

piddly twice-a-weeker who does whatever school of yoga she can find. So I'm an impure, multi-disciplined mess and I've got to stay outside the gates with the rest of the dirty shellfish eaters.

Lots of middle-aged American yoga bunnies with obviously very strong core muscles were waiting to be seen by the secretary, Mr Rao. He wielded his power using an exquisite mixture: by withholding time, denying admission to future courses and by just plain ignoring people. Everyone had the deference required when dealing with a difficult member of the administrative staff who makes all the decisions. One young Frenchman who had what looked like Parkinson's was there to put down his deposit for next year.

'Oh, you should wait and come the year after,' said Mr Rao, with unchallengeable breezy certainty. 'You should do alternate years.'

The Frenchman looked as if he was about to cry, or perhaps it was just the shakes.

'But I haven't been for six years before this and *He* said this morning, "I'll see you next year", so I assumed that I am to come back next year.'

'Oh, well,' said Sri Rao, beaten by the only person there with more authority than him, Mr Iyengar himself. 'If *He* said so . . . Come back this afternoon at about four o'clock. I will see you then.'

The shaky French chap scuttled off, relief flooding his face, before Mr Rao could change his mind.

I went on the offensive and love-bombed him. Sparkly sparkle charm quarks pinging out of my eyes, gosh he was the nicest man I had met all day ping ping, I would be so grateful for any help he could see his way to giving me. Ping pada ping. It worked – I got lots of numbers of people who had trained at the Centre but who taught outside. I called a woman who teaches from her apartment near the Boat Club. I start in a couple of days.

What's a nice boy like you doing in a place like this?

Thursday

I am starting to feel a bit like I am drifting. Becalmed in a gossip lagoon. The Amitabh that is emerging from these magazines is really weird. It is like trying to piece together a person's life from articles in *Heat* or *Now*. It's difficult to see how the man they describe has any relationship to who he was *then* either. It's all like this, which I found in *Stardust*:

> Amitabh, in a half-sleeved foreign jersey (obviously bought on honeymoon) has put on weight, which certainly suits him. Makes him look less like a famine victim.

Amitabh Bachchan was a posh boy in trashville when he first arrived in Mumbai. The film industry had some classy acts and some extremely good film makers, but Amitabh was from India's intellectual elite and one didn't leave a well-paid job as an executive in a shipping company to become just another 'two-bit *filmi aadmi*'. Amitabh's choice was totally unprecedented in the history of Indian film. Clearly he liked it once he was in. Today I found this:

'It's funny,' he says, 'because if I did give up films I wouldn't know what to do. It's difficult to leave the circle once you get into it. Your life style changes, your attitude towards *everything* changes.'

Why did he do it? Well, obviously he wanted to act, but I think in his leaving everything and going to Mumbai for a part in a film (*Saat Hindustani* not *Reshma Aur Shera*, OK?) you can see evidence of his heritage. His family did have a history of making less obvious or more risky career choices. Amitabh's father, Harivansh Rai Bachchan, probably should have become a clerk like his father but he became a poet instead and indeed was a leading light in the Chhayavada movement (romantic Hindi poetry). It was not the most promising of career choices, but his most famous poem *Madhushala* was reprinted every year for fifty-four years and has sold more than 100,000 copies.

Amitabh's parents wanted him to join the army, making use of his mother's Sikh heritage and strapping build. He became a shipping company executive because it was the only job he could get, but his inherited determination – to do whatever it was that his heart and not his head told him to do – would ensure that he wouldn't stay mouldering in the club lands of Kolkata for long.

Is this me mythifying him? Hmmm. Probably. But, *kaf kaf*, there is a textual source for my assertions. His father's real surname was Rai; Bachchan or 'child' was his pen name. These two names kind of shifted and flowed about him, depending what he was doing. It wasn't until he put Amitabh into school that the matter of how he would be registered became an issue. Harivansh Rai decided that the family would be defined by his success as a poet. He declared:

> My sole wish now is that each generation of this family should break away from the old conventions and forge ahead, recognising the strength of being alone, establishing themselves and expressing themselves fearlessly; and that they should develop the qualities that are associated with the *bachcha* or child.[63]

But of course the gossip magazines only care about what he was wearing or who he was seen with. He is coming across as a bit of a lad, which is par for the course, but I am contin-

---

[63] Harivansh Rai Bachchan, *In the Afternoon of Time: An Autobiography*, p.357

ually beguiled by his *levity*. Perhaps I am so used to sober patriarch Amitabh that a frivolous youthful Amitabh seems like a different person. I can't imagine him going on benders with Shashi or shaking it up at discos. It is quite charming to find more evidence of it in *Stardust*:

> He was quite the jetsetter in his pre-acting days (when he used to move around with Sheila Jones and clique) and even now he gets into the mood sometimes to 'live it up'. . . . 'I never plan my dates. They just happen. Sometimes when I find myself free and feeling like doing something I ring up any of the girls I know and ask her out. That's why most of my girls grumble that I don't give them time to deck up.' Mumtaz and him have gone off on spontaneous dates when shooting was cancelled and it was 'great fun'. Amitabh is also fond of breaking the monotony of routine life by 'shaking it up at discos' occasionally.

I wonder if I can get anyone to go on record to confirm whether Amitabh had indeed been a bit of a player, or if it was all talk to create the right kind of cheeky-chappie publicity to help with his image as a hero. Newcomers to the industry often like to suggest that they are a bit of a one with the ladies, eternally available yet impossible to pin down.

The gossip mags are often just nasty though:

> When trade circles started asserting that by 1975 Amitabh Bachchan will be the Number 1 Box Office star, outrunning even dear old Garam Dharam, a pudding-faced hero commented dryly, 'See how success brainwashes people. Until *Zanjeer* clicked, Amitabh had been written off by the industry as "that castor-oil-faced hero". In fact, one top producer, after seeing *Bombay to Goa*, had commented, "Can you imagine that spindly man singing a romantic duet?" and today Amitabh has suddenly

become "handsome". How? He hasn't had plastic surgery. Neither has he been reincarnated.'[64]

The good news is that I have changed rooms in an attempt to escape the mozzies. They've given me room number 9. It still overlooks the river so I am wondering if they think it will be less infested because it is a 'good number' in numerology. I remember once meeting Amitabh in Hyderabad when I was gathering information for my MA dissertation (on the über-nerdy topic 'Changing Patterns in Production and Distribution in Hindi Film'). I went up to his room where he was having a meeting with the director Ramnathan.

'Wow, you're in room 666!' I said as I walked into his massive suite.

'So?'

'It's the number of the beast in Revelation, the final book in the Bible that talks about the end of time.' I held up my hands in a heavy-metal salute to the monsters of rock.

Amitabh looked at Ramnathan. 'I don't like this room anyway. Let's move,' he said.

I hadn't realised that my flip comment would have such an effect. Another hotel was booked across town. Amitabh's servant Praveen came and packed up all his stuff and we shifted.

But the largest room they had available wasn't large enough for Amitabh's needs. A megastar has to be able to hold meetings and maintain his privacy wherever he goes. So we packed up and shifted back.

As Ramnathan told Amitabh, '6 + 6 + 6 = 18, 1 + 8 = 9, and that is a very good number.'

So let's hope it works for me too.

---

[64] *Stardust*, May 1974, 'Neeta's Natter'. 'Hot Dharam' was the name they gave to Dharmendra the Punjabi star who, according to one magazine, had muscles that rippled like fields of wheat in his native Punjab. *Garam* indeed.

More yoga

Friday

Today I started my yoga classes with a vengeance: I did two, one at nine and one at six o'clock. Fantashtic *yaar*, but as a result I feel mighty strange now.

I found the lady's house OK. It's always a bit touch and go with addresses in India but not anything like as confusing as Venice. At least you are helped by the fact that there are watchmen at the gateway to each compound, and they often know who everyone is in the blocks of flats. So if I can get them to understand my Hindi, it's often quite straightforward. The front door was open so I took off my shoes, walked into the flat and found myself face to feet with an anaemic-looking white girl who was strapped to the wall upside down in full lotus, just hanging there attempting to look serene. I was taken aback to be honest; I mean, I know this is what Iyengar is famous for but it was alarming to walk into Madam's House of Pain at 8.30 a.m.

The oh-God-everyone-is-way-better-than-I-am-I-am-going-to-look-like-a-twit panic I had while changing into my gym clothes (all the other whities had their special yoga *salwar khameezes* – *blurgh* – all sparkly and colourful and *horrible*) was quickly dispelled by the arrival of the teacher, a large jolly lady who wanders around everywhere with her special Iyengar shorts rolled up so we can see that her thighs are like two sacks of oranges and feel better about ourselves. Such a relief after all the teeny-tiny yoga teachers in London (where to be taken seriously as a teacher you have to be living proof that Geri Halliwell wasn't lying).

The morning class had a lot of earnest *goras* all attaching ropes to different parts of their bodies and ratcheting limbs into improbable shapes. This is much more like one of those traditional Indian wrestling grounds than yoga as we know it. She just barks the orders at you and lets you get on with it, unlike the softly softly approach that we have in the UK. There's no, 'don't push yourself-this is not an ego thing'. Here the teacher is more likely to come and yank your limbs into the required shape and clonk you on the head with a Helpful Positioning Block. The morning class was a little short on humour, but it did set me up for a day sorting through Amitabh's alternative life.

The evening class was more fun – packed with mad old Parsees. Our teacher spent a lot of time ribbing all the old men and forcing us younger people into painful positions. She keeps threatening to whack us if we get things wrong.

The librarian and I smiled at each other a lot today. And the ladies in the documents section offered me a glass of sugar-cane juice. Which I politely declined without reacting like someone had offered me poison. Sugar-cane juice! Sugar juice! Hello? I mean, does anyone, other than migrant workers on the streets, actually drink that stuff? Do you not all suffer from terrible hyperglycaemia, flooding your body with sugar like that? But I did appreciate the gesture.

I found the story that was one of the reasons that the relationship between the Bachchans and *Stardust* soured:

WILL THE BACHCHAN MARRIAGE SURVIVE IN SPITE OF ZEENAT?

Then there is a five-page article on Amitabh and Zeenat – how they were together on foreign shoots, having adjoining bedrooms, etc. The story is supposed to have come from Neetu Singh who said that when she was friendly with Amitabh it made Zeenat furious. They are described as being perfect for each other and Jaya gets dissed so badly. Reading it with a twenty-first-century Western brain it is amazing that they didn't

get their asses sued. But then as Amin Hajee once told me the Indian legal system is such a slow-moving leviathan that, 'The only suing we do in India is *su su*.'[65]

But get this:

> I don't know how it is in other countries, but in my country it's not easy for a married man to have an affair with another woman. Particularly when the married man's wife is (in alphabetical order) clawing, clinging, demanding, dissatisfied, ill-humoured, short (in stature and temper), unsporting and all the other related qualities. In one word you could call such a wife a nag. Or a snag.[66]

'Foreign bought velvet parallels'

Monday

I can't help but be constantly amazed by *Stardust's* chutzpah! I love the way that it plays with language – it delights in the possibilities of 'Hinglish', that unique Bambaya mixing of Hindi and English. It's kind of like a low-rent version of Salman Rushdie's style although, of course, there is no comparison. He is, after all, the Grand Master Flash Dash of Hinglish, taking it to Great Literary Heights and International Acclaim, and all. *Stardust* just uses it to rubbish film stars: 'Jaya – so-o *faltu* (out of work that is).'[67]

They gave everyone a hard time but they really seem to have had it in for Amitabh from very early on. Perhaps De was nastier to him because he was from a similar social stratum as

---

[65] Pee.
[66] *Stardust*, August 1975.
[67] Usual translation for *faltu*: Useless, unnecessary, unwanted.

she was, but had done something socially unacceptable by going over to the other side. Perhaps not, perhaps he just asked for it by being such a fashion disaster and wearing mustard yellow jackets with huge bow ties.

But there is very little stuff about Amitabh and Rekha. I was expecting more. The impression I had always been given by helpful people telling me about the whole Amitabh–Rekha thing is that *Stardust*'s 'coverage' of the affair was what soured Amitabh's relationship with them. Maybe it's because Rekha didn't become the sumptuous screen siren we know and love until the late seventies, going on into the eighties. It seems to really kick off as the topic *du jour* in 1977. This is the most extreme article I have found so far:

Fact is, Jaya was convinced that this Rekha passion was just a temporary infatuation with her husband, and she waited for the day when it would blow over. But, eighteen months later, when the affair still continued, Jaya on an impulse reportedly phoned up Rekha one night and called her over to dinner. Jaya's husband was not in town.

It was with confused, nervous feelings that Rekha went to meet Jaya. She expected Jaya to rave, rant, and curse, or to beg, plead and cajole. But Jaya did none of this. Instead she talked to Rekha in a most normal manner all through the evening. They talked of all possible subjects under the sun except the one that was uppermost in both their minds. Jaya acted the gracious hostess, offered Rekha an excellently cooked dinner, and talked of how she planned to decorate her bungalow.

When Rekha went home that night she suffered the first pangs of guilt and shame at what she had done. 'I have not been fair. Why did I get into this in the first place?' she asked herself tearfully, and before going to bed, she prayed, 'God, help me do what is right. After all, she has nothing but her husband and her home – and they are *everything* to her.'

A few days later the press censorship was lifted, and the husband himself had second thoughts about carrying on with Rekha. He told her, 'Now that the censorship has been lifted, you know the press is going to be at me again. I think it's best if we don't meet each other at all apart from when we're shooting. You know I love my wife and will never be able to leave her for anything.'

Perhaps it's this assurance that will see Jaya through her marital crisis. Let's hope this assurance is strengthened and re-inforced. For, if what her close friends say is true, Jaya is on the brink of a breakdown, and the slightest misunderstanding could tilt the balance. WHO WILL BE TO BLAME THEN?

How filmi is that?! It's all a bit much really. I am missing the Amitabh that I know. I feel a bit grubby reading these magazines. Although this snippet from *Star and Style* in 1978 made me laugh:

'Jaya reported to be relieved to have her husband back in bed even if it is with jaundice.'

Back to Mumbai

Tuesday

I have decided to return to Mumbai to interview some of the journalists who created this mythic Amitabh. I just called Shobhaa De, Nari Hira, Khalid Mohamed (editor of *Filmfare*) and Bhawana Somaaya (editor of the trade weekly *Screen*, and author of *Amitabh Bachchan: The Legend*). Perhaps if I talk to them I will get more of an understanding of why Amitabh was painted in such garish colours by the press. I mean, let's face it, during the seventies Amitabh was all that it meant to be a man. He was strong, handsome, he kicked some seriously villainous butt wherever it needed kicking, and he was romantic in a slightly dangerous way. I think that this dangerous edge was aided and abetted by the man created by the gossip magazines.

When I told Shobhaa De what I was doing and why I wanted to meet her, she said, 'I really have nothing to say about the man.'

'OK,' I said, unwilling to let her get away that easily. 'Well, maybe you could clear up a few questions I have?'

'I guess,' she said, sounding bored out of her mind at the thought.

After that exchange how can I feel anything but excitement at the thought of having what will no doubt be a truly illuminating conversation with her? Nari Hira has scheduled in two meetings with energetic, efficient helpfulness (Why two? Makes me a bit nervous and suspicious . . . Total paranoia is perhaps closer than I thought). Khalid Mohamed couldn't *understand* why *I* should *want* to talk to *him*. And Bhawana, who had told me at a party at Manisha Koirala's house to call her and that she would help me, was almost impossible to pin down. So. Here we go. Back on the Deccan Queen for a quick trip to the big smoke.

Sunday

Wiped out by that. Not sure if it was worth the effort but hey. Maybe. OK, here's what happened.

Shobhaa De

Meeting her was a *trip*; it was like being granted an audience with a Great Man of Letters. Except that she is a Great Woman of Gossip Magazines and Sex and Shopping Novels. The woman is colossal. Not one of the male actors I have met in the industry likes her; indeed, whenever I mentioned that I went to meet her they would launch into yet another Monologuing-Male Moment, which of course I listened to like a good girl. But I admire her: she is strong, opinionated, hugely prolific, ground-breaking and what's the female equivalent of ballsy? Ovariesy? No, makes her sound like a fried egg . . . gutsy, she is gutsy. Most importantly, as far as I am concerned, she was the editor of *Stardust* during the ban on Amitabh and during the period that it promoted all the Amitabh and Rekha stories.

Shobhaa De lives in one of the hideous seventies tower blocks built on reclaimed land at Nariman Point. This is a very 'des res' area, but it has a feeling of being totally dislocated from the city in which it is situated. I was shown into the living room which had a view out over the sea and was filled with the obligatory collection of antique Indian stuff. If you're rich there are a few ways to do interior design in India: the camp baroque favoured by people like designers Abu and Sandeep, or the white marble and raw silk sophistication, like Amitabh's houses, or there's bright colours and wildly expensive hand-spun ethnic chic, like Shabana Azmi and Javed Akhtar's apart-ment. But no matter which look you go for, the key is the tastefully chosen antique 'pieces'. It's a wonder there is a thing left in any of the old palaces, so much old stuff has been squished into clammy salty apartments in Mumbai.

I am told by De's house peon I will have to wait. No prob-lemo Kemo Sabe – this I can do with aplombo. Waiting for people in Mumbai, especially in conjunction with Ego Management, is one of my key skill sets, right there at the top of my CV. Anyway, I appreciate having a bit of time to come down. I think they mixed a bit of cocaine in with my coffee this morning. I am speeding so fast I have got the shakes. I don't want Shobhaa De to think she is making me nervous.

(I remember going to see Amitabh in Birmingham once years

ago. I was really tired so I drank a Pepsi Max on the train up. When I met him I was shaking badly.

'Wow,' I said, 'look how much I'm shaking!'

Amitabh looked at me sympathetically and said, 'Don't worry, people often shake when they meet me.'

'I think it's the Pepsi actually.'

Amitabh looked unconvinced, as well he might – people regularly *faint* when they meet him.)

I was waiting with two Mumbai Ladies who had come to see if Shobhaa De would like to attend their art show. (I don't think they have actually produced the art themselves, but they've organised it. Ladies definitely lunch in Mumbai.) They are not happy at being made to wait. They talk to each other in grumpy little tisky-shisky whispers and pretend, as do I, that they aren't getting really fed up of pushing De's dog off their laps.

'Ooh gawd, please!' they flutter, giggling.

Some women in Mumbai have developed a very odd way of talking; it's all high and in the throat, wispy lilty like a five-year-old Welsh-Indian girl. I smile in sympathy at them as the dog once again deposits hair all over expensive *khameezes*.

We wait and we wait and we wait.

And then we wait some more. Looking cool and aloof and chilled is getting more and more difficult as gravity starts to tug at me and the caffeine wears off and I start to crash. I feel like curling up and having a nap. De is making the film stars look punctual and considerate.

Finally De wanders into the room an hour and a half after I was scheduled to meet her, wearing a pink shirt and jeans and looking much more in shape than anyone who has had five children has any right to. She is still beautiful, although it has become a stridently scary beauty as the years have progressed.

After she dispatches the art ladies and gets the house peon

to remove the dog (yey!) we settle down to talking. She says again that she has nothing to say about Amitabh.

'I find him very dull. People talk about this charm and charisma, but I just don't see it. I am sorry but I just don't; he is extraordinarily polite, but dull.'

'Can I ask why you decided to stop writing about Amitabh in the seventies? It does seem to be an odd thing to do.'

'Everybody unanimously said that he was responsible for the harassment that the press was being subjected to,' De replies. 'Maybe it was just a completely false perception, but in that case there were a lot of seasoned veteran film journalists who were completely fooled, is all I can say. Amitabh said he was subject to a big conspiracy, but I am not willing to buy that.'

'So was there any evidence that Amitabh had asked the government to do this?'

'There was no evidence; it was simply the perception at the time. It was the Emergency; it would have been stupid to look for evidence. He was not getting the best press in the world, and then there were these censorship rules that came just bang out of nowhere. He did have family ties and was close to the Gandhi family, so . . .'

This sounds an improbable argument, but in 1975 the Prime Minister Mrs Indira Gandhi had decided that the security of the country was under threat because of actions planned by the opposition party. So she placed the country under martial law. It didn't seem to bother De at all that these days almost everyone has decided that Amitabh didn't have anything to do with the Draconian censorship placed on the gossip press. I can't decide whether this is because De actually believes it still, or whether she just continues to say it because it is not the prevailing trend and so grabs people's attention.

One thing that I do concur with is that during the Emergency it would have been silly to look for evidence. People used the time to settle old scores and personal grudges. It was a dark time for India – and at the apex of this darkness was Amitabh's childhood friend, Sanjay Gandhi.

Amitabh was getting pretty nasty press at this time but he is not the sort of person who would go and get his *burra admi* ('big man') mate to go and duff up the bullies. I think De and friends underestimated the love of power that petty officials have, and the delight that one such official must have experienced in being able to boss about a room full of people who were more than likely (and especially in De's case) of a much higher social standing than he would ever be.

'Can we talk about Rekha?' I ask.

'Sure,' she says, stifling a bored little yawn.

'I don't understand why the Amitabh–Rekha story refuses to die. Whenever I tell anyone that I am writing about Amitabh they get this naughty cheeky look and say, "Are you going to write about Rekha?" like they're little school kids. What happened?'

De smiles knowingly and says, 'No one has a real fix on it, no one is really sure whether it's all Rekha's fantasies, whether it was created by the Rekha myth factory, or what. She invents a lot of stuff.'

'You're suggesting that it might not even have happened?' I feel what shaky ground there is under my feet start to slip away.

'Yes. She should have a PhD in image manufacturing; she controls her image very well – evidence of that fact is that she is constantly in the magazines and hasn't had a film to speak of in years. I don't know if he made her his project and decided to transform her, or whether she did it to herself to regain his affections – if there were any in the first place.'

'You're the only person I have talked to who has suggested that it didn't happen *at all*, that the whole thing is just a huge self-perpetuating lie created by Rekha to help her image.'

De smiles, happy with the effect she has had:

'She talks of him as "the air, the colour, the sky" – he is this godlike image, which means he doesn't have to have a physical reality. He has never acknowledged her – any other woman would have had the self-respect to back off, but she has nothing else in her life. Not that this gets in the way of all her younger men.'

Shobhaa De is like 99.9 per cent of people who talk of the Amitabh–Rekha story in that she gives no concrete proof that they were or were not having an affair. Instead, like others, she offers circumstantial evidence: Rekha's transformation.

In her autobiography, *Selective Memory*, De's description of Rekha when she first arrived in Mumbai is snobby and mean:

Rekha was an unknown when she walked in with Vinod Mehra (dead now). Let me see . . . First impression? Gross. She was overweight, loud, giggly, and ridiculously dressed. Her face still had baby-fat deposits on it, her plucked eyebrows formed artificial arches over small eyes. Dusky – well . . . dark, and dumpy. Nobody could possibly have visualised the Rekha of today – Sultry Siren . . . Seductress Supreme. She chattered incessantly in a distinctly 'vernie' accent, much to everyone's amusement.

'Everyone' being the rest of the *Stardust* staff, a group known for their perfect Sanskritised Hindi.

It is said that the key indicator that Rekha was having an affair with Amitabh was that she suddenly transformed herself from the *kaali aur moti*[68] loudmouth southie slapper into the most glamorous and sexy heroine of the age. It is said that her desperation to please her man, to be worthy of him, manifested itself in a radical change in how she dressed and acted in front of people. This change is seen as being the result of Amitabh's

---

[68] Black and fat.

influence over her; his innate upper-middle-class north Indian good taste rubbing off on her. The magazines often used a phrase that was first coined to describe Fred Astaire and Ginger Rogers: 'He gave her class, she gave him sex appeal.' It is one of the key 'facts' of seventies Indian film history.

Thoreau said, 'Some circumstantial evidence is very strong. Such as a trout in the milk.' Rekha's make-over is the ultimate trout in the milk. It proves, to most, that the affair happened.

Personally I would prefer to see Rekha as being able to effect her own transformation independently, and not as the Eliza Doolittle of Bandra, moulded by a man into his own image of what a lady should be, but still lapsing into, 'Come on, Dover! Move ya bloomin' arse!' whenever she feels that no one is listening. But who knows.

One thing that I do know for sure is that Rekha has an astounding effect on men. All the boys that I have taken to meet her, regardless of their cultural background and sexual orientation, have fallen under her spell. Suddenly they want to do nothing but photograph her endlessly.

Travellers, bless 'em

I left Shobhaa De's house reeling a bit. I needed some food before I went to my next interview so I went and hung with the sick-looking travellers sheltering from Mumbai in the light, airy, safe Leopold's. I try and gather my thoughts before meeting Khalid Mohamed. I distract myself by watching the traveller couples who clearly ran out of things to say to each other weeks ago, and are now secretly counting down the days till they get the plane home.

A rake-thin boy in the standard loose cotton traveller trousers and an incongruous Ralph Lauren Polo shirt sits down at the table next to me. He is clearly stoned out of his mind but tries to hold it together. After studying the menu with extreme care he orders a banana milkshake. I smile at him and feel warm and protective. Poor chap. Banana milkshake is a beverage that should be praised by the World Health Organisation for keeping a lot of travellers alive during their attempts to get around India on 10p a day. A weak smile like curdled milk snakes its way across his mouth. He brings out the book that he is reading, *A Severed Head* by Iris Murdoch, and stares at the first page, his head shaking back and forth a bit. A gang of loud aggressive post-National Service Israelis berate the waiter about their food. I tense up. The Severed Head Guy looks at them pained and confused. I know that British people abroad are often shockingly behaved, but there is something so angrily rude about the young Israelis who seem to deal with the pressures of military service by going around the world and bullying people.

My food arrives. Banana milkshake and chips. When in travellerville . . . Me and Severed Head Guy exchange a weak smile and he kind of waggles his book at me, looking at it in confusion. This is both an explanation and an invitation to start to talk.

'Is it good? I haven't read that one,' I ask

'Yeh, it's . . . you know . . . mmmm, heh . . .' He stares at the first page some more and then suddenly jerks his head up and looks at me in wild desperation. He is showing me the first page. I guess the words won't keep still. He jabs at a word. 'Kashmir.'

I feel like patting him and telling him to go back to his hotel room. I have never understood the whole come-to-India-to-take-drugs thing. Stuck in Luton? Go ahead, take shed-loads of drugs, best idea in the world. But India is such a head fuck as it is; I can't see how you could possibly need to get any more out of it.

Two more Israeli girls in bikini tops and really short shorts come in and shout their way across to a table.

Time to get out. Leave this unappealing scene. Go meet Mr Khalid Mohamed.

Khalid Mohamed

Khalid is the editor of *Filmfare*. He is a slight man with curly hair that sits high above his forehead. He wears little glasses that emphasise his darting eyes and he never opens his mouth very wide when he speaks. We have met several times and even went to a couple of films together last summer. He was a satisfyingly acerbic movie-watching companion, but I have never felt remotely comfortable with him. It always seems as though he has about ten other agendas going on.

He was very pleasant when I arrived; we kiss-kissed and he softly lisped that I shouldn't have brought him some wine if I wasn't going to drink it with him. But as soon as we sat down he made it really clear that he didn't want to say anything on the record! He simply refused to help me. Why? I was confused and a bit thrown, if, somehow, unsurprised. So it was a really weird forty-odd minutes. It felt like official diplomacy: the two of us sitting and drinking tea in a civilised fashion, knowing that outside the diplomatic compound, the land is full of anti-personnel mines and snipers.

Actually, now I think about it, he did spend quite a lot of time telling me that people keep urging him to write a book on Indian cinema. When I agreed and said hey! the more the merrier, we've got to get the word out, he instantly started to demur, which led me to tell him that he could write a *great* book, until I realised he was loving it.

I did ask him why the rumours of the affair between Amitabh and Rekha refused to die, and he fixed me with a look out of the corner of his eye and said, as if he were imparting the most delicious piece of gossip, 'Embers linger on . . .'

At the end of the interview he said, 'Well, I am so sorry I have not been any help or said anything.' I could have laughed out loud at how smug and self-satisfied he was obviously feeling.

'Oh, *no*,' I gushed with glistening insincerity, 'you *have* helped me. I was so *unclear* on certain things and you have helped straighten them out in my *fuzzy head*.' I roll my head about like an imbecilic loon.

A fleeting smile plays on his thin lips. 'I can't see *how*, but that's good if I have.'

He shows me to the door of his cabin, we kiss, muah-muah, on each cheek, I exit. As the door closes behind him I look back and a chill runs through me.

So that was all very odd.

Bhawana Somaaya

I first met Bhawana Somaaya at a party at Manisha's place. She stated that she was supportive of my endeavour. I was pleased. There are so many factions surrounding Amitabh that it is easy to become paranoid that they won't be supportive.

'Oh, I am so happy that I have done *my* book on Amitabh,' she had said. 'It is *such* a relief to have got it out of my *system*.' She smiled at me sympathetically. I realised that she saw me as having Amitabh coursing around my system, but until then I hadn't thought of this as being something that would make me an object of *pity*!

This meeting wasn't very uplifting: I spent about an hour with her, during which she made no effort to concentrate on me, but continued her job as editor of the weekly trade paper, *Screen*. Any conversation that we had was conducted in snatches in between different phone calls and meetings. I realised that she had no intention of talking. Had she asked me to come and meet her at the office so that I could see how busy she was? I became paralysed and confused by the rapid fire of banalities and the stupendous sense of self-importance that she demonstrated.

In an attempt to create an entry point, I started to talk to her about the way that everyone treats Amitabh as if he were a giant.

'But he is so *tall*!' She stared at me, shocked – whatever was I saying? 'When I first met him I was terrified that he was going to crush me, he is so massive,' she shrank back into her starched and artily opened *duputa*, the mass of girly diamonds and gold shivering and glittering as she demonstrated how tiny and feminine she was.

She wouldn't have stood a chance against all that towering masculinity, clearly.

Yes, Amitabh is tall. He is not, like so many actors, driven by Short Man Syndrome.[69] I guess this is something that deserves comment, but not the amount that it gets. It's one of the areas of his life where myth and truth nestle quite happily together.

FACT: Amitabh Bachchan is not a giant. He is in fact 6 ft 2 in.

FACT: The whole of India talks of him and thinks of him as an enormous yeti of a man.

FACT: People often talk about his 'stature', meaning both his height and his social standing.

FACT: His tiny wife's nickname for him is *Lambuji* ('Tall-o'. Or, 'Big Boy', I guess). The press call him 'The Big B'.

FACT: He has always had excessively long legs. When he was a baby his parents had a hard time convincing ticket collectors on trains that he was under two, and so didn't need a full ticket.

---

[69] You've got to ask yourself though, why is it that so many film stars are so short? Perhaps it's just that once you're a film star, the fact that you're a tiny pocket-person stops being your most prominent feature. After all, Pablo Picasso was never called an asshole.

FACT: In his films he is more often than not shot from his feet upwards when he enters a room. He often fights with his feet and legs in amazing grappling moves.

FACT: It is always the shortest 'spot boy'[70] who wants to hold the umbrella up to shield him from the sun on set, thus causing much hilarity amongst the crew.

FACT: Nobody, and I mean nobody, can wear white flares like he can.

FACT: In the land of the vertically challenged anyone pushing 6 ft has a cracking good chance at being king.

Another meeting commenced. I said I would go. Ms Somaaya told me to stay. I felt claustrophobic and trapped, like my brain was filling up with pulped paper. I stared, transfixed by her diamond earrings in the shape of little flowers. Her meeting came to an end and she turned and looked at me.

'I think you should go away and write a really simple structure for the book. You have the composure of someone who hasn't started to write. Then you can come back and I will help you with your book.'

I glared at her.

'I have a structure,' I said coldly, 'I have started to write. You are obviously really busy and we haven't been able to talk properly. I understand – that is why I look calm.'

We parted company. I took another bloody stinking taxi to Nari Hira's house in Breach Candy. I did not arrive in the best frame of mind.

---

[70] A 'spot boy' is the lowest person in the film-making hierarchy – a general gopher he is shouted at to do all odd jobs. The cry, 'Spot!', with the 't' plosive to the max, can be heard on all sets. Usually teamed with some command like, 'Spoat! Kursi lao!' ('Bring a chair'). The spot boys are often very conscientious about making sure that guests have a place to sit – this is only offered to the highest of the hierarchy. A gentle nudging of plastic against the backs of the knees is often felt if you should wander away from your chair to watch a shot.

Nari Hira

This was my second interview with Nari Hira, the owner of *Stardust*. He had invited me to his home this time. He said that he wanted to talk to me 'without his *Stardust* hat on'. Wearing it he had told me pretty much what I have read elsewhere, about how and why he started the magazine and his developing relationship with Amitabh, so I was looking forward to what he might say now. I had been totally disarmed by him: he was intelligent, open, engaging and easy to talk to. I was a bit unnerved by the fact that I actually quite liked him, something I hadn't expected to do at all. Nari Hira lives in the *top four floors* of Millennium Towers, almost directly opposite the Breach Candy Club. Gossip has made him muchos dineros.

He is small, slightly orange and so full of energy that he shakes slightly. He scoots into the room on my arrival and offers me some coconut water. This is my favourite drink in the whole world and I am instantly in a much better mood. I tell him that I have been in a bad mood because Bhawana Somaaya was so difficult.

Hira is smooth orange sympathy itself and puts on some music. I go out on to a balcony turfed with impressively flat grass, a tiny semi-circular bowling green suspended above the city. From his terrace you can look down and see the swimming pool in Breach Candy, built in the shape of India before partition. If you have a British Passport you can get into the Club and swim in the over-chlorinated watery jewel in a long-lost crown.

Hira comes and joins me on the balcony.

'Why do you like Mumbai?' I ask him.

'Who says I like Mumbai?' he quips.

Nari Hira is Gossip Lord of all he surveys, from Nariman Point to Madh Island. The All-Seeing Eye of Rumour who can look into bedrooms and dressing rooms, and from whom no film star is safe. Even my question is turned into malicious hearsay that he must refute.

After I duly admire his view we go back inside. Hira has put on orchestral versions of Queen. We start to talk about Amitabh and he tells me, first off, that he doesn't like his acting.

'Don't be silly,' I say, '*everyone* likes Amitabh's acting. It's just a given. Saying you don't like Amitabh's acting is like saying that you don't like, I don't know, Heinz Tomato Soup or something.'

'I don't! But I am very fond of him. Don't tell him that I am very fond of him. I don't want him knowing that.'

I ask him if there are any stories he wouldn't publish, no matter if he knows they are true.

'All our stories have to be based in fact. We need to get things confirmed by two separate sources.'

I raise my eyebrows. He is insistent: 'If a story is found out to be untrue it damages our credibility. During our ban on Amitabh producers would come to *Stardust* with stories that were slandering him; I am glad we didn't run those stories. We would never publish a story that would harm a star's career.'

'What kind of stories are those?' I ask.

'Stories about homosexuality and black money.'

'I do find it strange that so many men in Mumbai are so very demonstrably gay, and yet are married with children.'

He smiles and says, 'That's just the way it is.'

'So then, what about Rekha?'

'Oh well, she was totally obsessed. I heard that when she was shooting for one film down in Goa she used to write Mrs Bachchan on the little sign outside her bungalow.'

'Huh. So who planted the story you guys ran about Amitabh and Zeenat Aman getting together when they were shooting for *The Great Gambler* in London. Neetu Singh still denies she said anything to anyone.'

'It was Rekha.'

'Rekha?! Why would she plant a story about a married guy and another woman?'

'Perhaps she wanted Amitabh and Jaya to split up over Zeenat so that she could move on in.'

'That seems a little warped. Not to mention far-fetched.'

Hira shrugs and orders us some more coconut water. 'Perhaps she was throwing up a smoke screen.'

Later on Hira suggests that I should talk with Amitabh's rich and powerful male buddies.

'Amitabh will be his most natural around them. *You* will not see him how he really is,' he says.

I get irritated and say, 'Why do men assume that men are only themselves around other men?'

He smiles at me.

A violin plays 'Can you do the fandango?' behind us.

An affable-looking teenage boy arrives in the room.

Hira introduces us: 'This is my son, Vikram.'

I stare at Hira, my eyes widening slightly. He smiles.

Do I believe that the man Amitabh is with his buddies is the real Amitabh? Not really. Another Amitabh, yes, the '*Yeh dosti ka* Amitabh'.[71] Anyway, I want facts. Which nobody seems to be able to give me. Hira just wanted to be the guy with the inside story, which of course he doesn't have; he just has stories told to him by third parties.

But here I am back in Pune, determined to get as far as the point where they all start to talk to each other again. I am not sure how any of this is going to help with the book, although I have a hunch that even if everything they said was untrue, the impact of this unique dynamic was crucial to Amitabh's story.

---

[71] '*Yeh dosti*' is a song from *Sholay* – a classic male buddy song. It has a *Butch Cassidy and the Sundance Kid* sensibility.

There is no doubt that the Amitabh that is emerging from the magazines is very mutated! They make him out to be a kind of marauding Heathcliff/ Don Juan, systematically working his way through the lovely leading ladies of the industry. I guess they must have thought that this would damage his popularity. I know that it certainly hurt him as a human.

When I told him I was going to read all the stuff in the magazines he protested, 'They made me into a monster and I had no way of contradicting them.'

But I am not sure that it *was* such a bad thing for his popularity. An affair with Rekha was the appropriate form of love for the Angry Young Man. On screen during the late seventies he was the embodiment of the all-powerful male, so off screen it should be OK if he's portrayed as the male dream of the potent, dominating phallus that no woman can resist, whose sexual appetite is as voracious and indiscriminate as a virus.

All writers have agendas – if they insist that they are objective then you should be deeply suspicious. *Yeh hai Mumbai meri jaan*,[72] so all of it's real and none of it's true – and nobody believes a word anyone else says. None of their Amitabhs is the true one, but all have a stake in insisting that they are telling the truth ... Could it be that they all want to write their own books?

Nothing strange in writers insisting their version of a subject is as close to the truth as you are likely to get. Traditional male biographers often maintain that what they are doing is presenting the truth, in all its virginal glory. How virginal and pure it actually *is* is of course one more area where the vanquishing men, all swashing buckles and bloody sheets, are desperate to be right and the rest of the world has a good chuckle into their scented hankies.

---

[72] This is Mumbai, my love.

These days it seems everyone is determined to present Amitabh as a Great Man. Not Shobhaa De, granted, but then her role as the Great Debunker makes for a more interesting editorial stance.

CHAPTER SIX

*'Lead me not into temptation, I can find
my own way.'*

Rita Mae Brown

Monday

I felt I needed to reconnect with something resembling reality
so I called Amitabh and told him he was right, there was nothing
here but a 'load a shite' (said in a strong Geordie accent).

'What did you expect?!' he said, barely able to disguise the
exasperation in his voice. He makes an indecipherable noise.
I can't deny that part of me hoped to find *something* here that
would be like a key to him, that would allow me to feel more
comfortable with the huge amounts of stuff that happened to
him before I knew him.

I asked him when he thought he might be able to schedule
some interviews. He told me there was a chance he would have
to come to Pune for business. I was thrilled and gushed a lot
at him. But then he said he wasn't certain because his father
is very ill and he wants to stay with him. I said that of course,
I totally understood – family comes first.

After I hung up though, I couldn't help but feel really . . .
how? Shaken isn't the right word. Disconcerted? I realise that I
have been immersing myself in the Unreal Gossip Amitabh.
I have gone back in time to inhabit, for better or for worse,
the bitchy-witchy world of *Stardust* in the seventies, so a quick

injection of the Amitabh that I know is a bit of a reality check.

Stardust does inhabit a parallel universe to ours, one which can be desperate and depressing, and yet that is true of gossip magazines the world over. Should I even be bothering with this? The man they have created is so far removed from the man I know that I am unsure how much relevance reading all that stuff could possibly have. But . . . a key thing that seems to legitimise my endeavour amongst other people I interview and the population at large is an in-depth knowledge of Rumours Past. Being able to 'out-gossip' people seems to afford me an odd sort of respect. Of course, a certain distance from your subject is necessary to be able to write about them. Lytton Strachey never had his Eminent Victorians rock up and get all complex and contradictory on him, did he?

Two insecticide coils going at night now. I can't breathe for the smoke but it doesn't seem to deter them mozziefuckers. They're huge, like little whining ponies. When I go to the loo in the night and bump into them I find myself apologising! Something's got to give. I think the smoke is affecting my brain.

Indian beauty parlours

I took the afternoon off to go and have a manicure/pedicure/ wax. In yoga this morning I was embarrassed when I looked at my feet (you become really well acquainted with your feet doing yoga). My toes were totally jacked up – my scarlet nail varnish had more chips in it than the entire Harry Ramsden chain; and my soles were positively *dirty* . . . I looked like a HIPPY. Ugh. It's hard to keep your feet clean when you're wearing sandals and everywhere is so dusty-dirty – but Indian women manage it. So I decided that work could wait, I needed to attend to some personal grooming.

In India the women scrupulously remove almost all the hair from their bodies. It is not seen as a luxury: 'New Year Pamper Package!' Or a seasonal thing: 'Get your feet ready for summer!' It is an eternal life-long battle against body hair and street grime. This is why India has a plethora of excellent beauticians and male pedicurists who really put their backs into pumicing your feet.

So, action stations – can't let yourself go, even if you *are* hot in pursuit of Lies and Rumour.

I swished like an Afghan hound into the huge two-storey-high lobby of the Mariott, the cold air eddying through my leg hair, making it move about like weed in a slow-moving stream. Ahh. Five-star hotels. Nothing like them. Utterly alien and removed from whatever culture happens to surround them. Outside is India. Inside isn't. I feel scruffy and dirty compared to all these immaculately ironed people. I hurry to the beauty parlour and tell the beautician I want to look like the people in the lobby.

'Shall I thread your arms too?' asks the beautician, running her hand up my furry forearm.

'Err, no, I like the hair on my arms.'

She looks slightly disgusted. I instantly go into my default setting of Extreme Deference to beauticians and start apologising for my gross hairiness and foul British ways. I think it is always best to be nice to someone who is about to inflict pain on you.

Once, in Jaipur, I was waxed by a girl who had clearly never been near a waxing-kit in her life. I was in a rush and was a bit impatient with her. In her nervousness she spilled the entire pot of scalding wax over my calves. I cried out in pain and tried to get up off the bed but couldn't because I was stuck to the sheet. I had to wait there while they got rid of the wax, any hair that I had on that part of my legs, most of the skin and the follicles, thereby removing any chance of future hair growth. I had blisters for weeks.

Tuesday

By lunch time today I'd had enough of reading gossip about people I don't care much for. Still, I forced myself to stay till four and then went to the gym at the Meridian where I paid an extortionate Rs 250 for the privilege of using one of their running machines – but it was worth it. I have to run my brain back into action. I had a long loungeabout in the sauna afterwards, feeling the blood in my muscles and creatively visualising all the auto-rick grime emerging from my pathetic *gora* pores. It's quite a trip back and forth each day, clutching my lovely iBook of joy and shrinking away from truck exhausts. Why are Indian truck exhausts placed at exactly the height of car windows? I think if you had a house here, set back from the road and surrounded by trees, Pune would be lovely. Away from the roads the air does once again have that amazing sweet smell that you only get in India – not like Mumbai, where it is always kinda foetid. You would have to be away from the river too. The mosquitoes are really getting me down.

Me delivering flowers to Rekha.

I have been phoning Rekha (and sending faxes and notes attached to divine red orchids) ever since I arrived. She is being all hard to get. I need another good-looking young male photographer to come and seduce her with his big lens. I can never get in touch with her when I want to meet with her for something, but as soon as there's someone who wants to photograph her she is the most charming, helpful and easy-going person. It's a bit frustrating, but it's in keeping with her role as screen diva so I don't really mind.

I feel a bit odd to be honest, trying to meet with her. I mean, basically I want to talk to her to see how she deals with the whole did-you-have-are-you-still-having-an-affair-with-Amitabh question. I don't particularly like the feeling of prying. But people here are really fixated about their presumed love affair.

Wednesday

I think I am suffering from a surfeit of gossip.

I think I have trivitis.

Look, feel my forehead . . . all clammy, right?

Plus I had my eyebrows threaded by the Depilator the other day, and now the skin around them has reacted really badly. I think I'm just going to leave my eyebrows alone from now on. Every time I've made an attempt to change their shape or colour or something it's gone dreadfully wrong. Last month I got beautician-bullied into having them dyed. Such a mistake – I looked like Mr Potato Head wearing his angry eyes.

Feeling a little out of whack actually . . . The mosquitoes are really really bad. I am being eaten alive each night and not getting enough sleep. I have those coil things, but I think they are just using them as landing lights.

Still, I did find this today which made me laugh:

So now it is Rekha's turn to play Jaya's real-life role and she is doing *pura* justice to the character of the neglected woman. Not only does she sob on every shoulder (preferably male) privately, but she is also seen sniffing and sobbing in public, when she goes for her early morning walks. This *natak* (or perhaps it is genuine grief for a change!) does not arouse any pity in the other morning joggers. In fact they have given her a special name – the red-nosed Rekha![73]

People get really odd when I ask them about the end of the affair. Everyone has a theory, from the simple (she talked too much)[74] to the thoroughly weird; that they were instructed to give it up by the then Prime Minster of India, Indira Gandhi, because it was a threat to national security!

I need a break.

Academic Amitabh

Thursday

Spent the morning drinking cold coffees and re-reading M. Madhava Prasad's book *The Ideology of the Hindi Film: A Historical Construction*. It was a good antidote to the wild and

---

[73] Stardust, 1981, 'Neeta's Natter'.

[74] Which would make sense. I found this in an interview with Shabana Azmi: 'There's absolutely no double standards about that girl. A lot of us may be a lot of things, but we will always try to project a near-perfect image. But Rekha is not ashamed of anything she has done, or does [*sic*]. Nor does she talk about it in hushed tones. For instance, she is allegedly having this affair with a married actor. I am friendly with the actor and his wife, and so you could say that I could belong to the hostile party. But when she met me, she just talked and talked about the man without any hesitation. For a moment I was a bit startled but then I had to laugh at her sheer audacity!'

whacky world of *Stardust* with its endless *pointless* politics-volitics. The guy behind the coffee counter was *choo chweet* (my brain is being Hinglishised) – he kept trying to get me to take sugar in my coffee, offering me syrups and other disgusting things. He couldn't quite deal with the fact that I just wanted straight coffee. Indians must collectively have the sweetest tooth on the planet.

I worked out what is missing – for me, at least – from these worthy works about Amitabh and the mobilisation of the working classes and the unification of the film industry, etc. etc. NO ONE MENTIONS HOW SEXY HE IS! I mean, *come on guys*, I know this isn't exactly theoretical but it's obviously of key importance, no? Not *one* academic mentions this when they talk about the appeal of the Angry Young Man – it's all politics and veiled discussions about 'masculinity'. Nowadays, of course, everyone is too reverential and will only say that he is a Great Actor. Which I happen to agree with – the man inspires conviction. But this isn't all he inspires.

For example, let's look at Amitabh's movement throughout *Deewaar*: it is remarkable. He may enter the film as a lowly dock-worker, but you sure as hell know there's more going on than that. All action has slowed right down; there is a heavy liquidity as he fights, almost like he is underwater. His physicality is in direct contrast to the cringing, jerky, learnt subservience of people who actually *have* grown up on the streets and spent years working long hard hours as dock loaders. This surety of purpose translated into deliberate and economic movement immediately makes you feel that you are in the presence of a very powerful male. Vijay (Amitabh's character in the film) is angry, but it is an intelligent anger. If you want to sum up an era, all you have to do is show the shot of Amitabh in the *godown*, leaning back in his chair, hands behind his dirty head, a half-smoked oily *beedi* clenched between his teeth as he sizes up the gang he is about to pulverise; he is all coiled male energy – like a cocked gun.

This is one of the reasons that he became such a big star: Vijay is one of the sexiest film heroes of all time. During the seventies Amitabh was the only actor to play adult male sexuality, when the script allowed it. This was the real break with the heroes of the past, vaguely neutered fellows who liked to skip about amongst the flowers – about as sexual as Barbie's eunuch boyfriend Ken. In *Deewaar*, he is actually shown in bed having a post-coital cigarette with Parveen Babi and discussing how, because of his childhood traumas, he is hardwired bad. Nothing sells like sex, and sex outside marriage in slidey sheets and fake-fur covers, with cigarettes and the possibility of violence always simmering beneath the surface sold like hot buns. He was an irresistible package, and India loved him for it.

Perhaps this is why the Amitabh in the magazines, Amitabh as Love Terrorist, was such a secret hit amongst his fans. It was a manifestation of the unspoken sensuality behind his performances that, since he was married and had children, it would have been unacceptable to indulge in thinking about otherwise.

Silsila

Saturday

I watched *Silsila* again yesterday. The very fact that this film exists I still find quite perplexing.

When I interviewed Yash Chopra and asked him about his film, he grinned and said, '*Silsila! Chel raha hai!*'[75] After he had rearranged himself he went on, laughing, 'It was a very complicated affair, but it was the most fantastic period of working together.'

---

[75] 'Silsila! Let's go!'

In this movie Amitabh is married to Jaya and has an affair with Rekha. Strange but true. Chopra and Amitabh came up with the idea of this casting together, and it was Amitabh who got the women to agree. I have always wondered *why* either of them agreed and thought that perhaps this was evidence that the affair was just a rumour. Why didn't Chopra think it a bit weird that a man would want to make a film about an affair, starring the two women in his life? Naturally people want to make films about the subjects that are uppermost in their minds. But wouldn't that have been a supreme act of ego?

Chopra said, 'Everyone was very nervous about it, but they were happy. Everybody tried to put their best foot forward. The two girls were exemplary. It was very stressful.'

There is one point in the film that seems to weirdly echo the apocryphal meeting between Jaya and Rekha, so salaciously reported in *Stardust*:

J: Let him go.

R: I cannot do that. It is beyond me.

J: Amit is my husband, my religion.

R: He is my love and my love is in my destiny.

J: You will lose this game.

R: I am not playing a game.

J: Why are you breaking up my home?

R: I am breaking up my own home too.

J: If you think you can take him from me then you are wrong.

R: Is this your faith?

J: Yes, this is my faith.

R: Live with your faith and let me live with my love.

J: If this is going to be a battle of love and faith, I accept the challenge.[76]

---

[76] Rachel Dwyer, *All You Want Is Money, All You Need Is Love: Sex and Romance in Modern India* (London, Cassell, 2000), p.156.

In the film it is a very stylised encounter: the two women stand back to back in a foggy wood.

Silsila was not a success. It was almost as though they had all decided to give the public what it appeared to want. The endless stream of gossip had reached a torrent by this time; surely a film about it would go down a treat? But of course no one likes to be confronted with their own snoopy behaviour. It is fun to twitch curtains and make judgements from afar, but really embarrassing to be presented with someone's underwear drawer and told it's OK to rifle through it.

Axel Bernstorff

Rekha

Sunday evening

Oh my God! Finally I get a call from Rekha! And she has agreed to see me and to talk! It's unbelievable da *daaa*! Years and years and years and *years* of chasing her finally pay off.

'I don't need any credentials from you,' she said, when I explained again what I was doing. 'I feel that I have a connection with you, and after spending as many years in the industry as I have, this counts for something.'

Then she said she had a lot to say about Amitabh, and that she wanted to make sure this was the right time and the right person to say it to. She thinks it is, and I am. (!!Hurrah!!)

'You were an Indian in a past life. You have a deep love for the country. You are more Indian than most Indians,' she pronounces.

'Maybe I was.' (What is one supposed to say to this kind of statement?) 'But I know I'm not Indian in this life because I don't like mangoes.'

Then she said, 'Everyone reveres him. They have all learnt from him, learnt from his indifference. If he has spent time with someone and imparted some of his knowledge to them, then they become better humans.'

I agreed. Wholeheartedly. She told me to phone the next day so we could set up an interview for when I get back to Mumbai.

Learnt from his indifference but? What does *that* mean? I tell you what though, I am so totally starstruck by her and gushy, I have to calm down or I will not get the best from her . . . How to do this?

Monday

I was really whizzing this morning. So I called Farzana, Rekha's PA, who seemed furious that Rekha had called me. She knew nothing about it. She told me that it probably wasn't going to happen because Rekha was so busy and that I should call back to confirm. So I did. All afternoon and all evening. Now I have stopped. Given up. I can't be dealing with that shit, not now. Rekha will have to wait till the next time I come to Mumbai and feeling fresh and up for the Thirty Years War II: Son of War. Sorry, delirium approaches like a welcome friend. I think I have ingested too much lead. What am I saying? – too much starry bloody bullshit more like.

181

All this Rekha-chasing is quite depressing. I keep thinking about something that happened when I was in Mumbai last summer.

After a preview screening of *Dil Chahta Hai* ('What the Heart Wants', 2001) everyone congratulated the director Farhan Akhtar (son of Javed Akhtar and Honey Irani) on his 'milestone debut'. Finally Amitabh, Jaya and Abhishek Bachchan departed in their white Mercs. The second show was just starting when out from another big white Merc rushed Rekha, looking beautiful and understated in a white shirt and jeans. She had been sitting in her car waiting for them to leave for over an hour, and was full of the drama of it all.

'You should have just come in and sat here,' said Shabana Azmi sensibly.

'No, no! I couldn't have!' said Rekha, looking horrified and smiling simultaneously, all of a flutter at the thought. She then rushed into the film.

I felt sad that she could still be locked in the same dance some twenty years later.

And then I started to realise what a lot Rekha must have invested in this, and what a lot she seemed to gain from the little drama.

Perhaps my having to chase her to do interviews is just evidence of her need to keep the spectacle going. If she actually agreed it would become spoken, and once put into words become a fixed thing, no longer in the nebulous realm of our imaginations. If she were to talk about it, it would just become another story, the great romance of her life reduced to a few paragraphs in Times New Roman (twelve point), that others are allowed to own. This way it is as if the high emotional drama of the affair continues.

Rekha is seen these days as a recluse. A bit *mad*.

'Why is Rekha mad?' I asked Nari Hira when I met with him.

He paused to think, and then caught himself and looked at me: 'You ask me as if you know for a fact.'

We smile at each other. He knows the power of such a statement. I could have gone on and reminded him that he had said it to me earlier, in a throwaway 'she's *barking*' kind of comment. Now he checks himself and then says, 'Because she is a recluse. People say that it is Amitabh's fault. But I don't buy it.'

Why wouldn't you want to become a recluse in Mumbai? Why would people expect her to be anything else? After a certain point wouldn't anyone get exhausted by the round of constant inane film meets, *mahurats*,[77] bir'day parties.

Tuesday

Oh, thank the Lord glory glory glory I am the resurrection and I am the light. Today I got to the accident. 1982. Watershed. After the accident even *Stardust* came back on board and started to write about him. Everyone loved him officially and unofficially, and his long exclusion was over.

Somehow this makes me feel that I can now be released from gossipdom. Nari Hira, who doesn't officially write for *Stardust*, did the editorial:

Okay, you win, Amitabh Bachchan. I am too shaken up by his accident to sit on my ban any longer. No doubt we've had our share of *jhagdas* and *katti-kattis*[78] and backbiting, but I would never wish what happened to him, on anyone. As we go to press, I'm keeping my fingers crossed that Amitabh will

---

[77] *Mahurats* are the ceremonial canning of the first shot, carried out at an auspicious time decided by priests often months before the main shooting commences.
[78] Fights and arguments.

soon be fighting fit – even if it means fighting with us all over again!

This wasn't the only piece of humble samosa being eaten about town. Get this:

I am standing in this shop buying toothpaste. This guy (there) knows I am connected with the film industry in some way. He says to the shopkeeper 'Why haven't you put the shutters down?[79] Don't you know at 9.05 this morning Amitabh has . . .' (God I can't even use that morbid word). Hell with the toothpaste – the girl next to me puts her face in her hands and sobs – reminds me of the American girl at Hotel Hilton who went hysterical at the news of President Kennedy's death. There is a pounding in my heart – Oh hell, why the hell do I love to hurt the people I love – why the hell did I have to go and involve myself in the Ban Amitabh movement two years ago – Oh God I hope the guy is wrong. No, he couldn't already know if it happened at 9.05. Heart pounding – Hands trembling – 577049 – Amitabh's residence. Pnoo – Pnoo – Pnoo – Phone engaged.[80]

I love it. Pnoo pnoo, pnoo pnoo – it's exactly how phones sound in India. And then, these days, you have the electronic holding music: 'Greensleeves' played by a rhythmically challenged robot . . .

I mean, I guess the mags *had* to start writing about him, didn't they? You can't remain all pissy about someone who is so obviously a frackin' god. For a god he was, even if it was only for a few months . . .

---

[79] Standard form of protest or show of support is to have a *bandh*, to pull the metal shutters at the front of shops down and close up for the day.
[80] Umesh Vyas, 'Pages from a Photographer's Diary', *Super Weekly*.

Wednesday

I called Amitabh today. He was feeling much relieved because his father's surgery had gone well. He was totally underwhelmed by the fact that I had got to the accident. I told him I was ready to interview him. So guess what? He has invited me to go with him to Malaysia. He said, 'I am sure I will have some time to devote to your needs.' I love how formal he can be – formal in a jokey, fond sort of way.

I asked why he was going to Malaysia. He told me he had been invited for the press launch of the International Film Federation Awards, India's newest award ceremony. These are held in different places each year and this year his film *Aankhen* ('All the Best', dir. Vipul Amrutlal Shan, 2002) is premiering there. I am so looking forward to seeing him again.

I have to say that this exit is coming not a moment too soon. The mosquitoes have started to coalesce into different shapes in front of my eyes at night; they form almost corporeal shapes. I think that my coil-addled brain is starting to be able to understand the words they spell out.

AYM. AYM. AYM. AYM. AYM

The Real Amitabh is not to be found in the gossip magazines or academic texts. The man that I have found here is a shadow cast by his film characters. The magazines and his characters and the academic theories need each other; they feed off each other and grow into a thick impenetrable wood of 'facts' and cross-referencing. I feel further away from finding him than I did before I disappeared into Gossipville, but at least I no longer worry that everyone else knows something I don't because they were brought up on a diet of this stuff. As for the affair, as Gore Vidal says in *Burr*, 'Eventually all things are known. And few matter.'

Now I'll try to go to sleep, but in reality I know that it will be another night where I lie slapping myself like a medieval monk with Alzheimer's, who periodically remembers what it was he was meant to atone for.

Malaysia. Cool. Verdant. Without bugs!

Part Three

MALAYSIA, LONDON, DUBAI, JAIPUR

CHAPTER SEVEN

'I mistrust those hopes that can give
murderers a clear conscience.'

Raymond Aron

Malaysia

Friday evening, March 2002

Shhhh . . . got to type real quiet – Amitabh is sleeping next to
me. I don't want all clatter patter to wake the poor man. I know
I am supposed to be Objective Biographer but he does look sweet
and heartbreakingly vulnerable. His mouth is slightly open, his
baseball cap is getting all squiffy and his jaw is relaxed. He spent
ages getting things just right, arranging and rearranging his pillows
and his blanket and woozling about, sighing at me a lot in a
pointed way. But then he seemed to press some internal button
and switched off. Powered down. 'Don't do it, Dave. Daisy,
Da-is-y.' And now I am free-floating next to him, waiting for the
lights and the big black oblong to take me to the next level.

It's strange, suddenly being next to the Real Amitabh after
all this time being with the Gossip Amitabh. He is such a solid,
large, statesman-like presence. And he smells so good. Mmm,
mmm, mmm – is that a hint of the new Bulgari Mr B? And
what have you mixed it with this time?

He is real and complex – so much more than the man in

the magazines. I feel like I have made myself smaller by spending so much time on them. Lies are so seductive; the possible worlds that you can invent with even partial lies are endless. I shall be like Gustave Flaubert from now on. Apparently he had such a fear of the false that he would be unable to get up from his couch for weeks or even months in case he wrote something that wasn't true. He was convinced that everything he had already written was dreadful errors and lies and he feared that the spread of stupidity – which was afflicting humanity at large – had entered his own head.

If he knew what was going on today 'truth sleuth' Gustave would turn in his grave. Or at least, since his fear of falsehood seemed to result in a very nineteenth-century paralysis, throw up his hands in horror and ask to be moved so he could see the sunset better. Perhaps the twentieth century did away with the idea of being able to attain an objective truth. But some truths *must* have more weight than others?

When I am next to Amitabh his physical presence is the only thing that is real. He is so *weighty*, it's like I go into orbit around him. I can't transpose that feeling on to paper though. Anyway, it's just another subjective experience of him: nothing objective about me, mate. If I write down the words he says to me I just add to the Print Media Amitabh – more paper to wade through for the next poor bastard who decides to write a biography of him. Nothing that I write could ever communicate what it feels like to watch his hands – with their long thin fingers decked out in HUGE sapphires and emeralds and remarkably smooth fingernails – tug his blanket up to his chin. If I stare at him long enough perhaps I will somehow be able to get the essence of Amitabh by osmosis, or perhaps the cosmic rays that are bombarding us right now will pull bits of him into me, and vice versa . . .

Cosmic smoshmic baba please to be waking up and smelling one item koppie – ooops. I moved about too much. He just opened his eyes and glared at me balefully, like a disappointed bloodhound. And then he went back to sleep.

Poor chap, he worked right up till he had to get on the plane. The least I could do is let the man catch a couple of hours of shuteye. Anyway, now we're about to land so he's going to have to get vertical soon. Malaysia, here we come.

As you can probably tell from my little rant I haven't really talked to anyone much. I got back to Mumbai and then spent the day rushing about trying to get the stuff for my curtains and then get it all to the nice tailor lady before her soft furnishings guy went home for the evening. Sounds like I am making molehill mountains, but things just take more time in Mumbai.

Plus I had everyone commenting on my face which is covered in red spots from both the bastard mosquitoes and the eyebrow-threading disaster gone wrong hello thank you very much not again no way.

Mumbaiwallas are very blunt. If you have a spot they point at it and say, 'Oh, what an enormous spot!' If you look tired, they will say, 'You look really exhausted.' If you have put on weight, they tell you even before they have finished kissing you hello. Rani Mukherjee does this without fail every time I meet her. 'Jess!' she says in her wildly sexy husky voice, 'Have you lost or put on?' She then looks at my paunch and pronounces, not unsympathetically, 'You've put on.' Which, since she always looks divine, just adds to my feeling like the Abominable Snowman next to her. But women here seem to take it in good grace. I was in a lift once with Manisha Koirala. A woman who knew Manisha also got into the lift and, after some initial pleasantries, told her with delighted horror that she had, 'put on so much of veight!'

'Yah,' said Manisha sweetly, 'I had an accident horse-riding.'

The woman got out a couple of floors before us. I was bristling.

'Well, at least you don't look like a bloody walking anorexic skeleton-witch like her,' I hissed.

Manisha looked confused. She had indeed put on weight so she had thought it a fair comment. I guess I am just used to the deep insincerity of English politesse.

But the best example of this bluntness has to be the time when Rachel Dwyer introduced two friends to each other and the Mumbaiwalla said, 'Hello, how nice to meet you.' And then, without even pausing for breath, 'Why do you have such tiny raisiny eyes?'

Anyway, the lady at the tailor's was really great and yet again translated my confused ideas into a workable pattern. I am glad to have finally found a good tailor. Women in Mumbai will often say something like: 'You should get a tailor to stitch it for you.' But when you inquire where such person may be found they get all misty around the edges and say, 'Yah, I will introduce you.' But you know they never will. Somehow, for reasons I haven't yet fathomed, it's an intimate sharing one step too far. It's like I'm asking to borrow their roll-on deodorant or something.

Amitabh and I have taken the night flight to Kuala Lumpur. Travelling with Amitabh can be quite fraught. I have flown internally with him many times and it requires total concentration; you have to be more prepared than Baden Powell (no fumbling for passports or dib dib, dub dub where the fuck's my boarding pass stub allowed) and an Olympic scuttler.

Amitabh has to get through public spaces in India fast. The idea, I think, is that if he creates enough velocity the populace will be repelled away at about the same rate as they are drawn towards him. This will allow him free passage until the compulsion towards him by the body of people through which he is passing reaches critical mass, and their combined momentum overwhelms him and they all pour in on top of him.

So, here is how to travel with him. Get to the airport earlyish – he won't arrive till the plane is ready to take off, so no point getting there too early – I mean, how many books on how to efficiently move your cheese can you read?[81] Wait for Praveen to arrive with Amitabh's ten enormous bags and give him your two small ones. Then position yourself just in front of the entrance to the departure lounge. You will be able to tell when Amitabh is about to arrive because, just like before an earthquake, the birds fall silent and the horses get restless. And then he is there. He will nod and say a curt, 'Hello Jessica'.

And he is gone, just his scent lingering.

So, making sure you have your boarding pass ready, you whizz through, flinging your bag at the X-ray machine and dive into the booth where the bored dykey policewoman cops a feel in the name of national security, and languidly stamps your pass.

'Come on! Time's a-wastin' lady,' you silently scream at her.

Then you go and get your bag from the pile, elbowing businessmen in the face in your haste and scuttle after Amitabh who will have managed to stride on and be almost at the boarding gate. No matter how fast I am he is always faster. I don't know how he does it. I think that his superstardom has allowed him to be able to slip in and out of dimensions that we can't see – Superstringy Amitabh. Anyway. Then you get on to the bus that takes you to the plane. During this ride he never makes eye contact or says anything – he is still in the zone. Then he levitates up the steps and takes his seat, always 1A, at the front next to the window. He then busies himself with his phones and his palm pilot and various bits of paper in his big leather briefcase. He clearly loves wizzling the lock combination around. He then reads the papers, rearranges his briefcase a bit more, and finally he's ready to talk to you.

---

[81] Airport bookshops in India are predominantly stocked with management self-help books.

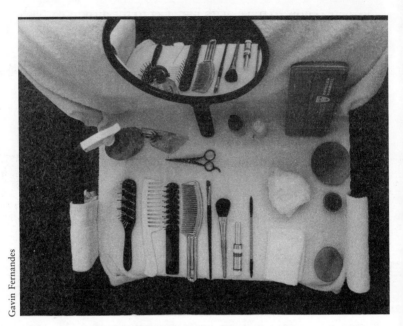

Gavin Fernandes

Amitabh's immaculate make-up table.

Amitabh loves order. He loves things to be in the right place. He loves clean, organised, calm rooms with everything arranged just so. He is always telling me that my life is too chaotic. I think that *everyone* is too chaotic next to him. You really have to wonder why he works in the film industry which is chaos only, *baba*. Mandelbrot Mumbai. Or perhaps this need to create a still point in his turning world has developed because of the nature of his work.

Anyway today, it being an international flight and all, I went ahead and got on the plane before him. I was surprised when a man came and sat down in the seat next to me. Didn't he know this was Amitabh's seat? It turned out he was in charge of the food at the Oberoi and we had a nice conversation about where to find the best *paani puri*[82] in Mumbai. I have a passion for *paani puri* after I was introduced to them a few years ago. This guy reckoned the best is to be found at a place in Pali Hill, so I've taken the address and I'm going to try it when I get back to Mumbai.

Suddenly Amitabh energised on to the plane, all the excess power from creating his Public-Passing Vortex in the departure lounge flowing out of him. He was chewing gum and looking quite rakish in jeans and a loose silky knit jumper. He looked at the Oberoi guy and then at his seating stub. The Oberoi guy's head snapped back as if Amitabh had just staked him to the headrest.

'Oh! Hello Sir! Is this your seat, Sir?' he asked, suddenly all unsure of himself.

'No,' said Amitabh simply. 'Jessica. How are you? Glad you could make it.' He nods, smiles at me and passes on to his seat next to Guarang Doshi, who produced *Aankhen*.

'You're travelling with *him*?' whispers Oberoi *khaanawalla*, all his my-*paani-puri*-place-is-the-best bravura gone.

All was rectified after the plane took off when Doshi came and asked the poor guy to move so that Amitabh could be polite and sit next to his guest. And she could watch enthralled while he organised his briefcase, waiting patiently till he turned to her and said, 'Oh! What happened to your face?'

And then feel guilty when she woke him up. Come on plane, hurry up. Bored now.

Saturday

Oh my dear life, where am I? I have been transported to a Chinese-Malay gambling and entertainment megalopolis perched

---

[82] Snacks made from small puffy *puris* which are punctured at the top and then filled with spicy chick peas and tangy tamarind water.

on a hill in central Malaysia. The resort is called Genting Highlands and it is, according to all the literature, the product of one man's vision in the late 1960s. He must have been tripping is all I can say.

Genting Highlands. I am spinning out badly. I thought Malaysia would be all happy orang-utans and . . . well, that's as far as I'd got actually. Bugger. Amitabh is in his room sleeping and then having meetings. I am, yet again, waiting for Amitabh. Left to my own devices in a humungaloidous hotel. Not even some irritating sidekick to have existential debates with. This place is doing my nut. It is, without a doubt, the strangest place I have ever been to. I'm really not sure I'd ever be able to describe it. But I will try. This is what you're supposed to do with trauma victims, isn't it? Get them to talk about their experience so that they can own it and not be owned by it.

OK. It's basically an enormous casino with, I am told, 3,140 slots and 426 tables. But around it have been built three vast hotels with 7,000 rooms each; so it's like a mini city. The whole thing sits on top of a mountain 6,000 feet above sea level, so clouds and mist permanently surround us. The organisers of this little shindig think this makes the place really romantic. If you are Cornish you do not think of rain as romantic. If you are Indian, you do. And never the twain shall meet. As you approach it from the airport it suddenly appears, looming above the jungle, sparkling in the sun and seemingly suspended in the clouds like Cloud City in *The Empire Strikes Back*, or the Emerald City in *The Wizard of Oz*.

As you can see, I am desperate to find things to link it to in my brain so that it doesn't feel so goddam alien. For alien it is, or rather, alien I am. Everyone else seems to think this place is just Jim Dandy. But it's the décor that's really whacked out: they have taken EVERY style from the whole of history across the globe and just thrown it in together in no order, or at least with no discernible linking feature.[83] For example, Amitabh is in the Egyptian Suite. Which means an eighties take on Art Deco goes Egyptian, and the walls are filled with prints of Impressionist and Modernist paintings. My sensibilities are so offended I feel, for the first and hopefully the last time, like Ruskin.

For God's sake Jessica, you snob. Sigh.

But it hurts my eyes and my brain. I can deal with the idea that there is no such thing as objective truth, but I am not sure if I am willing to capitulate over the suggestion that there might be no such thing as good taste. I can't help it, I am hardwired this way; my grandmother Clockwork-Oranged me from birth. As soon as my back muscles were strong enough, we would sit together and go through *Homes and Gardens* and she would point to things and pronounce judgement: 'Yes, yes, no, yes, no, no oh God no, ah yes, wow – how's that for colour! No, ah look – classic design. Remember Jessica, John Lewis for the everyday, Liberty's for the soul . . .'

Amitabh thought the place was a little OTT. I know because he looked about at the décor on our way up and then looked at me and widened his eyes and smiled an amused smile.

I think I need to have a nap. I shouldn't have drunk so much coffee when I got here. But I was having a Compulsive Oral Moment – I felt panicky so I needed to stuff something in my mouth. It is a miracle that I don't smoke. Nap later.

I am here for the next two days with about fifteen Indian journalists, none of whom I know, and a bunch of production boys from Wizcraft (the events management company)

---

[83] I have since discovered how to describe it: it is the same as the décor in the bath house of the spirits in Miyazaki's *Spirited Away*. If you have seen that film you will have believed it to be a fantasy. It is not. It is Genting Highlands.

who just want to watch the floor show, gamble and get drunk.

Now I am unsure about the possibility of the interviews happening. Amitabh probably thought that we would have some time, but then Bollywood stars are used to trying to fit twenty-eight hours into twenty-four. Did he underestimate the amount of work that he would have to do when he got here?

I talked with Amitabh a bit during the car journey here, but it was gentle *time-pass* chat. He had not been impressed that on our arrival I waltzed through the immigration line with nothing more than a passport that is valid for six months, whilst he had to wait in line with every passport he had ever owned stapled together and all relevant visas displayed.

He met me on the other side and growled, 'It's only because you guys ruled the world.' And then he and Guarang Doshi rolled their eyes at the discrimination in global immigration policies.

I smiled, savouring my one moment of non-scuttling grace.

Perhaps it's the fog that's depressing me. It's all a bit *Wuthering Heights*. I keep not being able to see the huge hotel opposite, then it appears briefly like a stage set for the *Multi-coloured Swap Shop* and I feel an inexplicable panic as I look down at the cable car that takes off to God knows where from its base. Perhaps I am just getting vertigo and I should stop looking out of the window and have a nap. But there is this child trying to get in, keeps saying she's come home – what to do?

Still waiting for Amitabh. He has called me to say that we are all going out to dinner in one of the Chinese restaurants here. But first he has to have another meeting. It turns out I am not the only person who has come all the way to Malaysia in the hope of getting some time with him. Insane but true, people have travelled here just to have meetings with him. I had forgotten this. Sigh. It's not his fault really. The way this industry works means that spending time – real time, like hours at a stretch – with anyone involved in film is almost impossible. So sometimes meetings have to travel with him.

Why? It's all about money. Of course.

Why it is impossible to spend any real time with Amitabh in Mumbai

As John Travolta says in *Pulp Fiction*, 'It breaks down like this . . .'

The use of black-market money in film financing began during the war when smugglers and gangsters realised that to launder money made by smuggling etc. they should invest in films about smugglers and gangsters. Making films is a great way of laundering your booty because you can pay for so much in cash. It's only a couple of steps from black to white, and after a few hit films you can be a pukka film financier. It was the beginning of a beautiful friendship, made all the more piquant because it also allowed everyone to stiff the British. In those days, not rendering unto Caesar was very patriotic. This symbiotic relationship still continues today although, if the industry is to be believed, to a much lesser extent. None of the bigger production houses will have anything to do with it. Or so they would have us believe.

The introduction of black-market cash had various effects on the way that films were made.

For a start it meant that the practice of having all artists and crew under written contract went out of the window.

Why?

Let's say that a Producer pays a Star half his fee in cash so that the Star doesn't have to declare it all to the Taxman. It is in the Star's interest not to sign a contract for the official amount (i.e. the amount he is declaring).

Why?

Should the Producer turn out to be an unscrupulous fellow, the Star could find himself in a situation in which the Producer could refuse him the remainder of his money.

And the Star would not have a leg to stand on.

So the way Stars make sure that they get all their money is by maintaining as much power over the production of the film as possible. How can they do this? Well, my friend, as a Star you have the ability to withhold 'dates'. If a Star does not put aside any days on which to shoot the film, he can stop the film from being completed. So, the blackguard Producer has to stump up the rest of the cash and do anything to keep the Star sweet so that they give dates to the film.

Another downside to film stars not having contracts is that there's no guarantee a film will be completed. This makes 'official money' unhappy about putting up the whole amount for a film – unless it's by one of the few 'big banner' production houses (established director/producer combos). So a film gets made as and when the money comes in. A producer secures an initial amount by signing up some talent: the stars, the music director and the director. He then goes to a financier and says something like, 'Please Sir, I have so and so and such and such, please give me the money to make the film.'

The producer will then use this money to make a couple of exciting scenes – a dance, a car chase, some punchy dialogue about a son's love for his mother. He will then go to another guy with cash to launder and say something like, 'Please Sir, see what I have made so far. I am asking you to help to complete this film.'

Very rarely is there a signed agreement between financiers and producers. A verbal agreement in Mumbai is binding; all business is personal and all relationships are business. A bad reputation is worse than the threat of legal proceedings, which could take years anyway.[84]

Another problem with raising finance by this method is the level of interest payable. This ranges between 24 per cent and 36 per cent, depending on the risk assessed by the financier.[85] So the producers are desperate to get the film finished as soon as possible. However, even if they give their stars all the cash they agreed on up front and everyone is like family to each other, they are often still thwarted in their goal of swift completion by the problem of dates.

Dates are to the Hindi film industry what guilt is to the Catholic Church. The rather fractured nature of the financing means that actors cannot rely on any one film at a time – it simply might never get finished – so they have developed the practice of working on several films at once. This way they are not sitting around waiting for the producer to get the next lump of cash; instead they are maximising on their ability to earn money.[86]

This multi-film phenomenon has resulted in the film industry developing a shift system. In Mumbai there is a morning shift, an afternoon shift and a night shift and stars shuttle their way through the traffic jams, perennially late and, more recently, permanently on the phone, placating and arranging. The multi-film trend reached its zenith in the 1980s, when Anupam Kher reportedly had twenty films on the go simultaneously, although

---

[84] Another way to raise finance is to pre-sell the film to distributors. The amount that you can raise this way is determined by your standing within the film industry and the type of project that you are known for.

[85] These figures were given by Aamir Khan in an interview on 11 September 1998.

[86] Actors and actresses sign as many films as possible while the going is good. After a hit they are often deluged with producers hoping they are going to be the Next Big Thing and make them lots of cash. In India it takes a long time for a star to die completely; the general dearth of icons compared to the celebrity-saturated west means that magazines and fans are loyal for much longer.

in the early 1970s Shashi Kapoor set the record by 'taking the signing amount' for fifty films.[87] These days if you want to show that you are a serious actor, and so successful that you have no worries about getting the next role, you only do one or two films a year.

Such are the insane demands on a star's time that his secretary becomes one of the most important people in the industry. A good secretary is the gatekeeper, the front line between the star and the chaos and the demands of the producers and directors. They look after the star's personal needs/desires/whims, and are often the chief ego massager too. The insanely intense type of fame that the stars are subject to, often overnight, means that they can very quickly lose contact with any reality other than that of their own subjective present. They feel that the world revolves around *them* and *their* wants and needs because, while they are famous, it *does*.

This is emphasised by the many *chamchas* (literally 'tablespoons', but 'yes men' is a better description) that dance in attendance around a star. For these people the sun rises and sets when a star says it does. They include the secretary, managers, drivers, make-up people and the ubiquitous 'man Friday' (whose job it is to anticipate the star's every need and undertake the essential duties of holding cigarettes and phones, etc.) as well as others who rely to a greater or lesser extent on their association with the star to secure work, be it in the star's next film or in a related project. So, hoping at the same time for a chance meeting with a director or a producer, they all sit around waiting for the star.

Like I am now.

---

[87] The signing amount is the portion of the star's fee that is given to them by the producer when they agree to do the film. This was Shashi Kapoor's way of protesting against his shoddy treatment at the hands of producers and directors. By doing this, he said, he was not reliant on any of his films ever doing well again.

I'm waiting for my man, $26 in my hand, he's never early he's always late, first thing you learn is that you always got to wait.

Hmmm . . . can heroin really have been that cheap?

The myth of Amitabh the Punctual

By and large Amitabh is punctual, but I have spent most of my twenties waiting in the sun on different dusty film sets for the Always-on-time One. It is such a strong thread in the Amitabh litany – he is on time, no one else in the film industry is – that when he isn't on time, which is quite often, nobody seems to notice. 'Amitabh's late!' I say. They look confused and shake their heads wordlessly. It's like their brains cannot compute such a radically different type of data and so they just revert to the old programme.

When he started working in the industry his timekeeping was dramatically better than that of the average star. In those days, being sometimes *days* late was all part of what it meant to be a star. When the director Manmohan Desai began to make his first film, *Amar Akbar Anthony*, he asked his actors not to give him any trouble during filming. One of them (Vinod Khanna) 'informed him in no uncertain terms that there would be no warning before such behaviour was displayed. If they wanted to act up they would just do so in the middle of the film.'

Ahh, come on pusher man, needing that crazy voodoo jive. Feel sick and dirty, more dead than alive.

Later . . .

Well, that was quite remarkable. I just saw a great magic show. These two very strange-looking guys turning lots of tigers and lions into lovely dancing ladies and back again. I was impressed. Amitabh wasn't.

'I have played a magician in two of my films. I was told how this is done.'

'How is it done then?'

'I am not telling you.'

'Why not?'

'I was sworn to secrecy.'

The audience was invited up on stage afterwards to have their photos taken with a tiger. We all left but I realised that I badly wanted to pat the cat so I told everyone I was going back. Amitabh said that he had wrestled a tiger in *Mr Natwarlal* and didn't want to do so again.

He's the king of the jungle, they call him the tiger-man . . .

'Yeah,' I joked, 'I've seen the stills. There's one where you have him in a headlock, your face is all *grrrr effort wrestle wrestle*, and the tiger's looking straight to camera. I have never seen such a bored, drugged animal in my life.'

Amitabh is rankled. 'They took its claws out but it was still terrifying.'

They took its claws out? Aren't tigers like, *protected*? Isn't that against some international law on the treatment of animals in films? Come to think of it, I can't remember ever seeing the 'No animal was hurt during the making of this film' thing at the beginning of a Hindi film. I told Amitabh I would see him back at the hotel.

I was allowed to go and stroke the tiger's flank. It was extraordinary, all muscle and short hair like a horse, but so much more powerful. As I stroked him he turned around and stared at me. I felt seen. It was both moving and terrifying. This tiger's claws were definitely still in. But I wouldn't try my luck with him even with them out.

Later I tried to interest Amitabh in my tiger connection while he channel-surfed. It is one of his least endearing features, but there is nothing that can be done about it. I tried years ago:

'*Must* you surf?' I asked through gritted teeth one afternoon.

'S-u-r-f?' asked Amitabh, staring at me in disbelief.

'Yes. Channel-surf. You flicking through the channels like this. It's called channel-surfing, and if you're not doing it yourself, it's torture.'

'Fine.' He stopped on the channel showing cricket.

I sighed. Surfing is better than bloody boring bloody cricket. 'Who's winning?' I asked.

He slowly turned and looked at me in disbelief, again: 'No one.'

Which just about sums up cricket.

What can I say? I am pre-new-ladette British girl – I haven't the first clue about cricket. Or football. I can say the right things for football: 'Referee!' or 'Get up you big girl' or 'Come on son, get it in!' if I have the misfortune of being forced to watch a game, but haven't a clue what these phrases actually mean.

Amitabh was still surfing. I think it's how he switches off. I have learnt to zone out while he does it – lie back and think of England.

I did ask him about the interviews.

'Yes,' is what he said. 'Don't worry, we will do them.'

'When?'

'Some time soon.'

I took a big swig of wine to stop myself from badgering him too much and making him mad. It's hard to know when you're about to reach that point, and I often overstep the line. Amitabh says that when I want something I have a particular tone of voice: 'So, um, Amitabh . . .'

He says that this makes his blood run cold as he wonders what I'm about to ask him for. Often this will trigger Amitabh's sudden transformation into a Black Hole. In the blink of an eye he has more mass and gravitational pull than is strictly normal. I grip the arms of my chair and hear the sound of unattached objects whizzing past my ears into the void.

So, now, I drink my emotions.

Tomorrow is the press conference, and I'll really have to push for the interviews. Nicely nicely isn't working right now. Straight off I'll ask him when, and I won't let him drift away into watching cricket or psychologically cripple me by telling me how tired he is. I am finding this transition from being a friend to someone he is supposed to be working with almost impossible to achieve. Somehow I have to shift the dynamic and not let either of us slip back into comfortable patterns of behaviour. But how?

I'm going to raid the minibar for a well deserved entire bottle of champagne.

Sunday

I got a lift in a limo down to the other hotel for the press launch. I was grateful for the lift because it's actually cold up on this mountain with the permanent clouds. I just don't see how people can think that a hotel that looks out at wet car parks can be anything other than depressing.

The launch was a bit of a non-event; mainly lots of people saying that Malaysia was indeed truly Asia. They showed some clips from Amitabh's latest film *Aankhen* in which he plays a criminal mastermind who gets lots of blind people to rob a bank. He looks darkly bad and sexy on the clips and says, 'Dangerous game . . . Exciting' in a very enticing manner. Journalists asked respectful but inane questions.

Amitabh is being treated as if he is the only person eligible to be ambassador to the Hindi film industry. It's remarkable how things have changed for him in the last couple of years – Amitabh is definitely becoming something else, shifting into a different role yet again. He used to be 'Angry Young Man' –

now what? He's not exactly hiding his head in the sand, but I wouldn't say the fires of righteous anger against the system are burning very strongly. If they ever did. He has said over and over again that the Angry Young Man was created by the scriptwriting duo Salim-Javed. They were the ones who fashioned this new type of character, and it was one that most actors were scared of playing. Not Amitabh. This is always taken to be an indication that he was somehow part of the widespread civil unrest that characterised the early and mid 1970s in India. But beneath the swagger and a tendency to light his ciggie with a burning dynamite fuse, he was actually a middle-class man who wanted to make lots of money for his family.

The crucial point is that Amitabh could act. He is a damn good actor, so you believed his anger and his pain. And since these were not common emotions in the beautiful, sparkly world of Bollywood, it was assumed – if subconsciously – that Amitabh the man was somehow similar to Amitabh on screen.

From Angry Young Man to game-show host

Amitabh is now Mr *Kaun Banega Crorepati?* (the Indian version of *Who Wants to be a Millionaire?*, *KBC* for short – Indians love acronyms). He is the source of all wealth and knowledge five times a week at 9 p.m. Who wants to be a millionaire? Well, just about the whole of India it seems, and they love it that Amitabh is the guy who can take them there.

Amitabh says that at the time he wasn't sure that becoming a game-show host was the right thing to do. He asked his family and they weren't too convinced either. He told me what he was about to do and I said that I thought it was a terrible idea – shows how much I know.

Three days after the show began he went on a pilgrimage to Amarnath in the Himalayas: not traditional Bollywood territory.

The crowds there were not screaming, as they usually would, the names of the characters from his films, they were shouting: '*KBC! KBC!*' The range and penetration of Amitabh as Mr Crorepati was way bigger than anyone had expected.

KBC was the first really good game show on Indian television and, although *Who Wants to be a Millionaire?* has been huge around the world, in India it was a phenomenon. It was, believe it or not, the first time people had been given the chance to win big money on television.

This is compulsive viewing anywhere, but in a country with no welfare state, where the slum beckons all those who fail, and where people regularly starve to death, it was magical.

By Christmas 2000 everyone had stories of the hapless fellows who had not been able to answer the simplest of questions. Javed Akhtar told me with great glee about the contestant who hadn't known how many lungs there were in the human body and had to 'phone a friend' who turned out to be her mother, who was a doctor. Or the woman who didn't know the name of Basanti's horse in Amitabh's biggest film, *Sholay*. You could feel the nation tense: what would Amitabh Bachchan do to someone who didn't know this simple film fact (it's Dhanno)? He was, of course, gracious and kind.

When Amitabh had to 'phone a friend' for people and told them who was speaking, the show would often be held up while the whole family came on the line. In the background there would be a lot of 'Aunty! Aunty! Come quick, it's *Amitabh Bachchan*!' Amitabh smiled and said hello to everyone respectfully, and thank you when they told him how much they loved him. The nerve-racked contestant would be temporarily happy and relaxed listening to their friends and family going bananas. Cinemas had to shift their screening times because no one was turning up to their nine o'clock show. The whole country was united in egging on their fellow Indians to win and make everyone proud.

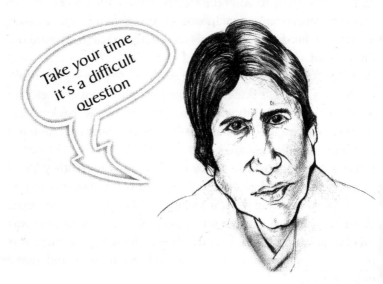

KBC became a celebration of the middle-class dedication to education. Some people watched the show just to hear Amitabh speaking his chaste Sanskritised Hindi. No Bollywood-shollywood Hinglish and all on *KBC yaar* – it was as pure as the snows that feed the Ganges. Such are the Subcontinent's self-improving tendencies.

1999 was a remarkable year because it marked the start of an outpouring of love for Amitabh from all over the globe. The BBC held an online poll to discover who was the greatest star of the millennium. To their utter amazement the response was overwhelmingly in favour of a man known to very few at Bush House. Amitabh Bachchan got many more votes than any other actor, including Laurence Olivier, Charlie Chaplin and Marlon Brando. When he's asked about it Amitabh is self-deprecating, often saying that it must have been a computer error, but it was a unique example of the democratisation of the net; an email was sent around the globe – from one Indian to another to all friends and relatives in the address book – telling them to log on to the BBC and vote for Amitabh. *Desipower* [88] proved itself more than a match for complacent western voters who, to be fair, hadn't realised their national honour was at stake. India ensured that her biggest star was recognised by the world. The BBC website said to its surprised users:

> Many people in the western world will not have heard of Amitabh Bachchan, fifty-six, but he remains one of Bollywood's biggest stars, having appeared in more than a hundred films in three decades. He made his name in the seventies and eighties as an action hero, a swashbuckling star of Hindi films.

Amitabh was then ushered into another very British hall of fame: Madame Tussaud's made a wax figure of him, resplendent in

---

[88] Indian power.

Italian suit and expensive Kashmiri shawl. He was the first star from a totally different sky who had made it into the collection, an indication of just how far the Indian film industry had managed to penetrate the British psyche. Amitabh inspected his effigy and then said: 'I want to thank the people, my fans, who have continued to be with me for over thirty years now. I am just so overwhelmed by their enthusiasm and this is indeed the most wonderful gesture.'

Giving awards to Amitabh Bachchan became something of a national pastime, and his biodata records all the major ones. Before 1999 he received eight but since then there have been more than thirty. The craze took off not only in India; we are told: 'He has been decorated by countries like South Africa, Mauritius, Egypt, Russia, UK, USA, Holland, Guyana, Trinidad and Tobago and Afghanistan for his achievements in the field of cinema. Mr Bachchan has also been the recipient of several other citations worldwide.' In 2001 he received the Padma

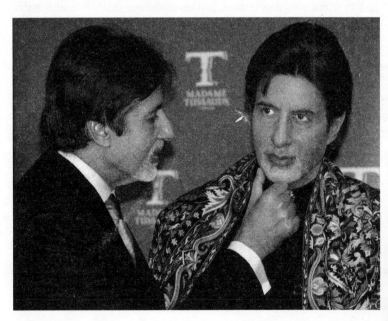

Bhushan, the third highest honour to be bestowed by the Indian government on its citizens (after the Bharat Ratna and the Padma Vibhushan).

This all reached a peak when some particularly admiring fans in Kolkata set up a temple to Amitabh. The Amitabh Bachchan Fans Association carried out a full day's *puja* to inaugurate the temple, starting at 8.30 a.m. They worshipped Lord Ganesha, moved on to Narayan and then to the main focus, Amitabh Bachchan. Hundreds of devotees dropped sticks of sandalwood into a small fire, addressing a picture of Amitabh as 'Lord', 'Guru' or 'Boss', and prayed for blessings. Apparently the priests chanted Vedic hymns and thanked him for making mankind see the difference between good and evil through his movie roles.

Do they actually think that he is a god? This is a bit hazy, but as one fan pointed out: 'A person who has touched so many lives, can he be any less than a god?'[89]

The Fans Association undertook good works in Bachchan's name to celebrate their month-long Amitabh Festival. One thousand people were given surgery at microsurgery eye camps, and blood was donated for thalassaemia patients. The first five hundred donors were rewarded immediately in this life with a ticket to *first day first show* of Amitabh's next big film, *Aks* ('The Reflection', dir. Rakesh Omprakash Mehra, 2001).

The temple was unique in its focus on Bachchan's screen personas as a way to personal salvation. On entering the temple a devotee would have to recite dialogue from his films, which the 10,000 members of the Association insist are full of sublime messages from heaven. These recitals would replace prayers, and songs would be playing instead of hymns.

---

[89] Which of course proves precisely nothing except that goal posts are made to be shifted and to do so is a fan's unique prerogative.

It is easy to lampoon images of men and women earnestly chanting '*aum*, I can walk English I can talk English *aum*, because English is a very funny language *aum*', but Amitabh's life – and by that I mean all his film lives too – is so fixed in the national consciousness that it has become a reference, a series of stories and examples that can be used by others to help them live their own lives.

Amitabh says:

> It's overwhelming to have been voted BBC Actor of the Millennium, to have one's wax statue at Madame Tussaud's, to have a temple in your name in Kolkata. What can you do about these things? The building of this temple for example . . . Somewhere inside you, you obviously don't agree with it but you cannot question the affection of the fan. How do you stop somebody from drawing your portrait in blood or walking backwards for several hundred miles as a 'mannat' for my recovery? You can't do anything; you can tell them not to do it when you meet them, but how can you stop them?[90]

This shift of Amitabh from Angry Young Man to the Great Patriarch is often perceived as a sellout, but Amitabh was never invested in the idea of the Angry Young Man in the first place. And he is only into being the Great Patriarch for its cash-generating possibilities. He is open about this, and always has been. In the first interview he did after the press ban was lifted by mutual consent after the accident, he described himself as basically still being a clerk, albeit a well-paid clerk. He reported to the sets, did what he was told, collected his cash and went home. Acting was a job. It was one that he loved and was good at, but it was still a job and he would be whoever they – the producers and the fans – wanted him to be. He had to

---

[90] *Outlook*, 13 August 2001.

reinvent himself and succeeded, even if it took him a little time to work out what it was that he was supposed to become.

Amitabh Bachchan surfs public desires. The public gets what the public wants. Dangerous game: exciting!

After the press conference Amitabh went off to do some interviews. Grrr. With other writers. Irrational anger. I decided to have a little wander around the hotels and found myself in a fake jungle filled with shops selling ginseng, and Chinese families engaging in that universal sport: trying their best to have a happy family holiday. And then, nestled beneath some vines, I saw a Starbucks. Ha ha, oh how I loved the post-modern globalised culture banal multinational irony of it all . . . so I went and had a latte with an extra shot. And yes, there is something oddly creamy about Starbucks milk everywhere you go.

Later . . .

Waiting again.

Tap tap tap tap tap tap drum drum drum drum drum, check my make-up, get depressed about my mozzied face all red and spotty, God damn them, tap tap tap tap tap drum drum, come on Amitabh, call.

Anyone would think that he is trying to avoid giving me the interviews . . .

This Awards *tamasha* that we are all here for – the organisers keep saying how international it is, how international Hindi films have become these days. Well, that's the word on Film City Main Street, but I am not sure what that means. There is definitely a sense that the rest of the world is somehow becoming aware that India actually *has* a film industry, but beyond that no one in the west really has a clue. They know that there is a lot of singing and dancing about, they know that it's big, and they know that Bollywood Style – this season's must-have – means lots of sequins and chiffon tops.

'International film' and 'crossover film' are words that are being bandied about a lot in Mumbai. It's less that people are excited about the artistic possibilities of creating something in a new genre, and rather that a new revenue stream has opened up which they hadn't thought of before. Everyone is particularly psyched at the moment because *Lagaan*, which has played to both Indian and mainstream audiences abroad, is up for Best Foreign Film at the Oscars. These days, when producers try to get stars to do their films they no longer say, 'It will get all the awards!' but instead they cry, 'Oscar winner! It's an Oscar winner!' Will all this internationalism mean that film making takes a radical new turn? The west is so goddam fickle that I fear this love affair could turn out to be just a quick knee-trembler behind the Curzon Soho. Let's see.

Later still . . .

Ohforgodssake. Got the call. Amitabh has decided to go back to India tomorrow so we're leaving for KL now. He says it will be more fun.

Fun to funky.

Wednesday

Well. No interviews. Amitabh went shopping in KL and then we caught the night flight home.

Party last night at Manisha's. She has this fantastic garden on the roof of her flat. Her own private oasis. Good food, good music, good people. All good. I'm really ill today because I made the mistake of drinking her punch.

'What's in it?' I asked when, after my fourth glass, I found I had to hold on to things.

'I mixed vodka and red wine,' she giggled. I gasped in horror. 'And fruit juice!' she assured me.

'Ah, good. For health.'

But before it all unravelled we had a fantastic time playing Holi, covering each other in coloured paint. Manisha's mother taught me some Nepalese dance moves, although I lack her innate grace in my execution. And after too much of Manisha's special punch, it all started to look a little *Lord of the Flies*.

It could be the hangover but I am feeling exhausted with Mumbai. With Amitabh. With everything. Totally burnt out.

I am not sure if I will ever be able to find anything that even remotely approximates the truth. I know I keep saying that I don't really care about the truth, and that what is interesting are the stories and how Amitabh is perceived, but I have realised that I kind of assumed there might be something there that I could stick a pin into and say, '*This* is a truth!'

Would another biographer be more tenacious? More driven? Perhaps, but they would have to be less of a friend and forgo the unique joys and frustrations that this friendship brings. And yet I am now not sure this is the added bonus for the biographer that I thought it would be. How *do* I shift the dynamic? I am at my wits' end. Or my 'end wits', as Jerry Pinto's father used to say.

Right now I am just looking forward to getting back to London and seeing my friends. They are normal and nice and I can have conversations with them about things other than Bollybloodywood.

Shazaam!

CHAPTER EIGHT

'We have seen the best of our time:
machinations, hollowness, treachery, and all
ruinous disorders, follow us disquietly to our
graves.'

William Shakespeare, *King Lear*, Act 1, Scene 2

London

Friday, April 2002

Ah, to be in England now that spring is here! London is so blessed colourful right now. So many different types of green! I now understand why green is the sacred colour in Islam – if you live in a desert the sight of green trees is paradise. If you have been in Mumbai, as the heat increases and the dust gathers, then London in April is a garden city, a paradise of fresh sweet air and flowers. My eyes cast out sight lines and reel the blossom and the tender new leaves into my thirsty soul. (Wa frackin' wa!)

I love London.

As soon as I arrived I went, as is traditional after my trips to India, to my grandfather's flat to eat bacon and eggs and an entire packet of Jaffa Cakes, and to talk at everyone. Then I came home to my lovely flat in Hoxton toon.

It is *so good* to be able to look out of my window and see

six different types of mullet and any number of deconstructed fashion items being worn with charming self-consciousness by the next generation of middle-class kids who think themselves special and different. (I just turned thirty. I get to be patronising.) *So good* to be able to walk home late at night through the rose garden behind the church on Old Street. To eat summer rolls and Bun Xa with prawns at Viet Hoa! To scuttle with irritated ennui past the hordes of trashed bridge-and-tunnel guys clotting the pavements around Mother and 333 and to be asked over and over again, 'Taksi lady?' To walk past cutting-edge furniture design shops and imagine how I would decorate my flat if only I had a gazillion pounds.

But best of all *so good* to be working once again in my own space, sitting in the Juggler Café with a large steaming latte to my right and a bowl of fruit and yogurt (for health) to my left, listening to the White Stripes on loop.

I feel a new rush of energy and have already bombarded Amitabh with emails and text messages about the frickin' interviews. You cannot escape me now Mr Bond, I will just take a bit of time out to explain my dastardly plan and stroke my pussy and then you will be mine, wooohaa ha haaaa haaa! Maniacal laughter emanates from Hoxton Square causing the web wankers to shudder, though they know not why, as they eat their £3 croissants from Catastrophe and try to navigate the roadworks formerly known as Old Street.

I have even managed to get my head round the trunks full of magazine and newspaper cuttings given to me last summer by Jerry Pinto's friend, an obsessive Amitabh fan. And I mean *obsessive*.

He started collecting anything to do with Amitabh in the early eighties and soon his house became so full of magazines, cuttings and photos that he had to use them as furniture. His bed was made out of magazines, his table rested on magazines. He has kept every picture that he ever saw of Amitabh. Didn't matter if he already had it, he just cut out another one and added it in. He is now safe in the arms of the Jesuits concerning himself with the finer points of Mariology.

And I deal with his legacy. Two huge steamer trunks full of crumbly bits of paper. They totally overwhelmed me before I went to India this time – all I could do was open a trunk every now and then, look at the unwieldy mass of musty magazines, sigh and feel depressed. But now, post archive, I am a hardened bits-of-paper-dealer-wither and have turned the sitting room into a series of piles that only I understand.

And it's great! – there's some really good stuff here. But it does give me an odd feeling, seeing Amitabh's face again and again: there are thousands and thousands of pictures of him here, which means that there must be millions and millions *out there* somewhere. It is beyond Warhol, beyond Diana, Princess of Hearts. Through reproduction and repetition the image has become something more than the sum of its parts. I don't know much about art theory (but I know what I like) so I'm not sure if there is a framework into which this fits. I guess I could ask my art-history chums, but I probably wouldn't express myself well and I might just sound like I'm losing the plot. Multibachchanitis.

It is the image of Amitabh that is important to Jerry's friend. Any picture of the Great Man should be cut out, treated with respect, and stored. Jerry told him I would laminate every picture he had collected. When Jerry told me this I stared at him in horror. Jerry stared back. I looked at the dusty hessian sack (that still smelt slightly of *dhal*) filled with thousands of pictures cut out from newspapers long ago, and sighed.

Amitabh is being responsive email-wise; he's like a different man when he writes. Then this morning at 4 a.m. I got a call from him. This is something he used to do regularly, when Amitabh Bachchan Corporation Limited was going down the tubes and he was depressed, but he hasn't done it for a while. I am rather liking the sleep-deprivation feeling.

He will be in town for the opening of 'Bollywood at Selfridges' and says we can chat then – he's being really positive and friendly again. I think this is because he likes it when I am in London – me being in Mumbai makes him panic. He likes to compartmentalise his life to an astonishing degree and I am definitely *not* in the Mumbai compartment. This used to freak me out a bit back in the old days when I was a young *ingénue* and wanted to be part of everything, but it doesn't so much now. I have a better understanding of how his mind works. Or at least I think I do today. Tomorrow he will go back to being a mystery again. I guess I benefit from distance too.

Wednesday

Amitabh arrived in London a couple of days ago. On his first evening, after a couple of hours of concerted effort, I managed to winkle him out of his hotel room to come and see a film with a group of us. Amitabh loves going to the movies; for him it is the ultimate freedom to be able to go to Leicester Square and sit incognito watching a film. Not that he ever gets to go anywhere all *that* incognito. There are always little knots of people who know who he is, and passing through Leicester Square with him you get followed by high-pitched squeaks as Indian after Pakistani after Egyptian recognises him. He doesn't create a Public-Passing Vortex here though; he's much more chilled and receptive to people, says hello, has photos taken and signs bits of paper.

Being with him transforms London.

It also transforms going to the cinema. I usually casually go and buy a ticket, get a bottle of water, perhaps some Revels, and take my seat. Amitabh buys *the shop*, every possible sweet/snack/soft drink combo gets purchased and then loaded on to me. He likes to make a big comedy of seeing how much he can pile on before I can't see where I am going. It's a little like being on *Crackerjack*. When we get into the auditorium he eats some of all of it and then passes the rest to me, demanding I hold everything so that when I move I crackle loudly.

This time we went to see *The Mexican*. Which he didn't like. Actually, thinking about it, I'm not sure Amitabh has ever liked a film I've taken him to see. After *Topsy-Turvy* he shrugged and said, 'This is what I do all day. Why would I want to watch a film about it?'

Today I got him to come to lunch with me and my glamorous publisher! It was stressful. I had forgotten what a remarkable effect he has on women, and also what hard work he can be with people he doesn't know or feel comfortable with.

After about two minutes of polite chat he transformed inexplicably into Unresponsive Amitabh. But he looked dashed handsome which, to my horror, made Glam Publisher just sit there and gently goldfish at him. This ability of his to provoke instant devotion and fawning from otherwise strong and intelligent women always makes me even more rude and bolshy with him than I normally am. It is not a good mode to get into, granted, but I can't help myself.

Whenever Amitabh appears in public men and women from the Subcontinent materialise as if by magic and stare at him. We all know that we live in a fantastically multicultural country, but you have no idea how many of the different races living in England are devoted to Indian cinema. You have no idea until you go out with Amitabh, that is. Today little groups of men began to cluster around the window of our humble Italian restaurant, waiting patiently so they could ask him for his autograph. Having seen this to the power of ten in India I have got much better at ignoring them. But the many demands on her attention were a bit much for Glam Publisher who kept darting incredulous looks at the men, not knowing whether or not they should perhaps be asked to move along.

In a desperate attempt to engage him in conversation she told Amitabh that we were hoping to have a big launch event: 'As big as we can really . . . perhaps the South Bank Centre?' she offered, sparkle-smiling at him.

Amitabh looked totally non-plussed at Glam Publisher's offerings. She had not been thinking filmi levels of pomp – she should have modelled it more on the Triumphal March in *Aida*. He made no comment whatsoever, he just stared at his cutlery until she began to flounder in his spirit-crushing gravitational field. I have watched too many fine men and women go down in flames when up against the impenetrable might of Amitabh Bachchan, aka the Death Star. I can see he has already fixed her with his 'tractor' beam and is pulling her to her doom on the cruel hard surface of male indifference.

Time for diversionary action.

'Yes,' I say to him, 'and then if you can come down through the hall on a burning crane with pyros going off all around and cold fire on your hands in a big gold and red cape with lights flashing at the bottom? I will of course enter stage left on an elephant.'

'OK. Sure,' he deadpans at me. We smile at each other briefly.

Being 'in it together' with Amitabh is a bit nerve-racking, but it does have its bonuses.

I can see that Glam Publisher's droid has managed to put out the fire so she can return to base and live to fight another day some place where her sparkle eyes will be appreciated.

Eventually, after two courses of pain, I tell Amitabh that he is free to go. The cluster of men with their hurriedly bought disposable cameras get to click their photos, and he signs their new notebooks and makes them happy before jumping into the waiting Merc and zooming back to the safety of his hotel room.

'Oh,' says Glam Publisher when I return to the table, 'that vulnerability! And that *need*! It's quite overpowering, isn't it? You would crawl on your knees over broken glass to get the smile, wouldn't you?'

'Shall I show you my scars?' I ask, suddenly feeling terribly worldly. 'Best have us some more wine then. Most are on my soul, daahlink, and are not the stuff of pleasant playground camaraderie.'

Amen to that.

Bollywood at Selfridges

Friday

I went to the Bollywood at Selfridges opening last night. There was gallons of alcohol but no food so everyone got absurdly drunk. Since I had been involved in the programming I wanted to look good. I wore the silver silk-jersey Alexander McQueen dress I got in the sale last winter, and very high black boots from Nicole Farhi (a gift from my ex). I bribed beautiful kind Ady, six foot five inches of solid American meat, with the promise of a chicken dinner if he came as my escort, held my arm and looked adoring.

In the end I had a great time because people came up to me and said either, 'This is so wonderful, and it's all thanks to you!' or 'This is so atrocious, but only because you're no longer involved!' so I was like 'yah, thanks *bhai*' to everyone.

Los Bros Moranis, the company from Mumbai who had done the production for the event, my knights in shining Versace, were there en masse; a group of tiny men branded from head to toe and wearing stacked shoes, their wives in designer saris and the world's largest diamonds. One of them was actually wearing bright red eye make-up to match her sari.

One of Selfridges' buyers from India (who with his white hair looks remarkably like the Kenzo man) was drunkenly expansive: 'Ah, I knew you were special when last summer I saw Aamir Khan kneeling outside the door of your hotel room at the Taj.'

'What nonsense,' I laughed. 'He wasn't kneeling in an act of supplication. He was crouching so that when I opened the door he could leap up and scare the crap out of me.'

He wasn't convinced: 'He doesn't kneel for people.' He waggled his finger: a wise, if a little pissed, *rishi*.

'Well, actually he'd do almost anything to play a practical joke.'

I saw Amitabh and Jaya trying to maintain their dignity and be regal: the King and Queen of Bollywood surrounded by a throng of uncaring PR girls. I lurched across their line of vision and Jaya started, as if I was about to belt her. When she saw it was me she looked relieved and smiled quickly as Amitabh said a formal, 'Hello Jessica.' And then they continued their attempt at a stately procession towards a private screening of the new *Devdas*, by Sanjay Leela Bhansali.

I left soon after that. Meeting a terrifically sober Mr and Mrs Bachchan made me realise that I was far drunker than I had thought. No food, man – it gets you every time.

Amitabh leaves today. So London – an obvious location, some might say, to do the interviews – wasn't right either. Funny that.

Monday

Today I got another 4 a.m. phone call from Amitabh. He suggested that I might like to join him in Dubai where he is shooting for a film called *Boom*, and we could do the interviews then. Finally! An 'out station' location! I was suddenly wide awake and agreed instantly, and now he is sorting it out. Bless him. I am loving having that pleasantly spacey feeling that phone calls from India in the early hours give me.

Dubai? I never imagined that I would go to Dubai. But then I never gave Kuala Lumpur much thought either. I will say this for Amitabh: I have seen more of the planet hanging out with him than I would have otherwise. And in a totally different way. Filmi travel is a whole 'nother ball game. In some ways it's amazing because there's no question of what can be afforded – production takes care of everything. But actually it's quite restrictive, and all you see is the Indian side of every city that you go to. If all you did was travel with Hindi film units you would believe that the planet had suddenly been repopulated entirely with Indians who like Bollywood films.

In 2001, just after 9/11, I got trapped in North America, so I joined up with the Morani brothers' star shows as they toured around. In these huge shows Bollywood film stars dance about on stage and mime to hit songs from their films of that year. This means that Hindi film stars interact with their fans in a way that Hollywood stars never do. With the *Lagaan* team I went to Calgary, San Francisco and LA – three great North American cities – and all I saw was stadiums filled with Indians. And the odd mall. But I liked that. I liked being part of a world that isn't mine.

So, off to Dubai next week.

Hindi 101

Tuesday

I went and talked to Rupert Snell at SOAS yesterday. When I was doing my degree he made a valiant attempt to teach me Hindi. I remembered trying to get Amitabh to help me with my pronunciation of the Hindi syllabary the summer before I started the course.

'Help me with my pronunciation?' I asked.

'No.'

'Oh, go on. I have to learn it in a couple of weeks.'

He sighed and looked at me in a long-suffering, exasperated way.

I grinned at him, knowing I had won, and opened my book.

'Tha,' I said.

'No.'

'THA,' I said.

'No.'

'Amitabh! OK, you tell me how it's done.' I passed the book to him

'Tha, dha . . .'

The plosives plosed off his tongue, the aspirates aspired no more and puffed out of his mouth like little silvery brown clouds and hung about his head. I could smell the rich loamy post-monsoon plains of northern India, could hear women singing as they batted kohled eyes at handsome men. In the distance I could see a camel train wending its way across the desert. I stared at him in awe. He finished and looked at me.

'That was beautiful.'

He looked surprised and amused. I took the book from him and made what could only be described as a stab at it. The clouds evaporate and we are forever in England.

'You'll never learn,' he said. 'Now we have to stop. I am busy.'

'You are not. You're channel-surfing. And I will learn.'

I tried and tried but I am not one of life's natural linguists, and Rupert did make a brave attempt to help me. Teaching me was clearly a seminal moment in his career, but more importantly he translated Amitabh's father's autobiography, *In the Afternoon of Time*, editing it in the process from four volumes down to one. Today I wanted to ask him if there was anything

227

about Amitabh in the Hindi original that he hadn't included, which might affect how I deal with the material presented. Because it really is an extraordinarily candid account of Harivansh Rai Bachchan's life and gives me not only the utmost respect for him, but also for Amitabh's mother who comes across as a remarkably strong woman. They lived through some extraordinary events, but no one has ever explored the impact these might have had on the young Amitabh. I intend to do this in my book.

Rupert was as urbane and charming, with just a hint of *smooooth*, as ever. Learning Hindi from him was like being taught by Rupert Giles in *Buffy the Vampire Slayer*. We had a nice little chat about this and that and he told me he hadn't left any of the Amitabh material out. I told him what I had got from the book and he agreed with my analysis, smoothly.

Dubai

Wednesday, June 2002

I arrived last night and was collected from the airport by Praveen and a hotel driver. The driver presented me with a rose, a nice touch which seemed to embarrass Praveen, who looked more tortured than usual. On our way to the hotel the two of them did a running commentary about the joys of Dubai. It sounded like a miraculous paradise, but I find that any city you arrive in at night looks like fairyland.

But our hotel, the Burj Al Arab, is like nothing else I have ever seen.

The outside is really beautiful, modern architecture at its most experimental and fun. White lights play over it all night so that it changes colour every thirty minutes. It's supposed to look like a sail of a *dhow* but to me it was more like a multicoloured pixie snood, and apparently the colour changes are meant to reflect the evening's progress. When you go inside it really is like entering the much-coveted sixty-four Crayola box. The atrium rises 180 metres and each floor is a different colour, so when you look up it's like peering through a rainbow. You go up an escalator to the reception through aquariums filled with incredible *huge* fish, and then at the top there's a fountain which does all this funky stuff. When I arrived, dazed and speechless with the opulence I saw around me, the thing started to splash water down in such a way that it sounded like clapping. I started and looked about but, strangely, nobody was heralding my arrival. The whole thing was really unnerving.

The funniest thing so far is that I have a duplex suite! The colour scheme in all the rooms is strictly gold and royal blue and yellow. Money – can't buy you love but can buy you a lot of gold carpets. In the downstairs sitting room there are the obligatory uncomfortable sofas in a colour that can only be described as hotel-swank-red, from which you can watch Al Jazeera on a TV surrounded by a huge gold frame. The hotel is on a man-made island; to get here you have to come over a little causeway. It is like a gross, modern-day St Michael's Mount, I guess, but without the beating heart of a mythical giant. Without any heart at all, as far as I can make out.

After I freshened up, I had dinner with Amitabh. Delicious. I love Middle-Eastern food and the chef here is terrific. I ate my bodyweight (which is quite considerable these days) in lamb and couscous. But I feel even more of a scruff than usual. It is like beyond rich here. Light years ahead of the levels of wealth and consumption that I have seen at any other point in my life.

Amitabh was tired after a day of shooting in the desert and seemed almost as uncomfortable with the level of opulence as I was.

'Doesn't being here make you feel guilty?' he asked.

'No. Because it's got nothing to do with me or who I am. It's all connected with you.'

'Right. Fine,' he said, clearly disappointed with my response. Then he rearranged his long *lungi*-clad legs and settled down to some serious surfing.

That was almost all I got from him this evening.

He was definitely depressed. I didn't get any response whatsoever about the film he's making. It can't be a good situation that he's got himself into. Ah, the joys of trying to second-guess Amitabh's moods.

Thinking about it now, though, I feel considerably less guilty staying here in this oil-rich country, where everything has sprung out of the sand, than I do staying with Amitabh in one of the five-star hotels in India, where people are starving to death at the gate. And I do have the distancing thing of knowing that I could never afford to stay here in a million years. I don't think I could even afford to get the golf cart across the causeway from the mainland.

Thursday

I thought we were going to be doing the interviews when Amitabh was shooting, but he called this morning to say that he doesn't want me to come with him to the sets today. He says it is hours away in the desert, and that I would be hot and uncomfortable. I will acclimatise today and then go tomorrow, I guess. This is very thoughtful of him, but what do I do today instead?

Luckily – cynically? wisely? – I expected to spend some time on my own so I have brought all the clippings and stuff I've collected on his years in politics. Today I found this quote about his experiences on the campaign trail:

It was an eye-opener. During the campaign, I discovered that those of us who live in the cities are incorrigibly cocooned. We are blind to the fact that the real India is in the villages. The

Indian there wants nothing, he only wants consideration, and he wants feelings. His material interests are zero. I've seen entire villages surviving on just a light bulb and a water tap. Women walk 30–40 miles for a pot of water. Here at the flick of a switch, 70 light bulbs come on, at the jab of a knob water gushes at you, hot or cold. I felt guilty about this, I still do.[91]

It does seem remarkable that Amitabh didn't have a concept of how the other nine-tenths of the country lived, but I doubt the really rich in Britain have any clue as to what it means to live on benefits.

Friday

Dinner with Amitabh again but he was even more tired than yesterday, even less inclined to talk about anything. He totally ignored me when I asked about the interviews.

I think I am going to have a whirlpool bath. There is a Bath Menu here; perhaps I should have something from the Bath Menu. What do we think that means exactly?

Perhaps Amitabh has brought me here so I can be part of a social experiment. Soon perhaps I will not be allowed to leave my suite, or I'll have my social interaction restricted. Or could it be that, *perhaps*, this is just my stunningly egocentric nature kicking in again?

But there is a huge gold mirror above my bed which doesn't bode well – all my paranoias come racing to the surface. I was in bed last night looking at my face, all small and two-dimensional, and thought that I should make use of this mirror over the bed thing. Isn't it supposed to be sexy? Well, when you're on your own suspended in a airtight box high above the

[91] Khalid Mohamed, *To Be Or Not To Be* (Mumbai, Saraswati Creations, 2002), p.163.

hot hazy gulf, swimming about on a huge bed with too soft, slidey sheets and the blankets tucked in too tight, it doesn't feel sexy, trust me – it feels threatening. I could be on a direct feed though to some website. Me reading in bed, prime-time viewing on pay-per-view in Qatar, or something. So I read Eric Hobsbawm's *On History*. Which really is like the Anti-Sex. I feel sure that it will make viewers switch to a more interesting channel. Of course, there is always the remote chance that they get off on historiography, but that would just be really sad.

Saturday

I am slowly becoming resigned to my fate: after working out in the extremely pink women-only gym (I was the only person in it and had a fab time kicking the pink Swiss balls around), I went and swam in the women-only pool. There was no one else there. The water is actually hot and the air scented by lots of aromatherapy oil burners.

The pool is in the most incredible room suspended above Dubai, and the water goes right up to the window which slopes down from a ceiling about thirty feet up. So when you swim you can watch yourself (amazing for stroke improvement!) and then feel like you're about to swim right out into the hot desert night and fall to earth amongst the illuminated palm trees and exuberant oil-funded architecture. The rest of the room is filled with huge, fat, pepper-grinder-shaped columns covered in blue and pink mosaic. I floated above the city.

Tonight, after yet another strained dinner with an exhausted and depressed Amitabh, I decided to explore the Bath Menu and so rang *my butler* and asked him if I could have the Zen Balancing Bath. *My butler* is cute with a very sexy smile, and is seriously eager to please so he instantly rushed off to get the necessary equipment.

When he came back with all his bits I was about to say,

'Look, I think I can put on the Enya-derivative CD and bung a bit of lavender oil in the burner myself, chum.' But then I realised that I liked the idea of him happily puttering about in my bathroom (perhaps getting a little bit of a damp cuff) *a lot*. I let him get on with preparing my bath for me while I sat in my white linen robe and drank special Burj Al Arab mineral water like a total princess.

Post Zen Balancing Bath I have started on the retox and am drinking champagne, enjoying the absurdity of it all, and soon I will go to bed and lie bravely under the mirror, staring down all the unseen eyes till they switch off in shame.

Politics: Part One

Sunday

Another day in paradise, going slowly mad from boredom. Already I feel myself losing mental traction, as if my synapses are trying to trudge through the Empty Quarter.

Amitabh always says that he was caught up in the fever that gripped the country after Indira Gandhi's assassination; that he wanted to help his childhood friend Rajiv now that he was being press-ganged into becoming the new Prime Minister. And I have no doubt that this is true. But today I found an interesting thing in one of the clippings. I think it's likely to be the underlying reason why Amitabh went into politics. In this article he says that ever since the accident took place on the set of *Coolie*, he had been wondering what it was that the people wanted from him; what it was that he could possibly give them.

> It was a kind of reaction that I could not understand. People just standing in front of you, not saying anything, just shedding tears. It worried me . . . All they said was, 'let me touch

you'. I used to talk to my wife a number of times and ask her: what exactly do they want? I feel they want something. I thought: maybe I will give them a better film, a better performance.

When this offer came about the elections, I suddenly felt that this was the time. Perhaps now I have an answer to the question that was bothering me.[92]

This fascinating passage is one of the few that gives anything like a true insight into who he is. I am not sure how it connects up with the other stuff I've been thinking, but it does seem to be 'key'.

For Rajiv it seemed an obvious choice, to insert the most popular film actor the country had ever seen into his newly formed coterie of bright young things. Amitabh would be perfect for Gandhi's fresh, new, anti-corruption stance. He was the man who had fought corruption in his films. He was the man who spoke as the underdog, fought as the underdog, and won.

Amitabh was accompanied on his election campaign in Allahabad by a loud and continuous soundtrack of songs from his films. All the cinemas in the city suddenly seemed to be partaking in an unofficial Bachchan retrospective. At his rallies he drew crowds bigger than even Indira Gandhi had. Everywhere he went he was followed by his films' real-life counterparts: the rickshaw wallas; the pickpockets; the *gully* toughs,[93] who by this time all dressed, talked and walked like he did in his films. This was their moment as much as his, their time to feel the excitement as their on-screen representative made it into the big time. He was a Congress colossus, still glamorous in *khadi*, and the people loved him. Reactions to him were, as always, intense. When he went into the villages

---

[92] Ivan Fera, 'Amitabh Bachchan MP', *Illustrated Weekly of India*, 3 March 1985, pp.6–13.
[93] Alley toughs.

old men would come up and anoint his forehead with a *tika* of their blood.

Amitabh won by a *huge* margin. In Rampur he got 100 per cent of the vote, and in the cities he got all the women's and young people's votes.

And so he went to Delhi.

Christmas the Bachchan way

Monday

Amitabh has become mute with exhaustion. He is so tired that he can hardly keep his eyes open during dinner. He won't even talk about the film. What is it that they make him do each day that is shredding him? I can't think that this is a good film . . . he would surely be in a better mood if he felt that he was undergoing all this exhaustion for a ground-breaking, career-saving film?[94]

I feel like I am losing him. I can't seem to get through to him at all in the evenings. I have to believe that this will pass, that there will be a right time to do the interviews. I am holding on to the memory that I was close to him in the past.

A couple of years ago I was in India for Christmas. I went down to Chennai where Amitabh and Anupam Kher were working on a film for the south Indian director Ramnathan. (They've been at it since 1997. Will it ever be completed? I think not somehow. But since this is the same Ramnathan who cast Amitabh in his film *Bombay to Goa*, which was seen by Salim-Javed, who then recommend him to Prakash Mehra, who then put him in *Zanjeer* and allowed the rest to be history, I think he feels obliged to make a show of working with him.)

---

[94] I was right. *Boom* was one of the worst films of all time.

My favourite picture of Amitabh because he is looking at me (messing about to the right of the camera) and smiling, honest.

On Christmas Eve I went over to Amitabh's suite to have dinner with him and Khalid Mohamed. I walked into the sitting room and was greeted with a 'Happy Christmas!' from the two of them. The place had been decked out with balloons and streamers. I had actually been suffering from homesickness having just got off the phone to my family – my father and brother had been arguing about how to stand the Christmas tree in a bucket full of rocks so that it didn't list. This display of sensitivity from them both made tears of gratitude and affection spring to my eyes.

We sat down for a Christmas dinner. They both insisted that I have some champagne and the Christmas Special Turkey Dinner offered by the Madras Taj. They would stick to the more traditional Indian Christmas dinner of Punjabi Chinese (Chinese food in India tends to go via Jullundar and end up remarkably like curry with the odd token bean sprout). My champagne arrived and the waiters uncorked it with great terror and poured it into my glass while we watched. It was all I could do to keep sitting, being very good (*quelle surprise*) at uncorking champagne bottles.

It was brown. Khalid and I looked at each other and laughed.

'What's this?' I asked

'Sampain,' they said, looking confused by our sudden ignorance.

'No. It isn't supposed to be that colour,' said Khalid giggling. I sniffed it. 'At the risk of stating the obvious, it's corked.'

Amitabh looked at them with his unique mixture of exasperation and amused affection used exclusively for dealing with staff shortfalls (and sometimes, come to think of it, mine too) and told them to take it away and bring another one, explaining with infinite patience that it had gone off. There was no more. Amitabh asked them to find more. The waiters looked stressed.

'It's fine,' I said, not really all that thrilled at the idea that

I was going to have to wait while Chennai was scoured to find me some champagne before I could have a drink.

'I'll have some of Khalid's wine – if that's OK?'

Our food arrived and they started to tuck into their vegetarian noodles and egg-fried rice (Amitabh is not a foodie), whilst I struggled to find some way of swallowing my dry, skinny-arsed turkey.

That was fun. I hardly see this side of Amitabh any more. I am not sure what has changed. Other than the inception of this book. Anyway, since I'm not going to the set with Amitabh tomorrow I'm off on a tour of the city with lots of other slightly bemused Brits.

What I learnt on the tour of Dubai

Tuesday

There was nothing here but a couple of mud huts and some boats until they discovered oil, and then almost overnight a city was born. It's thanks to the Crown Prince that Dubai has grown so efficiently – he had the nous to make sure that the sewage, water and roads were made first so that all the buildings *enormes* (built by migrant labourers from India) can function properly.

The old houses had very beautiful towers that would funnel air down into the living areas and so cool the inhabitants.

There is a huge, gaudy gold souk in which I saw nothing that I liked and a most tempting spice souk that has cool things like dried lemons.

That's about it on Dubai. Its newness and hugeness is very odd. It's like being in a Martian mining colony in a sci-fi short story.

I would wish for Sean Connery to join me in a seventies sci-fi fantasy tonight, but I am all maxed out on ageing action heroes.

Politics: Part Two

Wednesday

I find thinking about Amitabh in politics – how much it crushed him – very saddening. No one I have talked to seems to think that it was anything other than a personal disaster.

Prakash Mehra said, 'During and after politics he was depressed. I told him, "It's not your area. You are not having the temperament of Reagan. He was a stunt hero and so could adjust easily to politics." '[95]

Amitabh has told me that he doesn't think he is half as much fun as he used to be, and that this is primarily because of his time in politics. When I interviewed Yash Chopra he agreed:

> When he went into politics he became really boring. I invited him over to dinner. I told him we are not doing party-wartys, just you and Jaya come over. He sat for three or four hours and didn't say a word. He was on the wrong track. He was the youngest and everyone else was totally corrupt. So many blames on him: Bofors, anything; the press would blame him. If he comes to the functions – blamed, if he didn't come to the functions – blamed. He became so aloof.

Whale 101

All this serious thought doesn't actually jell with a sojourn at the Burj Al Arab. Luckily I have discovered the Assawan Spa

---

[95] Although by that reckoning Steven Seagal would be a prime candidate for the role of what Gore Vidal called the Oval One. No doubt Prakash Mehra wholeheartedly approves of the election of Arnold Schwarzenegger, *hai na*?

सर्वाधिक बिकनेवाली समाचार पत्रिका

साप्त

१५ जुलाई १९८७   मूल्य ४.००

रक्षा सौदों में दलाली

राजीव-
अमिताभ:
क्या दोस्ती ले डूबेगी ?

at the top of the hotel, so I've been having lots of essential treatments done while waiting for Amitabh to come back for dinner each day.

Today it all went a bit wrong because I was having a Thalgo seaweed mud wrap where they slather you in happy marine algae and then put you in a heated blanket so that you stay snug while all the healthy minerals find their way into your skin through osmosis. Unfortunately the therapist put my blanket on too hot and I was basically slow-cooked for fifteen minutes, like a baked potato in foil. On her return she was most apologetic and, as she wiped the rivers of sweat from my face, asked why I hadn't complained. I told her that I was trying to learn Whale. She looked at me like I was mad, but I know what it is that all beauty therapists are trying to keep from us: they are secretly learning Whale.

You may think that beauticians are just puttering about, placing hot stones on your back or extracting blackheads with deft – if demoralising – precision and verve, but they are in fact undergoing a secret indoctrination into the language and social history of whales. All that seemingly innocent whale music that they play? Not so innocent. Whales, who are, we must agree, demonstrably more intelligent than we are, have sussed that their dull dinner-party conversations about the best way to get to the Northern California coast without dealing with the LA traffic are being played over and over again in beauty parlours to a captive audience.

These days when they see a mike dangling from the bottom of a boat they start to decline verbs, or give a potted history of the Cambrian Whale Wars, or exchange theories on why some of their brethren decided to get legs, lungs and dry out. So now, when the polar icecaps melt because we are a really stupid and destructive species, and we are bobbing about in dinghies feeling like the game's up and it is only a matter of time before we start eating each other and wishing that we had Kevin Costner in our boat, they will come to us and smile at us with their tiny intelligent eyes and start to talk. And then the beauty therapists, who no one had wanted in their boats, will rise up and nod silently at our whale guides and *know what to do*!

So, just in case I end up in a boat that lacks someone who specialises in Brazilian waxes, I want to take any opportunity I can now to get me some Whale grammar locked into my subconscious.

Politics: Part Three

Thursday

Losing the will to do anything other than drink the minibar dry and work out ways to seduce *my butler*. Any more baths and I will turn into a squid. Sleeping too much. Staring out of my floor-to-ceiling windows at the flat, hazy, pale-blue sea. Nothingness. Feel unable to think about anything relevant. If I had a girlfriend here it would be fantastic but unfortunately they all work! Hey ho. Amitabh in politics. Does anyone care any more? Do I care?

I'm going to go and watch the England game in the huge hotel opposite us on the mainland, the Jumeirah Beach Hotel. Terrifyingly it contains an English pub. I need a mental health break.

Later . . .

We lost. The 150 Bulldogs *Thermidor*, their acres of flesh, rolls and rolls of love handles, burnt crispy-red by the Arabian sun, drinking endless pints, were not pleased. I left as soon as the game ended and mutterings were beginning, and hightailed it back to my Brit-free zone. I feel re-energised by that little bit of cultural tourism to an Arabic Benidorm and I'm ready to tackle Amitabh again.

The first time I met Manisha, when she was shooting with Amitabh in Jaipur, we had to leave the set one night because it had just got too crazy. It was too open an area and the police had a hard time asserting any control over the crowds. So it was decided that we would all leave and go off for a drive. The crowds would be told that the stars had gone, they would disperse, and then we would come back and Amitabh and Manisha would be able to do their shots unmolested. We went incognito, two cars per star with an escort of several police jeeps. The plan was to drive up to a fort on one of the hills that surround Jaipur and enjoy the view. As we got to the rough track that led to the fort Amitabh realised that Manisha was no longer with us. He decided that we should probably turn back too.

'Where could she have gone?' I asked, flummoxed.

'She is a leading lady,' he informed me. 'She is allowed her whims and fancies.'

So how much more is he allowed his? OK, more politics.

In 1987 Amitabh was accused of taking a kickback from the West German company Howaldtswerke Deutsche Werft to secure a deal for four submarines, even though the contract was negotiated in 1980 when Indira Gandhi was Prime Minister and formally authorised in 1983. The kickback was huge: 7 per cent or 21 million dollars paid in instalments between 1980 and 1987, during the time that Rajiv Gandhi had been Defence Minister.

It was judged to be too great a sum of money for one person alone: it must be for Congress or for the Gandhi family itself. Amitabh Bachchan was interviewed by the *Times of India* for an article entitled 'An actor, a politician or the PM's man?' The interview soon shifts to what the people really want to know about:

Interviewer: What about these 'shady deals' your brother is said to be involved in? Apparently he has about $500 million tucked away in Swiss banks.

AB: Which would mean that he owns 50% of total Indian

holdings abroad. According to a survey by the IMF the total estimated Indian holdings abroad are about $1,000 million! Why doesn't anybody specify the 'shady deals' of my brother? He is a non-resident Indian living in Switzerland, doing very well in his pharmaceutical business. What's so sensational about that? Even V.P. Singh's sons are living abroad![96]

But it was no good; a nightmare was about to engulf Amitabh and his family.

The *Indian Express* ran a front-page editorial which said that the worst suspicions about Rajiv Gandhi had been confirmed. It then claimed there was no way that V. P. Singh (the man responsible for investigating the allegations of kick-backs) could have embarrassed him unless he or 'someone dear to him' had taken a kickback.

Who was known to be dear to him? Who had only the year before gone on a luxury holiday with the Gandhi family to the Andaman Islands? Who had become, in popular terms, the only other member of Rajiv Gandhi's government worth worrying about? Who was India's greatest celebrity? Which name was guaranteed to sell newspapers?

Amitabh Bachchan.

There followed a media blitzkrieg. The possibility that Amitabh or his brother Ajitabh might be involved in taking kickbacks was manna from media heaven. By this time Ajitabh had become a very successful businessman and had recently settled in Switzerland. Having his brother dragged through the media mud was extremely galling for Amitabh. He was used to seeing himself lampooned and attacked in the press, but the fact that his family was now being abused too made him furious. And at no point was it suggested that the actions taken by

---

[96] The year before Amitabh and Jaya had also decided to send their children to school in Switzerland.

V. P. Singh might be seen as opportunistic and part of a larger plan to attain the position he coveted most – Prime Minister.

On 17 July 1987, Amitabh decided to quit. He says that it was the best decision he ever made. He wasn't cut out for politics; he didn't get it, and as a newcomer he didn't have what it takes to not be affected by the insults and harassment he was starting to receive from the press. He took it all personally, even if *intellectually* he knew it was part of a political game. He was not a natural politician; he was a film star. He had become used to adulation, to everyone agreeing with him. Let's face it, people had elected him not because he was a Congress Party politician, but because he was Amitabh Bachchan – they were choosing him, personally, and not the party that he stood for. So when the attacks started, they too were personal.

After the public slaying he received over Bofors and his subsequent exoneration in the courts, he went and visited each journalist who had been slagging him off in the press. He went to their homes, met their wives and mothers and children. He posed for photos and signed autograph books. He demonstrated that he was a real man, and made it impossible for the journalists to distance him or turn him into someone else, a star it might be OK to be horrid about because they were somehow less, or more, than real. As the photographer in *Roman Holiday* says, 'It's always open season on princesses!' That is, of course, until you know them as a human being.

Feel a bit sad for Amitabh. He has been so low. He told me last night that his father is very ill and he is extremely depressed about it. He wishes he were back in Mumbai making sure his father is being cared for properly rather than here doing a film he doesn't like. He does have a terrific sense of familial duty. I know that most Indians do, but his is somehow touching, I guess because you expect such a huge star to be all about themselves. Which, let's face it, most of the time he is, but perhaps the megastardom has made him even more aware of what is important in life. Like your parents.

Friday

Do you think that a true measure of power is how much boredom people are willing to take because of you?

Saul Bellow thinks so. He cites all kinds of examples in the never-ending *Humboldt's Gift*, which I have been reading as I wait. Hitler, Stalin et al they all seemed to mete out most exquisite torture by making their underlings sit through hours of home movies and the like. Perhaps this just proves that only really dull people get to the top. I have to admit it struck a nerve when I read it. I have endured endless hours of five-star ennui, pacing about my room the television on/off, painful/pleasurable yet unable to stop it, the cities below these high-rise, hermetically sealed boxes sparkling and distant. I press my body against the sheets of liquid sand and bounce gently against the emptiness.

If I got out will I miss him? But he is always late . . . except for the times when I go out and he is early, etc. etc.

I am getting used to my life o' luxury now. I'm not sure how I will function without my beautiful sweet butler and daily spa treatments. Surely this is how my life is meant to be? Would buttleboy be happy doing the same in Hoxton? Or would he sulk and start to pull out his feathers like a grey parrot? I don't think I can do without the special spring water I have in my fridge. I have never seen it anywhere else and it feels *life giving* when I drink it. The hotel chef has been told which of the delicious mezzes I like best, and so makes extra ones for me. Am I not supposed to have a private hot pool and daily milk whirlpool baths?

Re-entry will be hard this time.

17—23 SEPTEMBER 1989 □ AN ANANDA BAZAR PUBLICATION □ RS 7.00

WHO WILL GET THE MUSLIM VOTE?

SUNDAY

DON'T
WORRY
BE
HAPPY!
(Are you kidding?)

Amitabh Bachchan after
Jaadugar: a change of
style and no more politics

BOFORS
THE COVER-UP
UNRAVELS

Sunny side up

Saturday

I will be patient. As James Stewart says in *The Philadelphia Story*, 'With the rich and mighty, always a little patience.'

Amitabh isn't normal. He doesn't do things the same way as normal people. I remember being in London with him once and he was really excited about using the ticket machine in the underground car park.

Another time I decided to try and test him. He had always said that he was good at cooking omelettes and so I turned up at his apartment in St James Court with eggs and milk and challenged him to make me one.

To my amazement he agreed and disappeared off into his shiny black kitchen. After about five minutes curiosity overcame me and I went into the kitchen. He was standing at the counter holding an egg over a glass bowl, his fingers squeezing the egg really hard in the middle. The egg exploded, and egg and shell splattered down into the bowl.

'Shit,' he said and started to pick out bits of shell.

'Do you want me to show you a really great way of cracking an egg so you don't have this problem?' I asked, hopping from one foot to the other behind him.

'No,' he growled.

'But it's so much simpler than this,' I said gesturing, as he tried to slide the bits of shell up the side of the bowl.

'Go away.'

About half an hour later he appeared with two plates of what looked remarkably like a hubcap that had been struck by lightning.

'Wow! Amazing! Thank you!' I gushed, and started to tuck into the omelette. He had fried it in oil, lots and lots of oil – it was hard and rubbery and sickeningly greasy. I said nothing. Amitabh said nothing. We both emptied the salt and pepper pots on to its glistening, blackened surface.

'This hasn't turned out right,' said Amitabh glumly.

Then he smiled, we both started to giggle; he picked up the phone and dialled.

'Room service please,' he said. 'Yes, can I have two omelettes please? Yes, and toast with butter and jam. Thank you.' He replaced the handset.

'That is how to make a really good omelette.'

Sunday, on the plane home

Spent the day by the pool drinking fruit punch and spritzing my face with the Evian sprays that they place next to your lounger. As a result I stayed out longer than should I have, and now I think I have sunstroke. I am totally baffled by this past week. Very odd. Very odd. I feel strung out and in a strange mental limbo.

I managed to talk to Amitabh a bit before I left. He kind of rallied to be encouraging, so I wouldn't be too depressed by his non-presence over the past week. Perhaps this is just him stringing me along; perhaps I am a fool, but I care for him and I just hate to see him unhappy.

What do you do when someone shows you their pain? It can be a form of manipulation. If it's all about them and their terrible problems, after a while you begin to believe you have no right to your own feelings. Theirs become paramount and you must fit around them. At the same time this creates an instant and powerful intimacy that you feel privileged to have been allowed.

But it does feel different this time. Is he hoping that the

book never gets written? Does he not like this shift in our relationship, the fact that I am writing about him? Surely he would just tell me?

I think I need to go and just start writing.

CHAPTER NINE

'The human world flourishes best when refreshed by falsehood.'

Roger Scruton

Jaipur

Wednesday, late August 2002

Amitabh is selling tractors. He told me this was why he was going to Jaipur, but can I be blamed for thinking he was being ironic? Why is Amitabh selling tractors? Well, it turns out his son-in-law makes tractors, so Amitabh is being a good father-in-law and making an advertisement that will hopefully encourage rich farmers to buy this tractor rather than another type of tractor.

They're shooting the ad right now; Amitabh drives his shiny red tractor into a village square and is surrounded by lots of well-fed, contented peasants in bright Rajasthani outfits. Amitabh, the successful farmer in his *lunghi* and turban, is the focus of their communal joy and prosperity. It is a colourful, Subcontinental version of Eisenstein's *The General Line*: happy post-collectivisation peasants experiencing collective orgasmic happiness; but this time the cause of their happiness is a tractor rather than a mechanised cream-separation machine.

The ad is being shot in a five-star resort hotel called Choki

Dhani that pretends to be a sanitised village. It's like being in an Indian rustic theme park, like those places in England where everyone dresses up and pretends that they're living in a nineteenth-century mining community or something: 'Time passes slowly at Morewelham Quay.' You can just imagine the people who came up with it: 'You know what, rural India would be lovely if it wasn't for those unsanitary peasants.' So here at Choki Dhani you can stay in 'quaint mud and thatch dwellings' with the promise of a 'blend of rustic environment and modern amenities' (i.e. your room has a toilet; you are not forced to go off into the fields with your little pot of water).

You can even bring your company here to use the facilities in one of their two conference centres. I wonder if the evening entertainments include some of the traditional village pastimes, like making baskets or patting cow dung into rounds to burn on the fire. Or for the senior management, hunting trips deep into the surrounding countryside, culminating in the rape of real-life low-caste women.[97]

That would encourage corporate bonding, no?

I am on track with the book and feeling reconnected to Amitabh who is, apparently, ready to do the interviews. This time I am inclined to believe him. Why? Because he's just read the introduction. His response?

'It's genius *yaar*!'

I arrived in Mumbai in the early hours of yesterday, and spent the day visiting friends and telling people what Amitabh had said. Everyone was overjoyed for me. Well, almost everyone. Aamir Khan said:

'Now I am worried Jess. For the first time I am worried about this book you're writing. Bachchan has the worst taste; if he likes it then it can't be very good.'

I laughed at his hilarity and told him that if this film-star

---

[97] I think I have been reading too much J. G. Ballard.

thing goes pear-shaped for him, he could always find work on the Northern Working Men's Club circuit.

After I got back from Dubai, Amitabh and I didn't really communicate for about a month. Some time and distance to think in a way that at least approximates to objectivity. Enough of pissing about – I had to start writing this baby, with or without the help of the Almighty Amitabh. I couldn't sit about and wait for the equation to shift again, for him to come out of his slump, so I retreated to my cousin's home in the Cotswolds to draft the introduction. Crab Mill is a long thin house that looks out over what can only be described as 'the picturesque village of Illmington'. All a bit too picturesque for me really: I prefer the harshness of the Cornish coast to these safe yellow villages. Of course Crab Mill makes up for that by being the coldest fucking place on the planet. I spent the first half of August wrapped in layers of wool, gripping my coffee mug to unfreeze my fingers and staring out at the low dark-grey clouds sitting on top of the hill, gently raining as they made their way out over the valley. I warmed up each evening by running to Compton Scorpion through fields of corn failing to ripen in the cold, rainy English summer. Docs Luke Hodgkin and Jean Radford were excellent hosts and very helpful with things like first lines and clarifying multiple world theory. Luke, a mathematician, is from the science-genius side of the family (not my side) and is writing a history of mathematics.[98] So my whingeing about too much information and how I was suffering from overwhelmshon didn't cut much ice and I managed to produce the introduction in just over a week. Ha! At this rate I should be done with the first draft by Christmas! Perhaps Caroline Moorehead's work schedule is not so alarming after all!

---

[98] Luke Hodgkin, *A History of Mathematics: From Mesopotamia to Modernity* (Oxford, OUP, 2005)

Amitabh says he is going to show the introduction to Jaya and Abhishek. Feeling really pumped by it all now. Want to consume information. Want to absorb a ton of information. Bring it on! If Amitabh is behind it as much as he says he is, then it should be plainer sailing than it has been up until now. He has even started to talk to me differently. It is as if he had been secretly worried that perhaps I couldn't write anything longer than a text message. That might be me projecting on to him. I hadn't realised how anxious I've been, worrying that he may not like it, but now I feel a whoosh of energy knowing that it was well received.

I started the introduction with these mind-a-blowingly brilliant ideas:

Each morning at dawn during the winter of 1982 Amitabh Bachchan left his house to find out who he was.

His driver drove him into the fields of his farmhouse near Delhi, away from the concerned gaze of family, friends and staff. He set up a video and monitor, and put in one of his seventy films. In the thin, cold, winter morning light Amitabh Bachchan, still frail after his recent brush with death, watched the films over and over again. He obsessively studied and imitated the man he saw there. The man who he had so easily been and who now he felt he no longer knew, feared he no longer was. He slowly trained his body to do what he saw on the screen: to walk, to kick, to point his finger and to glower like Amitabh Bachchan Superstar.

Why did he need to find out who he was? *Everyone* from Fiji to Russia, from Morocco to Mauritius knew who Amitabh Bachchan was.

But not Amitabh Bachchan himself . . .

During the winter following Amitabh's illness, he was physically very weak. He had to relearn how to do the simplest physical tasks. Later he would say that the accident had reduced his physical capabilities by 50 per cent. To realise that you can no longer do what you once took for granted must be terrifying. More chilling would be to realise that you don't know who it is that your fans are devoted to; are willing to lay down their lives for.

At dawn each morning during the winter of 1982 Amitabh Bachchan left his farmhouse near Delhi to find out who his fans wanted him to be. What did he see? What did he learn? . . .

During his childhood his best friend was the boy he saw in the mirror.

> As long as I can remember, I've always wanted to be another person. My favourite comic-book hero was Lone Ranger. I dreamt of becoming brave, rich, very famous. I must have spent a good part of my childhood in the bathroom, before the mirror, acting as a king or a millionaire. The mirror was always my best friend.[99]

Here is the mirror self, the idealised self who says the things you want to say, who can be brave, cool and say the right things at the right time. The problem of having a strongly developed relationship with the mirror self, your 'magic friend', is that it can lead you to giving your power, your agency to a fictional person.[100] The person in the mirror can take the lead, or start to operate for you. If this happens, what do you do when they change? Or disappear?

Throughout the years of frustration and anonymity Amitabh had been confident of one thing: he could act, be someone different, someone special. On stage and then on screen, his alter ego, his mirror friend had slowly taken over and had taken

---

[99] Interview by Khalid Mohamed, 'Sometimes I feel I should roll up my sleeves and tell the world: Come along, I'll take you on', *Times of India*, 1 April 1984.
[100] Jacques Lacan, 'The mirror stage as formative of the function of the I', *Ecrits: A Selection*, translation from the French by Alan Sheridan (London, Tavistock Press, 1977), p.2.

him out of himself, away from his daily frustrations and limitations. For the past decade he had been able to be all that the mirror self told him he should be. He had become more successful than even he had dreamed he would; it had taken him to extraordinary heights – to demi-god status. But now, after the accident, the man he saw in the mirror had changed. Who did he see there now? The mirror self no longer looked back with such surety; Amitabh could no longer disappear into a more perfect version of himself.

At the same time the demands of his fan following had reached unprecedented levels. Now they waited outside his house each morning. Dirty white snowdrifts of men collected beneath his windows, stood and stared up at the blank, black screens, waited for him to come out and show himself, to raise his hands in a *namaste*; to see them.

What did they want from him? What did India, who had almost with one voice prayed for his recovery, what did India want from him? Could he deliver? Would he ever have a hope of measuring up to what was expected of him? What happens if *your* mirror self has suddenly become a *country's* mirror self?

When Amitabh was first X-rayed on his admittance to hospital he was proclaimed fine, nothing to worry about. As the doctor gave upbeat press releases, the toxic faecal matter seeped through the hole in his intestines, poisoning his blood and filling his abdomen with puss. One source has said that you could see a bubble of gas under his diaphragm.[101] This could mean only one thing, that he did indeed have a ripped intestine. Why could the doctors and nurses not see this? Was it because he had by that time become so invincible in people's eyes that the examining doctor – like the crowds admiring the Emperor's new clothes – was blind to the obvious?

---

[101] *India Today*, 31 August 1982, p.63.

As Amitabh lay in hospital and the country went into hysterical shock, the god-father of Indian comic books, Anant Pai, who had set up Amar Chitra Katha press to popularise and disseminate the stories in the Ramayana and the Mahabarata, created a new superhero: Amitabh Bachchan aka Supremo.

A year later he would be saying, 'They chose the wrong man to be Amitabh Bachchan,' but no one was interested in that sort of negative chat and he remained, firmly, the country's Amitabh Bachchan.

There is a story about the god Shiva and the goddess Parvati. They loved each other so very much that they wanted to become one being. And so they became one being.

After a while Parvati said, 'I have a problem – I can't look into your eyes, I want to look into your eyes.'

'Look into a mirror,' replied Shiva. 'I am in you. When you see yourself, you see me.'

It now seemed that when his millions of fans looked into Amitabh's eyes, they saw their idealised selves. When Amitabh looked into his own eyes, he saw their need for an idealised self and the reality of a physically impaired, deeply scared man.

As they say in Mumbai, 'Problem, no?'

The fear of losing 'it', the special quality that has set you apart from the crowd and made you a star, is classic film-star trauma. The elusive something that distinguishes a remarkable performance from a good one is the Holy Grail of all actors. There is the story of Laurence Olivier coming off the stage after just such a brilliant performance, the audience still standing and cheering him after he takes his final bow. Backstage he is in a foul mood and storms past a group of waiting friends.

'But Larry,' they say in their best Brit-thesp voices, 'Larry, what's wrong? Don't you know you were just wonderful tonight?'

'Yes, of course I know that!' He snaps, slamming past the thunder board, the dust rising from the backdrops, an actor to his eyelashes. Then he turns and faces them.

'I just don't *bloody know why*.'

I am hoping it was this series of blinding insights that Amitabh liked, and that it will spur him to delve deep within himself and trawl up memories and motivations to make my book richer than a rich thing.

Rajvilas

The monsoon is set to break and Rajasthan feels exhausted, like it hasn't got energy for anything other than sitting and waiting for relief. The rain hasn't yet arrived in Jaipur, but it should do in a couple of days so they are trying to get this ad done as quickly as possible.

A late monsoon is not good news for anyone: crops will fail and people will no doubt starve. But such pedestrian concerns find no place at our hotel, Rajvilas, just outside Jaipur. Here the vast grounds are constantly sprinkled with water that would probably serve several villages. It is a lush green oasis in the middle – quite literally – of the desert. The fact that Rajvilas exists at all is odd; there are so many palace hotels in Rajasthan, including two perfectly good ones in Jaipur itself, but someone has obviously felt the need to build a modern hotel that looks from the outside like a Rajput fort – huge oversized pillars and a kind of moat effect – but which then allows its guests to feel like they are special.

Once you're past the fortress walls/reception, the fort idea gives way to a kind of posh Butlin's concept. All the rooms are little bungalows, clustered in threes around a water feature. The whole place is landscaped with huge luscious plants and modern versions of classical sculpture and stuff.[102] I can't help but be entranced

---

[102] I have always thought that if you had water India would be an incredible place to be a gardener. Once I went to stay with the film maker Muzaffar Ali and his wife the fashion designer Meera Ali at their old *haveli* north of Lucknow. They had bound the soil around the main buildings together with damask roses, and it made the place heavenly: I will always remember

by this place. It is really beautiful, and I feel like I've been transported to a fairy-tale kingdom. I also *love* having a huge four-poster bed and a sunken bath that looks out over a little garden.

Amitabh was on good form today. We went and worked out together this evening. I ran like a bitch for twenty-five minutes and he walked at a leisurely pace. But then he is almost sixty and has several life-threatening diseases coursing about his body. This evening in his villa we had the most delicious food. I was impressed by my room but it's nothing compared to his. *He* is staying in the Crystal Villa. This is a vast bungalow with its own full-size swimming pool forchrissake. The rooms are huge, A/C-freezing and filled with beautiful *objets*. You could fit my little flat in Hoxton into the dining room.

Let's see how he is tomorrow when we start the interviews.

Amitabh on set

Thursday

When he is on form like he was today, Amitabh on set is a sight to behold. He strides in and stands for a while to chat to the director. He knows that all eyes in the unit will be on him. He knows that from the moment he arrives till the moment he leaves they will all be watching him. Even if he is with the hot heart-throbs of the moment, it is Amitabh that the technicians and the inevitable spectators can't quite believe that they are seeing. He is a legend, and finding that legends have some basis in reality is always a little surprising. He banters with the

---

[102] *cont.* walking through groves of rich, satin-red roses, all smelling beautiful against a backdrop of crumbling romantic *haveli*, on my way to enjoy a dawn *qawwaali* session. But then, you see, they were helped by having their own lake from which to pump the water.

lowliest spot boys and makes them grin silly grins and get a bit floppy from the adrenaline rush this invokes. If there are people he has worked with before, the banter can sometimes become more physical. I remember this one guy, skinny, cocky, with an over-confident grin. Amitabh used to pretend he was trying to hit him, and would suddenly lunge at him with his hand raised to strike. The guy would skitter out of the way with a huge smile on his face, while the rest of the unit laughed slightly more than was necessary.

He is the first to initiate conversation with his co-stars. They respond happily and respectfully. I have only ever seen one actor (who shall remain nameless) being snarky about Amitabh's acting during the filming of *Aankhen*, saying that he wasn't doing a fight scene very well. But the very beautiful model-turned-actor Arjun Rampal then jumped in and defended Amitabh, saying that he had 'taught us all how to do it. He is older now – give him a break *yaar*.'

Amitabh has been doing many more advertisements recently. Now that he is King again, everyone wants him to be the face of their product. Sometimes it's hard to escape from the wise bearded fellow who hovers over you with his half smile and encouraging eyes. He has been asked why he advertises everything from Pepsi to tractors, from pens to Reed and Taylor. He replies that he needs the revenue for his company. When ABCL was in trouble he took whatever work he could to pay off debts. Most of them have now been settled, but he still does whatever work comes his way. That brush with penury was, I believe, more terrifying than the whole Bofors debacle. It is this that keeps him relatively sane: he believes that at any moment all that he has and is could be taken away. He does not feel that he is special – he has had special things happen to him, but some really terrible things too. He told me once that every time something great happened he would wait for the bad thing that would inevitably accompany it.

Fulfilling your dreams

ICICI Bank

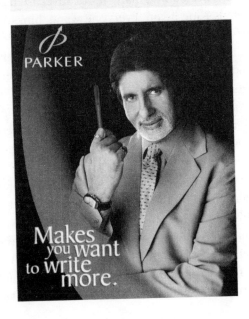

PARKER

Makes
you want
to write
more.

There are some people who spend their lives skirting around the things they are not good at, and then there are others who seem to need to live in them, to be right there pushing their perceived inadequacies over and over again till they can escape into them. Amitabh is really quite a shy person but, like a lot of actors, he decided he only felt 'alive' when he was on stage or in front of a camera, in the most nerve-racking and stressful place of all. Is this how Amitabh escapes from himself? Is this what pushed him towards acting during his young adult life?

Today I started at the beginning and asked Amitabh about his childhood. He was utterly engaging and seemed pleased to talk. We sat and he chatted and we laughed and the film unit watched us, and it felt good, like being part of some private club. It is amazing when this happens.

I try for a more informal approach to interviewing, but I am not sure how effective this is. Looking back through my notes this evening I realise I haven't got anything all that new. I have read similar things in interviews he's given.

How would you describe your childhood in an interview? How would you get across the smells or the colour of the light in the morning that one Diwali when you couldn't stay in bed, or the struggle to keep warm (or cool) on the way to school? Just before his accident in 1982 he gave an interview in which he was asked about his childhood for the first time in a few years. He goes some way towards a description by saying, 'More than my studies, what I remember of my childhood are the kinds of trees on the road, my box camera, the swing in the park, the warmth on the faces. They were my real sources of learning.'

But even this only gives us more fragments: the slow-motion, video-grainy clips of kindly adults looking down; the exhilaration of upwards movement through the air: a small child's point of view of trees: leaves rustling in the hot summer wind;

the satisfying weight and solidity of a box camera, the first adult item he possessed.

Today he remembered playing children's games of *gilli-danda*,[103] endless rounds of marbles with the *mali's*[104] son and *kabadi*.[105] His father's friend, Sushil Kumar Bose, was a fireman and would come around with his fire engine and let Amitabh ride on it, which was of course thrilling. Bose was Amitabh's superhero, the man he wanted to be when he grew up. He recalls the fierce competition of kite flying, the necessity of having the right kind of string covered with ground glass to slice his opponents' string and send their kites tumbling to earth. The panic and rush to rescue his own kite from neighbours' roofs, gardens, trees. The indescribable pleasure of owning his first bike: 'It was the ultimate thing in life. Speed, independence. The best.'

Today Amitabh was electric. I wish I knew a way to continue this run of good luck and keep him in the expansive communicative zone that just spews forth information. It felt so great; I felt so happy and energised. When he is like he was today it is hard to imagine that the sad, depr∅essed Amitabh is not just a figment of your imagination that shimmers in the hot Indian sunshine, before disappearing when the real Amitabh, the confident star who is loved by all, marches on to set. But I know that he is there, and I worry about his return and what that will mean for the progress we are finally making.

---

[103] A game like rounders.
[104] Gardener.
[105] A game like British Bulldog.

Amitabh magnetism

Friday

Amitabh is often quieter on set on the second day. I think he makes a splashy entrance, gives 'em what they want like the old trooper he is, and then kind of feels it's now going to be OK for him to kick back a bit and sit moodily on his stacked chairs. Everyone around him is at a loss to work out what the hell happened to the guy who was so friendly and funny the day before. They tend to blame themselves, and you can see them casting about, desperate to find something to say that might engage him and allow them to bask in his warm beneficence once more. But it is not about what they do or don't do, it really isn't; it's just how he is. All of us who orbit him lie in the palm of his hand, like those Chinese paper fish – it is his temperature that dictates the shape we take.

It was more difficult to get Amitabh to talk today. We talked a bit more about his childhood, but it seems yesterday's openness may just have been part of his First Day on Set extrovert display.

One of the problems with remembering your past must be that the more you talk of certain memories, the more others become forgotten. So people who are interviewed all the time, or excessively analysed, will often not be able to remember much beyond what is needed to get through the interview. I am not sure how to access the stuff behind the stories he tells us all over and over again.

I watched him a lot on the monitor today. When he's in good spirits on set he is electric, but no matter how he's feeling, he is almost always electric on screen. Even looking like a right *goonk* on this tractor he manages to appear almost cool on the monitor. I mean, there have been times when he hasn't been that sparky; before he took his break in the late eighties and early nineties he looked miserable, a certain spark in his eyes had died. I find it quite hard to watch his films from this period, primarily because they are 99 per cent shite (that's a *Cahiers du Cinema*-approved film-theory term). But in his glory days he was just endlessly watchable.

The fans

Saturday

Today we were joined on set by two devoted fans, Laxmi and Neel.

I feel a bit aggressed by their single-minded focus on Amitabh. Plus they are so quiet and so small and so neat, they make me feel like I have nine arms and a rotating Ravana head. They are not professional coquettes like the South Mumbai ladies; they are genuinely feminine and gentle. I will never be like that.

Laxmi and Neel are best friends who, due to various circumstances, live together here in Jaipur. Ever since Neel was struck down with love twenty-seven years ago, Amitabh, idealised out of all recognition, is the man in their lives. This is genius: they get a man who is without any negative attributes. Amitabh for them is handsome, strong, kind, caring, decent, a devoted husband, father and son, courteous, disciplined, hardworking and conscientious. Laxmi and Neel take the examples set down by the idealised Amitabh and live their lives by them. They do not drink, smoke or eat meat. They try to imagine what he would do in any situation, ask his picture, think of past examples. Amitabh as they present him is the ultimate Boy Scout, the rightful heir to the description of a hero in the Sanskrit epics: 'modest, handsome, generous, prompt in action, beloved of the people, of a good family, young, intelligent, energetic, skilled in arts'.[106]

But of course Amitabh has a double life; he is also the characters in his films. He is a lover, exhilaratingly masculine, macho-fighting and tough-talking. Their chronic idealisation of him is slightly neutering – you can't be that good a person and still be sexy – but this problem is taken care of by the fact that they are in love with Amitabh in the films.

Whenever they are on set they sit together and tinytalk whisper to each other, nibbling at bits of information about him. I soon found out that any attempt to engage them in conversation about any subject other than Amitabh is met with blank stares. When they are in his presence he is all they can see or think about. Laxmi and Neel are, without a doubt, the ideal fans. They demand nothing of Amitabh but that they be allowed to watch him.

Today, before lunch, we were all sitting together in Amitabh's dressing room. He had gone to change out of his costume so that it could be pressed again for the afternoon shoot. On one wall there hangs a very long vest of his. (Vests are still encouraged for Indian men – Sunny Deol, the ultra-Punjabi male, advertises one brand suggesting that if you wear it you will enjoy 'the Sunny Confidence'.) They bend their heads together (I am not part of this: this is their personal, intimate talking which no one can be part of). They point to his almost knee-length vest and tinytalk whisperchew over it. Storing this piece of evidence, this *piece of him* to line their worldview later on: Amitabh Bachchan wears vests. They remind me of wasps (if wasps were harmless and sweet, that is) building nests from chewed up bits of paper.

---

[106] Rachel Dwyer, *All You Want Is Money, All You Need Is Love: Sex and Romance in Modern India* (London, Cassell, 2000), p.30.

After they have dealt with the vest they turn on me as another possible source:

'Tell us what he has told you,' they tinytalk, their mouths hardly opening so as not to disturb the air in this citadel. 'We want to know what he has told you.'

They are unfailingly polite, but today their eyes were full of resentment and a jealousy they cannot articulate. I carry information that they somehow sense is not rightfully mine. I am a grave robber, caught by the deceased's descendants, gold necklaces spilling from my pockets.

'I don't know what you don't know,' I say, lamely. 'Wait and buy the book.'

Which is mean. They will buy at least two copies, cover them in paper and plastic to protect the covers from time and the harsh Rajasthani climate, and get them autographed by Amitabh when they next meet him. Each time they meet him they come with a plastic bag full of different memorabilia for him to sign.

It is my lack of visible output that arouses their suspicions. When we first met, when I came to Jaipur with Amitabh on one of the shoots for *Lal Baadshah* ('The Red King', dir. K. C. Bokadia, 1999), I was still doing my BA, writing my second thesis on brothers in Indian myths and films. That time we chatted a lot and they gave me presents and thanked me, totally genuinely, for writing about him.

Today they didn't smile very much and said to Amitabh when he emerged for his soup lunch that they think my claims that I am writing a book are bogus: 'We think it is a ploy so she can spend time with you,' they half joke.

He smiled and nodded, and then looked stern. No jokes like that allowed.

I feel odd when I am with them. I will never have their level of devotion and unquestioning love and acceptance. I am Black

Michael slavering after the fair Princess Flavia (a blonde Amitabh) in *The Prisoner of Zenda*.[107]

After lunch that day I continued to ask him questions about his childhood and the time he had spent at Sherwood College. Whereas over the last couple of days he had been almost playful, he suddenly became serious and started to lecture me on the lessons he'd learnt from being put in a boxing ring at school with opponents much older than he was. His constant willingness to step into the ring and receive a beating to gain points for his house eventually won him a prize for being the Pluckiest Loser. After he'd told me this story he started to expand, using the boxing ring as a metaphor for life: it is only ever you in the ring; it doesn't matter what those outside the ring are shouting, you're the one who has to take the punches.

He then explained to me exactly when he had put this lesson into action:

'When I left politics, everyone told me that I should stay with the party and let them do the fighting for me.' But he would have none of this. He would get into the ring and fight because, when it came down to it, he was on his own against a much larger opponent. He needed to know that, even if he lost, he had fought for himself.

This willingness to step up to a fight is definitely one of Amitabh's more admirable qualities – something that marks him out from the crowd. But when I looked at Laxmi and Neel gazing at him with a fixed intensity and nodding to every-thing he was saying, I got irked. It seemed as if Amitabh,

---

[107] As the granddaughter of Edward Hodgkin, a world expert on Ruritania and, in fact, the best Elfberg that ever lived, I must point out that I am referring to the 1937 version of *The Prisoner of Zenda* (dir. John Cromwell, prod. David O. Selznick) staring David Niven, Douglas Fairbanks Jr, Madeleine Carroll and C. Aubrey Smith. Not any of the subsequent remakes. To those, I bite my thumb.

however unconsciously, was acting the *swami*, giving his devotees what they wanted from him.

So I changed the subject and couldn't stop myself badgering him about a statement he'd made previously. He got mad at me and the Glass came down for the rest of the day.

I shouldn't have got stroppy, but I do find this recent Amitabh as Guru thing quite unnerving.

This past winter I had a discussion about religion with Amitabh and my friend Claire one time when he took a bunch of us out to dinner. Amitabh told us that the strangest thing had started to happen towards the end of his time on *KBC*. At the start of the show he adapted Chris Tarrant's introduction a little by adding a couple of lines about how to live your life: homilies and aphorisms on middle-class values such as honesty or the importance of family. The viewing figures revealed that people were switching on just to hear that portion of the show, and then switching off. Old people began to try and touch his feet when they met him when it should have been him touching theirs, as his elders. Unless they were meeting their Guru.

In Hinduism there is a tradition of going to see a Guru, not for any specific spiritual aim or for a service or anything, but just to sit with them while they tell stories, little extended examples of lessons to be remembered when life's day-to-day problems arise. Sometimes they're told in response to a specific problem, but often they're just stories offering illumination on some small or large Life Thing.

Why did I feel so weirdly threatened by Laxmi and Neel? Is it because we are so similar? Do I see myself in them, in their need to collect up and store information on Amitabh? His knee-length vests and soup for lunch? His stories about being the pluckiest loser? Do I feel guilty because my aims are not as pure as theirs? Or do I fear that there will be pressure on me to assist in the manufacture of this idealised Amitabh, especially now that he is once more so adored. It is as if the nation can no longer bear to have him criticised.

Am I expected to take a tone that is as reverential and devoted as his fans'?

Rajvilas again

The urgency I felt when I arrived in India, that *this* is the time I'll get the interviews, has ebbed. I feel submerged once again in India-time, Amitabh-time, endless and cyclical, with no stressy Aristotelian linear narrative structure – my inner Jerry Bruckheimer, who had been demanding a third-act climax, is taking a siesta. Whenever, *yaar*. What is all this rush-vush?

Or perhaps Rajvilas is beginning to have an effect on me. There is stillness and a sense of gently enforced leisure here ... I can feel myself being lulled into relaxation and a feeling of security.

Five-star hotels rot your brain.

We guests are encouraged to get little golf carts to transport us around the thirty-two acres of gardens and pools. I resolutely walk and look haughtily at the huge Americans that spill out of the side of the carts on their way from room to coach to ancient monument and back again. Last night, when we got back from the set, a whole coach-load had just arrived. It was as if the lobby had been invaded by an alien race of giants. They were all so much bigger than the Indian porters scurrying around them, like cleaner fish around a pod of whales. As they walked to their waiting fleet of golf carts they swayed back and forward, the males of the herd with so many cameras slung about their person that they bristled, and if they turned too quickly threatened to take out the little chaps that trotted behind them.

They have dressed all of the poor bastards that work here in long, quilted block-print jackets and make them wear the most absurd block-print 'heritage turbans'. I asked one of the waiters if he minded. He muttered something like 'not really'. Then I asked if his friends knew what he wore, and he confessed that he hadn't even told his parents.

These hotels are ideas of the past reconstructed to suit modern tastes. They will quite quickly become more real than actual palaces and villages. They will be what people envisage when they think of Rajput Rajasthan. Just as what other people remember of Amitabh's life as it is presented now in the media has become more real than the actual events. This is especially true of the accident he had filming for *Coolie*, which was low-key and un-dramatic at the time – just another minor injury on set.

A sandy place

Sunday

This morning I wrote up some of my interview notes. I arrived at the set at lunch time, but they were all packing up. They had managed to finish the ad just in time, as big clouds were starting to loom. Amitabh didn't look that impressed at my late arrival. I told him I had been working on some theories about his fame; he looked rather bored at the thought of it. We came back to the hotel and he decided he was going to enjoy a bit of relaxation before we headed back to Mumbai, so I was dismissed and he went and lounged by his personal pool. Amitabh relaxing? Miracles really do happen. I approved his course of action wholeheartedly and went and lounged too, *avec la populace riche ET blanche*, until it was time to get the plane back to Mumbai.

On the plane I discussed the introduction with Amitabh.

'So which films did you watch when you were off at the edge of your farm practising being you?' I asked.

'I didn't watch any films.'

'*What?!* But I read an interview that said you did!'

'No, I didn't watch films.'

'But! . . .' I was momentarily speechless. This was terrible; I was going to have to rewrite the whole bloody chapter.

'I went to a sandy place and there was this tree and I practised kicking. Seeing if I could move my body a bit more each day. Kicking a bit higher. Practising fighting, moving around, jumping. I had a tape recorder with some film songs on it. I didn't *watch myself on film*.' He wrinkled up his nose, 'Why would I do that?'

'*You went to a sandy place and practised jumping*? . . . This means that the basic premise of the introduction is totally wrong. It's based on something that didn't happen! All my extrapolations about the mirror and all . . .' My crest had fallen flat into a puddle.

'Na, that's fine,' Amitabh said. 'They're brilliant. I don't mind it staying like this. It reads well. Good dramatic opening.'

Truths can become myths, but when do myths become truths because they are believed by so many? What can your life have been like when a myth illustrated something about you better than the truth? When would you give up insisting on the truth?

I asked Amitabh when we could do some more interviews. 'Soon, soon,' was the response. 'Call me and I will arrange it.'

This is good. I won't get all the info in one go – it was silly of me to think that I would – but I will get it. This is going to work.

Mumbai

Monday

It is raining heavily. Everything is damp. I am reading *The Rings of Saturn* by W. G. Sebald. The pages have swelled up in the moisture-saturated air and it is now all puffy. I think that Sebald would have approved of monsoony Mumbai. The city is dissolving, leaving one painfully aware of the impermanence of human endeavour, oh yes. Perhaps it is not the book to be reading when I am trying to be all endeavoury. The pressure from the thunderheads that roll up along the Western Ghats makes it hard to think straight. Or at all.

I am staying with Manisha; she's going to have a birthday party so I said I would help. In my world this means doing lots of moving of heavy furniture and cooking endless bits of chicken. In Manisha's world this means sitting with her while she tells her staff what to do. The house has been literally filled with white flowers; they adorn and bedeck every surface and lintel. The place looks beautiful but I thought I would split out for a bit before everything gets crazy to allow the caterers to do their thing.

I saw Aamir, Charlotte and Amin this evening for a sizzler.[108] Aamir claims to be the world authority on eating sizzlers, but then anything that Aamir likes he has to become the best at. When it comes to sizzlers, however, I think I have to disagree with him: his technique involves a lot of lifting the food away from the hot plate as soon as it arrives sizzling at the table. This stops the bottom bits from burning. It is my humble opinion that his technique is just common sense, and that anyone who actually cooks with a frying pan regularly would do it automatically.

On the way home we had to drive slowly because it was raining so heavily – as if someone was chucking buckets of water at the windscreen.

'This is absurd,' I said.

'Once I was driving home from Film City and the whole highway just ground to a halt,' said Aamir. 'The flooding was

---

[108] A hot plate brought to your table, full of sizzling meats and vegetables.

so bad that no one could move. We all just had to sit there. Then the water started to come in through the doors and was slowly rising. There was nothing for it but to get out and walk home. I had to pull my hat down over my eyes and my valet had to hold my hand and we walked home with the water often coming up to our armpits.'

'Ugh,' said Charlotte and I.

Aamir laughed. He was in 'Aamir vs. Extreme Situation and Triumphing' mode. 'When I got home I just stood in the shower washing myself over and over for about an hour.'

We inched our way in his huge silver Mercedes through the back streets of Pali Hill. The shacks by the side of the road were all flooded, their hapless inhabitants standing knee-deep, holding on to their cooking utensils and other possessions. Men passed things to women who balanced them on their heads, children carried each other.

A line of pedestrians edged their way through the flood-water holding hands. In order to get rid of the run-off as quickly as possible, the authorities often just remove the manhole covers. This leads to fatalities when people walking through the flooded streets just fall in, *never* to be found.

'Falling into a drain. That has to be one of the worst ways to go,' I say. Everyone nods and murmurs their agreement. We all become quiet. The road has turned into a lake.

'It suddenly seems dangerous to have nineteen million people on this tiny spit of land. Surely it could just sink? Back to the rule of the mangroves and the pomfrets,' I think out loud. 'I have never understood why the monsoon is supposed to be romantic.'

'Perhaps the fact that we're from England makes it hard for us to equate rain with romance,' says Charlotte.

'Yeah. Maybe this is why I can ignore the unrelenting ugliness of suburban Mumbai when there is sunshine and heat.'

'Mumbai isn't ugly' says fiercely loyal Bandra bugger *men*,[109] Amin.

'Yes it is,' says Aamir. 'Mumbai is like a cockroach, tough, ugly – a survivor. If there was a nuclear war Mumbai would survive.'

'Ha, correct. Mumbai is a cockroach' says fiercely loyal Aamir Khan *ka dost*[110] Amin.

'The unrelentingly harsh climate does make the already aesthetically challenged concrete buildings hideous though,' I pushed. 'Coming into land it looks so blackened, so blasted. Except for the lush green hills of Film City of course.'

'Ah yes,' says Amin dreamily, 'our little mountains. They are always there. That is the funny thing about mountains – they never move.'

'But the monsoon is definitely romantic.' Aamir is determined on this one. Amin agrees.

I stared at the raindrops racing each other down the window.

'I guess I have never experienced the monsoon at its best. It probably would be romantic if you were in some beautiful Mogul palace with peacocks and jasmine and lotus and a really great lover. And you had a loyal servant bringing cardamom and black pepper tea sweetened with jaggery to revive post-sex sugar lows. Yes, I could get into that all right.'

'You are quite mad,' says Aamir. Amin agrees.

A couple of cars sounded their horns, more, it seemed, to see if they still worked rather than in expectation of having any real effect on the situation. A whole family edged through the stationary traffic on the back of a motorbike, wrapped up in plastic bags to keep the rain off, a baby perched on the handlebars, but not one of them had a helmet on. I stared out

---

[109] *men* – a uniquely Bandra-Christian colloquialism, a kind of Hinglish for 'man' as used at the end of a sentence.
[110] *ka dost* – friend.

of the window. There was a truck with 'Horn OK Please' painted on the back and lotus flowers on its diesel tank, as well as, helpfully, the word 'Diesel', in case someone at a gas station somewhere needed guidance. The non-helmet-wearing-plastic-bag-protected family had got trapped behind a taxi whose back window sticker stated bleakly 'Life is too short'.

I write this conversation down in full because it is one of the few I have had with both Amin and Aamir where we have talked about something other than their films (e.g. *Lagaan*) or the films they are about to make (e.g. *The Rising* or *Swades*). Everyone here just lives and breathes films. Amitabh lives and breathes films. All those around him live and breathe films. I am not able to live and breath films 24/7 – my brain starts to seize up. Perhaps this is one of the reasons Amitabh likes to hang out every now and then with me and my friends in London, we talk about everything *but* Hindi films.

Sebald is filling my mind with long empty stretches of the Suffolk coastline; its overfished waters and abandoned country houses. But there is one great paragraph about looking at the Waterloo Panorama which kind of sums up how I am feeling right now:

> This then, I thought, as I looked round about me, is the repre-sentation of history. It requires a falsification of perspective. We, the survivors, see everything from above, see everything at once, and still we do not know how it was.'[111]

But now time to bestir myself, stop being all thunkful and party-sharty! *I'm a Bombay girl, in my Bombay world, life in plastic, it's fantastic.* This time I will supervise the creation of my drinks. No sneaky-cheeky different-different combos tonight, Ms Koirala!

---

[111] W. G. Sebald, *The Rings of Saturn* (London, Harvill Press, 1998), p.125.

The Taj Café, Mumbai Airport

Tuesday

Odd that I keep leaving Mumbai hung over. Luckily I have discovered that you can buy Valium over the counter here, so will pass out on the plane.

11 October 2002
London

Amitabh is sixty today.

'Long live our living legend!' the nation cries with one voice. 'Get out those ubiquitous strings of fairy lights – he has made it to sixty and we love him more than ever!'

In India the media has gone into Bachchan Tribute Overdrive. Khalid Mohamed's book on Amitabh, *To Be Or Not To Be*, is just being released. It is vast, almost life-size – everyone thinks it is a very fitting tribute. He was followed all of yesterday and again today by two camera crews as he and his family made a quick, early-morning dash in a mate's private jet to the temple at Tirupathi. Radio stations have left the airwaves open for the nation to call up and wish him Happy Birthday. Internet servers have crashed with the bulk of mail being sent not only to his email address, but also to websites inviting people to write and say whatever they want to him on his sixtieth birthday. Tonight, at his family's insistence, he will have a huge party. The entire industry plus the Indian *haut monde* will arrive to pay homage and obeisance.

Not to be left out, the fans at his temple in Kolkata presented him with a six-foot-tall statue of Lord Bajrang Bali made out of paddy and spices. They also made a life-size cake of Amitabh, which I presume *they* ate.

He was born two months after Congress initiated the Quit India Movement, and five years before India achieved independence. While he did not quite have the elegant poetic timing of Rushdie's heroes, born on the stroke of the midnight hour when India awoke to life and freedom, he is, undoubtedly, a child of Independent India.

Amitabh has mutated once again. The shift that was beginning to take place in his public persona is now complete: he has become the Patriarch, the one unblemished figure of authority in India; politics forgotten, he rises again to be the unofficial Father of his People. After the accident, he had a hard time working out what exactly the people wanted from him (now that it was being decided by committee, as it were). But he has discovered it at last, and now a nuclear-bunker-thick wall of respect and deference and love protects Amitabh.

I am fed up with chasing him for interviews. My idea now is to just write the book. I will show him the first draft, and hopefully this will jolt him into going behind the myth, going beyond the litany and telling me what was really happening.

Hullabol!

EPILOGUE

'I don't know how he keeps it together.'

Salman Rushdie on Amitabh Bachchan

Part One: Finding the Angry Young Man

July 2005
Bangkok

How come I'm in Bangkok? Well, apparently *now*, three years later, Amitabh wants to talk to me about the book. He's here shooting for yet another film, so I've flown out to meet him. *Hang on just one goddam moment!* I hear you cry, *didn't you start writing in 2002? What the hell happened?* Quite a lot, actually, thank you very much. For a start, I have had personal experience of all of Amitabh's film personas. It has been an edifying experience.

It all started when I sent Amitabh a copy of the first draft of the book. He didn't like it. Well, that's a bit of an understatement. 'He went mental' would be more accurate. Threatened to sue me and anyone else it might be useful to sue. He would, I was informed in an email, fight me to the last drop of blood in his veins. A threat which, even at my most upset, struck me as a little filmi.

It was as if the real Amitabh had been replaced by one of his film roles. I had wanted to find the key to the man on screen for so long that I appeared to have manifested him. Abracadabra! A loud *poof*!, a heady nose of cordite *et voilà*: he was suddenly the Angry Young Man – Vijay in *Trishul*, to be exact. (Just my luck to get Vijay, the most extreme version, and not one of Amitabh's more lovable characters, like Anthony Gonsalves from *Amar Akbar Anthony*).

I replied that instead of fighting me to the last drop of blood in his veins he could just tell me what he didn't like and I would change it. *Mais non*. All communication cut.

To say that I was devastated would also be a bit of an under-statement. It was like being sucker-punched by your dad. It had never occurred to me that he might not like the book. But maybe I had been looking so hard at the past I had failed to recognise that he had changed again. Who he is in the minds of the public these days – man of the Millenium, the good man of India, a living demi-god, a goddam gen-u-ine hero – has so little bearing on the man he was in the seventies and eighties. Was it that he didn't want people reminded of it? It was his idea that I write his biography in the first place – was I supposed to help perpetuate the myth he himself had created? I had been a fool to think I could help him get behind his image, dig up hidden memories and present the whole story.

I felt I had become trapped in someone else's life; caught in some weird loop that appeared to have no resolution in sight. I wrote Amitabh; I lived Amitabh Gothic – all spooky portents and a dark brooding man curled up around my hard drive, my head, my heart and my life.

Or perhaps this angry Vijay–Amitabh is the real Amitabh, with his blistering white light of rage coupled with a determin-ation to get his own way, no matter what. Is this what lay beneath the Amitabhs I had explored over the last couple of years?

Then, in September 2004, Amitabh and I managed to reach a kind of uneasy truce. I had finished the second draft and sent it to him, asking if he was going to help me with the book. When he replied to my email in a reasonable manner I felt shockingly alive. Amitabh is a hard habit to kick – especially for an intensity junkie like myself.

It was bizarre: I went and saw him at his hotel and it was as if the last nine months hadn't happened; as if he hadn't threatened me with ruin, causing me deep depression and many sleepless nights.

We ate Chinese food.

We watched *Lost in Translation*.

Amitabh didn't enjoy the film, didn't really see the point. Ah, the irony.

The following week we talked about the book. He didn't like the fact that I had repeated what his father had written in his autobiography. He said that, in India, people were impressed that his father had been so open and honest about his life, but they had had the decency not to talk about it themselves (he also felt that I had used the source too heavily, which he thought ethically incorrect). I pointed out that in England a biography would be expected to include such information: his parents had *obviously* shaped Amitabh, and were therefore essential to the telling of the story of his life. Especially since it was all already in the public domain. I think he understood this but he still didn't want me to talk about it. He spun out again. So I spun too. And more angry words were exchanged. I felt he was trying to own my mind. I told him that if the past couple of years had taught me anything, it was that nobody owned me. (Me getting my filmi melodrama bit in too.) We both stomped off in a huff.

I'd always imagined that I was a true believer at the Church of Amitabh Bachchan within the greater religion of Bollywood. But now I am not so sure. Perhaps I was always just engaging in participant observation and 'methoded out'.

Part Two: Finding the Wise Patriarch

In March this year Amitabh *apologised*.

Stunned? I was. He said he was sorry for having been unnecessarily rude and for encouraging me with the book and then being only critical rather than helpful. I was gobsmacked and, once again, instantly and completely impressed by him.

He came to my house for dinner – the first time in *ten years*. We ate Chinese food.

We didn't watch a film. We talked.

He was *reasonable*.

It occurs to me now that something has happened to Amitabh since I was last in India. His father died in January 2003, and since then he seems to have morphed into a new persona: 'the last gentleman standing'. Now he somehow incorporates both Amitabh the film star, past and present, and a man who treasures and champions the values of his father's generation. And he is, I believe, almost totally genuine. Perhaps it is this self-belief that has made him so very powerful these days.

One thing I know for sure is that I am not the same woman I was when I started writing this book. Coming out to Bangkok felt like a chance to get back to my old self, zoom zoom across the world because Amitabh Bachchan has demanded my presence, yey yey. But I don't seem to belong to this whole scene any more.

I'm just waiting for Amitabh to call, and then we're going to get together to talk about all this.

Part Three: Finding Amitabh Bachchan

Later that same evening . . .

Now, minus the bit about his family, he likes the idea of the book again. Almost two years later. Is this what Jimmy Stewart meant when he said, 'always a little patience'? What about ten years of patience then?

He told me that now we've cleared up what is and what isn't OK to write about we could go through the book. Not this trip – we've run out of time – but next time we meet. He patted the manuscript of the second draft I had printed off for him when he was in London . . .

At that moment I suddenly saw myself in another three years, in another overly air-conned lounge filled with ugly furniture in another five-star hotel. I saw the shifting sands of Amitabh's fame moving once again, and the threat of legal action hanging over me if he didn't like what I came up with next time. Of waiting and waiting and waiting and being reliant on him for publicity and support. Everything, everything, everything always having to fit in with his endlessly crazy schedule.

Once, a couple of years ago, he wound me up on set as part of our double act: 'Jessica,' he pronounced solemnly, 'you have known me for seven years. My life has changed seven times. You will never finish this book.' Had this been a prophecy? I shivered.

A bird flew past the window. Outside the hotel room it was raining real rain. I knew there were hills and woods to run in, and freedom – I just had to want it bad enough.

I looked at him sitting in his tracksuit and baseball cap, kindly and methodically spelling things out to me whilst keeping his empire going by text and phone and fax.

'Do you want a drink?' he asked suddenly. Amitabh has that

teetotal thing of being really aware that we *sharabis*[112] might be thirsting for some hard liquor at any time of the day or night. Bless 'im. I grinned and shook my head.

'What's so funny?' he asked, once again flummoxed by my seemingly random sense of humour.

I have known Amitabh for many years and yet, to deal with writing about him, I needed to distance him. I almost needed to make him the man I fell in love with in the films in order for him to be Amitabh Bachchan. Why hadn't I had the courage to own what I knew? And to listen to him when he told me he was, 'an ordinary man to whom extraordinary things have happened'. What if I hadn't seen any of his films, if I hadn't read all those endless interviews but instead had studied the man I knew? Perhaps this would have been the really radical way to approach his life, a quiet, soft, feminine approach that moved from the inside out. I had tried, I realised now, to grapple with the enormous polyhedron of his exterior selves and force them to lead me to an interiority that I felt sure existed. I had thought this was how I would somehow make sense of the cacophony of Amitabh Bachchan Superstar. The star persona is false, not who he really is, and all I could find was a staticky hologram (like a dead Jedi), insubstantial and unsatisfying to all.

I took a deep breath and told him that I wanted to do something different; that I would write a book from my point of view, and try to get across the man I knew.

'Yes, you should,' he agreed. 'This is the only way you can write about me and the industry. You have seen so many amazing things with me. That's what you should write about.'

'It will be about me and my time in the Indian film industry.'

He shot me a quizzical look.

'Not everything that happened to me, obviously, but about trying to write your biography.'

---

[112] Drunks.

He was quiet for a moment and then looked at me and said, 'That sounds like an original way of doing it.'

'Well, what to do *yaar*, I'm an original kinda gal. What if you don't like it?'

'You can write what you want about me. It is your point of view.

He picked up the remote control, and then added, 'This is good. I have decided that the only person who is qualified to write my biography is –'

'Jaya.' I finished his sentence for him.

'No.' He looked over at me surprised. 'My mother.'

Amitabh filming the hundreds of people who had come to watch him.

A NOTE ON THE AUTHOR

Jessica Hines grew up on the Lizard in Cornwall and went to clown school in Toronto. She returned to study Comparative Religion at SOAS and do a M.A. in film at the BFI. She has achieved remarkably little in her thirty years having wasted most of her twenties inhaling pollution in Bombay. This is her first book.